Religion with/out Religion

Derridean deconstruction has been seen by its critics as nihilistic, relativistic, subjectivistic and and anti-religious. John D. Caputo's *The Prayers and Tears of Jacques Derrida* has changed all that. The Derrida that emerges in Caputo's interpretations of his recent, sometimes autobiographical writings is a man of faith, bridging Jewish and Christian traditions. Deconstruction, in Caputo's reading, is astir with deep messianic, apocalyptic, and prophetic tones. Deconstruction, as it turns out, is a way of doing the truth, of keeping things authentic, of living in faith, impassioned by a desire for the undeconstructible.

Written in response to John Caputo's *The Prayers and Tears of Jacques Derrida*, *Religion with/out Religion* gathers together the work of cutting-edge theologians and philosophers to examine the frictive relationship between Derridean deconstruction and religion. Including Caputo's own "Response" to his friends and critics, as well as a wide-ranging interview with him, the volume considers issues of the relation of justice to messianism, the tensions between determinate historical religions and the open-ended messianic structure of faith, between faith and reason, between the gift of forgiveness and balancing the books, between the tragic and the religious, between the logic of the "with" and the logic of the "without." Venturing into the uncharted borderlands between deconstruction and religion, *Religion with/out Religion* dramatically extends the boundaries of debate in new and dynamic ways.

James H. Olthuis is Professor of Philosophical Theology at the Institute for Christian Studies in Toronto, and a psychotherapist in private practice. His publications include *The Beautiful Risk: A New Psychology of Loving and Being Loved*; *Knowing Otherwise: Philosophy at the Threshold of Spirituality*; and *Facts, Values and Ethics: A Confrontation with Twentieth-Century British Moral Philosophy*.

Religion with/out Religion

The Prayers and Tears of John D. Caputo

Edited by James H. Olthuis

London and New York

First published 2002 by Routledge
11 New Fetter Lane, London EC4P 4EE

Simultaneously published in the USA and Canada
by Routledge
29 West 35th Street, New York, NY 10001

Routledge is an imprint of the Taylor & Francis Group

Typeset in Times by RefineCatch Limited, Bungay, Suffolk
Printed and bound in Great Britain by
MPG Books Ltd, Bodmin

British Library Cataloguing in Publication Data
A catalogue record for this book is available from the British Library

Library of Congress Cataloging in Publication Data
has been applied for

ISBN 0–415–26607–6 (hbk)
ISBN 0–415–26608–4 (pbk)

To all those who—in prayer and through tears—are filled with the passion for God, the passion of God.

Contents

Notes on contributors

John D. Caputo is David R. Cook Professor of Philosophy at Villanova University, Pennsylvania, where he has taught since 1968. His publications include *On Religion* (2001), *More Radical Hermeneutics* (2000), *The Prayers and Tears of Jacques Derrida: Religion without Religion* (1997), *Against Ethics* (1993), *Demythologizing Heidegger* (1993), and *Radical Hermeneutics* (1987). He is editor of *Blackwell Readings in Continental Philosophy: The Religious* (2001), *Deconstruction in a Nutshell: A Conversation with Jacques Derrida* (1997) and co-editor of *Questioning God* (2001) and *God, the Gift and Postmodernism* (1999). He and his wife Kathy, an art teacher who has designed the covers of many of his books, have lived in the Philadelphia area all their lives; they have three children and a new granddaughter.

Shane Cudney is a Ph.D. candidate in philosophy in the joint doctoral program of the Vrije Universiteit (Free University) in Amsterdam and the Institute for Christian Studies in Toronto. He is writing his dissertation on the anthropology of Soren Kierkegaard, and teaches courses in philosophy at Canisius College in Buffalo, and Daemen College in Amherst, New York.

Jeffrey M. Dudiak is Assistant Professor of Philosophy at King's University College in Edmonton. He has written *The Intrigue of Ethics: A Reading of the Idea of Discourse in the Thought of Emmanuel Levinas*. He is a Quaker, and lives with his wife, Julie Robinson, in Edmonton. They have recently said *bienvenue* to a son, York.

David Goicoechea is Professor of Philosophy at Brock University. His special interest is the philosophy of love in the existential postmodern movement. He examines Enlightenment reason and postmodern faith in its implications for an ethos that goes beyond *de facto* descriptions and *de jure* prescriptions to living exemplars. Two of his recent articles, one on the leap in Kierkegaard and Derrida, the other on motion in Kierkegaard, appear in *Philosophy Today* and in *Symposium, the Canadian Journal for Hermeneutics and Postmodern Thought*, respectively. He is a nature-lover and has a long-standing love of the poetry of Gerard Manley Hopkins.

Ronald A. Kuipers is a Ph.D. candidate in philosophy in the joint doctoral program of the Vrije Universiteit (Free University) in Amsterdam and the Institute for Christian Studies in Toronto. He is the author of *Solidarity and the Stranger: Themes in the Social Philosophy of Richard Rorty* (1997) and co-editor of *Walking the Tightrope of Faith: Philosophical Conversations about Reason and Religion* (1999). He is active in local housing and environmental initiatives in addition to academic work.

Avron Kulak (Ph.D., York University) teaches in the Division of Humanities of York University in Toronto. His dissertation was entitled "Origin and critique: reading Nietzsche's *On the Genealogy of Morals*." He has published studies in the area of religion and (post)modernity.

James H. Olthuis is Professor of Philosophical Theology at the Institute for Christian Studies, Toronto, where he has taught since 1968. His publications include *Facts, Values, and Ethics* (1968); *I Pledge You My Troth* (1975); *Keeping Our Troth: Staying in Love during the Five Stages of Marriage* (1986); *A Hermeneutics of Ultimacy: Peril or Promise* (1987), and *The Beautiful Risk: A New Psychology of Loving and Being Loved* (2001). He has edited *Knowing Other-wise: Philosophy at the Threshold of Spirituality* (1997) and *Towards an Ethics of Community: Negotiations of Difference in a Pluralist Society* (2000). He is a psychotherapist in private practice, a grandfather who rollerblades to work.

B. Keith Putt (Ph.D., Rice University, Houston) is Senior Pastor, University Baptist Church, Baton Rouge, Louisiana, and Adjunct Professor, Department of Philosophy and Religion, Louisiana State University. He has published "The im/possibility of a passionate God: a postconservative mani(n)festation of Caputo's Kingdom Christology," *Perspectives in Religious Studies* 24 (1997), and "Indignation toward evil: Ricoeur and Caputo on a theodicy of protest," *Philosophy Today* 41 (1997). Keith is the father of two fine sons, Jonathan Keith and Christopher Andrew.

James K. A. Smith (Ph.D., Villanova University, Pennsylvania) is Assistant Professor of Philosophy at Loyola Marymount University in Los Angeles. His research on Augustine, Derrida, contemporary French phenomenology, and aesthetics has appeared in journals such as *International Journal for Philosophy of Religion, Literature and Theology, ACPQ, New Blackfriars*, and the *Heythrop Journal*. He is the author of *The Fall of Interpretation: Philosophical Foundations for a Creational Hermeneutics*, and his next book, *How to Avoid Not Speaking: Theology, Language, and the Logic of Incarnation*, is to be published by Routledge.

Acknowledgments

The essays included in this volume were originally presented at a symposium, entitled "Religion With/out Religion," held at and hosted by the Institute for Christian Studies in Toronto, April 23–24, 1998. The symposium papers were all responses to John D. Caputo's *The Prayers and Tears of Jacques Derrida*.

I wish to thank Jeffrey Dudiak, who first broached the idea of such a conference, and Henry Friesen for his help in preparation of this volume. I thank Keith Putt for his interview of Caputo. And a special word of thanks to Jack, not only for his gracious participation in the conference and the lengthy response which he wrote for this volume, but for his encouragement and support in bringing this book to print.

Grateful acknowledgement is also made to the *International Philosophical Quarterly* for its permission to reprint in slightly revised form, with a new title, my feature review article "The prayers and tears of Jacques Derrida," which appeared in vol. 34(3) (1999).

James H. Olthuis

Introduction
Prayers and tears

James H. Olthuis

Jacques Derrida at prayer, bowing his head and saying amen, *oui, oui!* Derrida weeping! Derrida's *désir de Dieu* (his passion for God)! These are the pious images that appear in John D. Caputo's *The Prayers and Tears of Jacques Derrida: Religion without Religion.*[1] Venturing into the uncharted borderlands between deconstruction and religion, Caputo presents a compelling and original portrayal of Derrida as a religious thinker. He gives deconstruction an unexpected religio-messianic twist in which "the prophetic passion to let justice flow" and "the deconstructive passion for the coming of the other" (114) flow together. Deconstruction as "the passion for the impossible 'is' . . . the passion for God, the passion of God" (339).

This book is a collection of essays written in response to *The Prayers and Tears* by a mix of Canadian and American contributors who take up key themes in the work of French philosopher Jacques Derrida as seen through the prism of a leading American Continental philosopher. These themes— temporality, justice, religion, repentance, the messianic, the gift, faith and reason, the logic of the "without," iterability, the *khôra*—are of direct relevance not only for politics and ethics, but for such key theological concerns as repentance, forgiveness, prayer, and grace.

Originally these papers were presented at a two-day conference at the Institute for Christian Studies in Toronto with Caputo as guest. For this book, Caputo, with his usual wit and brio, graciously responds to each essay. An added treat is the inclusion of a wonderful, wide-ranging interview of Caputo by Keith Putt, one of the participants in the conference.

All of this gives this book a unique cachet. In it we see John D. Caputo not simply as philosopher, or even as a postmodern Catholic philosopher, but as caring friend, a passionate man of faith, prayer, and tears. "I write," he says, "with my blood, with my heart, passionately, from a deep concern, which Augustine and Derrida, each in his own way, call 'the love of God.'" Thus the subtitle—the prayers and tears of John D. Caputo—is a *double entendre*, referring both to his book and to his person.

Messianic/ordinary time

Jeff Dudiak's opening and welcoming essay immediately asks a seminal question: how does a structurally future justice—a justice always coming but never arriving—relate to justice today? For in tying the moment of justice to a justice to come, Dudiak fears that justice is rendered "im/possible," suspended between the ordinary present and the messianic future. If "justice" takes place in ordinary time, in Caputo's Derridean scheme, it cannot be just, because the structures of ordinary time are always unjust. On the other hand, if "justice" belongs to messianic time, it does not take place in ordinary time, and there is no justice there either. Dudiak wants to think of justice more humbly and less totally as momentary events and acts of justice—as cups of cold water.

In his response, Caputo rejects the idea that there are two different times, one messianic and the other not, and argues for a messianic conception of the one and only time there is, in which justice is never here, always to come, but also and at the same time, or in the same time, always required here and now. Caputo is quick to reassure Dudiak that the to-come of justice "does not consign us to despair but intensifies the demands" for justice here and now. Indeed, it is the messianic demand for justice now that "constitutes the present as 'lived' time." Moreover, if we come to a common understanding that ordinary time is always already messianically charged with the demand for justice, Caputo suggests that "then we could all spend more time in good works"—in offering cups of cold water.

Determinable faiths

In "Dangerous safety, safe danger" (Chapter 2 of this book) Ronald Kuipers is concerned that Caputo's book is one-sidedly negative in describing communities, especially concrete religious communties. Kuipers agrees with Derrida/Caputo that determinable faiths often instill a false sense of security in their adherents. And these religious institutions do have much blood on their hands. But, he asks, have they not also been at times communities of healing, channels of justice? Is any community—by its very constitution as community—inherently violent, a bastion of dogmatic exclusivism, an instrument of war—always, necessarily?

Caputo uses his response to reformulate his position. First, an immediate and forthright *mea culpa*: in *Prayers and Tears* I admit, he says, to having failed to maintain the pharmacological tension between poison and remedy which inhabits every institution. Caputo then recasts his views in terms of the constitutive tensions and torque that constitute anything truly worthwhile, like the tensions that beset the determinate historical religions, or messianisms, and the open-ended messianic structure of faith and expectation by which they are inhabited but which they cannot contain or restrict to themselves. The result is a more even-handed discussion of institutions that seeks to correct this "serious failure."

Shane Cudney's "Religion without religion" (Chapter 3) picks up a similar theme. Cudney is concerned that Derrida/Caputo's religion without religion, and the concomitant distinction between the messianic and concrete messianisms, dishonors particular historical religions, writing them off as "essentially poisonous," in favor of an abstract universal structure. For that reason, Cudney welcomes the move on Caputo's part to see deconstruction as itself a concrete messianism of sorts. Along these lines—more true to the deconstructive gesture—religions would be released to be pharmacological sites with potentials for both good and evil.

In his response, Caputo agrees that we begin where we are, in the concrete historical setting in which find ourselves, which means that we always inhabit and are inhabited by some concrete messianism or another, a point that extends all the way to Derrida and deconstruction itself. But the point is to keep our concrete form of life open to a horizon of expectation beyond itself, to an unforeseeable future. For, as Caputo writes, "we are all nourished, as also slightly poisoned, by our various traditions." And he goes on to describe deconstruction as "one more late modern messianism that repeats Jewish messianism with a democratic difference."

Faith and reason

In "Is deconstruction an Augustinian science?" (Chapter 4), James Smith argues that Derrida's critique of reason is "fundamentally Augustinian:" trust and faith are the commitments that precede knowledge and philosophy. This is reflected especially in Derrida's emphasis on a pre-originary pledge which precedes any engagement in language, and in Derrida's emphasizing that knowing or seeing is predicated upon a certain blindness. In this context, Smith wonders if Caputo doesn't undo the radicality of Derrida's faith-before-philosophy structure by reading it through a Thomistic, or at least Kantian, lens. And he suggests that, if the Augustinian–Derridean structure holds, Caputo needs not only to insist that the "religious" response is a "construal," but to emphasize that it is equally true that the "tragic" response is also a "construal."

Caputo responds to the first concern by arguing that while he too agrees that what we call "reason" after the Enlightenment is structured by a certain faith, it is still very important to distinguish the common faith we can all have in justice, democracy, etc. from the particular faiths that, for example, distinguish those who believe that Jesus is the incarnate God-man from those who do not. Such a distinction, he says, will "do the work" of the older faith/ reason distinction by "redescribing" it. In response to the second question, Caputo makes grateful use of the opportunity to remove possible misunderstandings about the nature of the tragic. The tragic—every bit as much as the religious—is a faith and an interpretation. He does not want to leave the impression that the tragic is the thing in itself, like a Schopenhauerian *Wille*, and the religious but a veil of illusion we lay over it. Everything is an interpretation. This involves working out what Caputo calls the "neutrality" of *différance*.

Confession, forgiveness and retribution

In his contribution "Prayers of confession and tears of contrition" (Chapter 5) Keith Putt is concerned that Caputo's radical hermeneutic of forgiveness, which is antithetical to an economy of retribution and satisfaction, "might lead to confusing the *pardoning* of sin with the *condoning* of sin." He insists that repentance requires some "orthopraxic manifestations of sincerity."

Caputo is quick to grant Putt's point. Yes, we do "require sorrow for wrongdoing." Yes, "grace always interweaves with grief in anyone who has turned around." However, Caputo, intoning the parable of the prodigal son and Jesus' forgiveness of the unrepentant Roman soldiers, questions whether "the gift of forgiveness [can] ever not look like condoning." Will not radical forgiveness always look a little mad and a little risky? It is always a question of maintaining a tension between the gift and economy, the gift of forgiveness and the economic exchange that reestablishes equilibrium and reconciliation, and balances the accounts. Isn't, he asks, "forgiving those who have not earned it" a paradigmatic case of forgiving? After all, "if you have to earn forgiveness, it is not a gift, not forgiving, but a fair exchange."

Caputo's Derrida?

In "Caputo's Derrida" (Chapter 6), David Goicoechea argues that Caputo's reading of Nietzsche, Heidegger, and Levinas is "not quite Derrida's reading." The difference for him amounts to the fact that Derrida is always "indecidable" between the "with" and the "without." In contrast, he reads

Caputo's Derrida as putting more emphasis on the "without." His religion is a religion "without"—"without certain aspects of religions such as the guide, the pope, the angels, the martyr, etc."

Caputo, in response, admits to being unconvinced that there is a logic of the "with" in Derrida which is parallel to the logic of the *sans*, the "without." "The logic of the *sans* is ubiquitous in Derrida's text." But, Caputo argues, the "without" doesn't decide anything; it only brings a necessary moment of "undecidability into what would otherwise be an uninterrupted positivity or identity (religion, faith, community, nation, etc.)" that rejects difference.

Is deconstruction Jewgreek?

In "Between biblical religion and deconstruction" (Chapter 7), Avron Kulak argues that "if the Hellenistic *eidos* or concept of origin is not iterable," then, since repetition or iterability is the heart of deconstruction, does it not follow that "deconstruction is utterly biblical and not Greek"?

Caputo grants Kulak that "[w]ithout its biblical heart, deconstruction would lack a messianic passion, a passion for justice." Nevertheless, he argues that, since every text is "structurally iterable and deconstructible," and since this is a point that follows from careful analyses and rereadings of Saussure and Husserl, having little or nothing to do with biblical texts, it follows that deconstruction "is nicely described as Jewgreek."

The test of the *khôra*

In the final contribution to this collection (Chapter 8), I raise concerns about the fact that, in the test of *khôra*, Derrida and Caputo show a preference for reading this non-place place as without, anonymous, barren, rather than as a with-place opened by God and vulnerable to rupture.

In response (Chapter 9), Caputo argues that the *khôra* is "neither the tragic nor the religious," but a neutral and necessary condition for both. He further claims that making the *khôra* a justice-friendly, loving matrix stacks the deck in favor of the good!

As Caputo argues throughout these responses—and this is an idea to which he returns repeatedly in addressing these questions—the point of a deconstructive analysis is always to keep the tension and the undecidability alive, to see that our beliefs and practices, our institutions and structures, are what they are only so long as they are exposed to their own undoing. The way to save the things we love is not to keep them too safe. The point is to see that things are made possible by the very conditions that threaten to make them impossible.

Doing the truth!

The book ends with a far-ranging autobiographical interview of Caputo—the first lengthy interview of Caputo to be published. In the interview (Chapter 10), Caputo comes across as a Christian philosopher, "very attached to Jesus," transcribing into "Greek"—that is, philosophy, à la Levinas—what he has learned from reading the Bible. Caputo wants to bring faith out of the *epoché*, remove the brackets, and situate faith within the "cloud of unknowing."

For Caputo, removing the brackets makes for a rethematizing, beyond the categories of logocentrism and phallocentrism, of an "incomplete, imperfect phenomenology"—a phenomenology of a gifting and forgiving God of grace who suffers with us.

What Caputo wants to stress in Derrida is not so much his interest in mysticism and negative theology, which is what tends to draw the attention of most religiously minded readers of deconstruction, but his recovery of "the voice of prophetic Judaism." And this is of crucial importance, for it means that deconstruction is a "radical call to justice," the " 'undeconstructible,' " an attempt simply "to say that we are always driven by an affirmation, by a desire, or a desire beyond desire"—a desire for which we "pray and weep."

In these essays, in his response and interview, John D. Caputo emerges as an engaging and engaged postmodern Meister Eckhart, hanging on *by* a prayer and *to* a prayer. He is a heretical phenomenologist whose first question—"what do I love when I love my God?"—is infused with an old Jewish prayer, "amen," and its postmodern translation, *viens, oui, oui*.

This unflagging prayer is also an invocation to all readers to come and join in, raising their distinctive voices in the ongoing discussion. Even more—hand in hand with Jack Caputo—it is my prayer, not without tears, that reading this book will inspire us to renewed zeal in doing what finally matters: the truth—visiting the stranger, comforting the widow, taking in the orphan, offering gifts of cold water to all who suffer.

Note

1 Bloomington and Indianapolis: Indiana University Press, 1997. Throughout this book, bracketed numbers in the text without further specification are page references to *The Prayers and Tears*. Bracketed numbers preceded by "p." are page references to the present work.

1 *Bienvenue*—Just a moment

Jeffrey M. Dudiak

Just a moment of *bienvenue*

I would like to begin for just a moment with just a word, just an opening word, for our guest, Professor John D. Caputo: *bienvenue*.

Allow me to repeat, this time with emphasis. I would like to begin for just a moment (in what I will argue is at least interpretable as a just moment, or a moment of justice) with just a word (which I will argue is a just word, a word of justice), just an opening word (a word that occupies in extending and concretizing a certain space and time for justice), for our guest, Professor John D. Caputo: *bienvenue*, welcome. And, to be just, I extend this word to our other guests as well.

Several months ago, we here at the Institute for Christian Studies in Toronto extended an invitation to Professor Caputo to come and discuss with us his newest book—another in a growing list of important and challenging books—*The Prayers and Tears of Jacques Derrida*. "*Viens*," "Come," we said, and he graciously replied: "*Oui. Oui.*" (Although my memory sometimes fails me, so he may have said it only once.) And, now that he is here (*il est venu*), on behalf of the Institute, the conference committee, and myself I say: "*Bien-venue*," "Wel-come." That is, in this very rough and ready fashion (wherein the terms of Caputo's Derrida[1] are being used and already a little abused—though I shall try shortly to make amends) I am suggesting that there is, perhaps, a certain gap between the "*viens*" and the "*bienvenue*," a gap that Caputo's Derrida[1] does not recognize (or that recognizes only in already traversing it—and this is what concerns me, although just a little, but since this little has to do with justice, perhaps this is no little concern), just a little temporal gap that nevertheless affects the way we think about the temporality, or temporalities, of justice. That is, there is something unsettling for me— and unsettling me would not at all unsettle him, as unsettling us is what he aims at—about this John, this John's Jacques, crying *viens* in the wilderness, preparing the way for a Messiah who is coming, always coming, but who therefore never comes. I would like in this chapter, therefore, among other things, to examine the temporality of the *bienvenue*, and I propose tentatively that we will find in it a temporality that differs from the temporality of the *viens* (in emphasis if not in "structure"), that messianic time can be alternatively thought of, and more justly thought of (or at least I shall propose), as just a moment, as a just moment or moment of justice, that makes of the messianic future correlated in a privileged way with justice by Caputo's Derrida, just a moment of justice, just a moment of messianic time, a just moment, without doubt, but just a moment.

That is, there seems to me a gap between the extending of the "*viens*" ("come"), and the extension of this "*viens*" in the "*bien-venue*" ("wel-come"), even if we sometimes employ the term "welcome" when we mean "come." Indeed, the "*viens*" and the "*bienvenue*" are not strictly separate, even if they are not, on my reading, synonymous, which it is, I think, the tendency of Caputo's Derrida to make them. As with a "welcome" on the mat of our doorstep, the "*viens*" is already a promise of "*bienvenue*," even if it is concretely only a word, and not the food from my mouth, that is given in it. The "*bienvenue*," the "welcome," transforms as it extends (in both senses) the "*viens*," the "come"; it says "come" again even as the one welcomed is come (and any good "welcome" ends by saying "come again"). The "*viens*" is repeated in the "*bien-venue*," the "come" in the "wel-come" ("*viens*," "*bien-venue*," "*viens encore*"), but repeated with a difference, for now, in response to *celui qui est venu*, it feeds the other, the *arrivant(e)*, by the flesh of the host, with the food and not only the words of my mouth, in the very moment of the other's hunger, with a promise not just made but kept, which is, I shall argue shortly, with a promise. And in accepting the hospitality of the host, the guest too must enter into a repetition, for the "*oui*" of "*je suis venu*," "I am come," must be sustained across the "*oui*" of "*je reste*," "I'll stay" (as across the "*je viendrai encore*," "I'll come again"), but a repetition, again, with a difference, which transforms the "*s'il vous plaît*" indigenous to the face into a "*merci*," which transports the other into a *merci-full* time, into the time of "*bienvenue*," into a just moment, for just a moment.

Now, across these terms that I am adapting from Caputo's Derrida, that I am attempting to repeat with a difference, a cynical reading is always possible. There may be no genuine hospitality in my "*bienvenue*," as there may be no mercy acknowledged across what I am perhaps presumptuously presupposing will be Professor Caputo's "*merci*." "*De rien!*" Perhaps I am merely using this occasion as a means to pad my CV in an attempt to secure an academic job (so you see, in case there be any doubt as I proceed, that I too dream the impossible), as Professor Caputo may be using this occasion to sell a few books. Indeed, a lot of economics are transacted across these terms every day. But let us presuppose for just a moment, across if not against these economies, the possibility of a just moment, of the "*bienvenue*," which I am interpreting as hospitality ("*Faites comme chez vous*"), and continue our inquiries from there.

A time for justice

From the introduction to *The Prayers and Tears of Jacques Derrida*, beginning with its own citation from Derrida's *Circonfession*, I quote:

> [Derrida:]
>   . . . you have spent your life
> inviting calling promising,
> hoping sighing dreaming,
> convoking invoking provoking,
> constituting engendering producing,
> naming assigning demanding,
> prescribing commanding sacrificing
>
> (*Circon.*, pp. 290–91/ *Circum.*, p. 314)

> [Caputo:]
> Six times three, eighteen ways to pray and weep, to dream of the innumerable, to desire the promise of something unimaginable, to be impassioned by the impossible. Eighteen ways to begin *by* the impossible, to be set in motion by the prospect of the unforeseeable, by the call of something that calls us before we open our mouths, to be sought by something, I know not what, that seeks me out before I seek it.
>
> (xviii–xix).

Across this *circonfession* with commentary, Caputo's Derrida confesses his perpetually, repeatedly, tearful prayer, his dream. And that of which he dreams is the impossible, namely, we soon discover, an impossible justice, an impossible Messiah, an impossible promise to come. So even while Caputo's Derrida acknowledges a certain implication of this "to come," this "*à-venir*," in a certain past (which I would argue is not insignificant, which I would argue is the very significance of what the *à-venir* signifies), the irremissibly futural orientation of this tearful prayer, this passionate dream, is firmly established.

Indeed, we read: "Derrida is dreaming of what is not and never will be present, what is *structurally* to come (*à-venir*). He is dreaming and praying over an 'absolute' future" (73, my emphasis), over an "absolute surprise" (76). This future of the futurity of justice is thus to be clearly distinguished from the future present, from a future that can be linked up with and anticipated from out of the present, a future that, in time, will flow into a present, a possible future, a future full of possibilities to, potentially (in potency), be realized in some future present. The future of the futurity of justice, that is, does not belong, as one of its ekstases, to ordinary time, but belongs to another time that Caputo's Derrida refers to, after a certain tradition, as messianic time. And messianic time, the time of the Messiah, is resilient to ordinary time, to being assumed to lived time with its past, present, and future, such that Caputo's Derrida will claim (in the context of a discussion of Blanchot on death) that

> the Messiah never comes, that the very idea of the Messiah would be destroyed were the Messiah, to everyone's embarrassment and consternation, to have the indiscretion to show up and actually become present. The very idea of the Messiah is that he is to come, *à-venir*, something coming, not that he would ever actually arrive. The very function of the messianic idea is to evoke or provoke the come, *viens*. . . . The messianic idea turns on a certain structural openness, undecidability, unaccomplishment, non-occurrence, noneventuality, which sees to it that, in contrast to the way things transpire in ordinary time, things are never finished, that the last word is never spoken. Were the Messiah ever to show up, that indiscretion would ruin the whole idea of the messianic, [or, as Caputo's Derrida puts it a few pages earlier] would ruin everything.
>
> (78, 74)

This futurity of the Messiah is so futural, we are told, that even were the Messiah to show up in presence, such that we could "poke him in the ribs," we would still have to ask, "When will you come?"

So, justice, and the Messiah upon whose broad shoulders justice is to be borne, are structurally *à-venir*, and this for good ethical reasons, for the sake of justice, "[f]or," as Caputo's Derrida claims, "the most unjust thing of all would be to close off the future by saying that justice is present, that the present time is just, 'to pretend that the last word is spoken, time completed, the Messiah come at last'"(81). And I, at least, wholeheartedly agree; this danger should not be underestimated.

Good enough, almost, but not just; that is, not good enough for justice, or, as such, too bad for justice. For while a structurally future justice, the promise of a deliverance always to come, might be quite acceptably à la mode at the École des Hautes Études, at Villanova University, or at the Institute for Christian Studies, it would be less well received, I suspect, around Pigalle, in north Philadelphia, or in Parkdale, Toronto. Justice, if it is to be just, must be justice today, because, as Caputo's Derrida rightfully recognizes, quoting Blanchot:

> Justice won't wait; it is to be done at every instant, to be realized all the time. . . . Every just act (are there any?) makes of its day the last day . . . a day no longer situated in the ordinary succession of days but one that makes of the most commonplace ordinary, the extraordinary [81, from *The Writing of Disaster*]. . . . That is why Blanchot says that merely saying *viens* would not be enough, if the call were hollow, full of sounding brass but unaccompanied by virtue and repentance. That call for doing justice is also signaled by the setting [in the story from Blanchot being commented upon here] of the Messiah's appearance—among beggars, among the poor, the widow, the orphan, and the stranger, those who demand justice now, for justice deferred is justice denied.
>
> (80)

So, and again for good ethical reasons, for the sake of justice, for justice to be just, in addition to a justice to come, to a messianic future, there needs to be justice today, a messianic today.

My question, then, is this: What is the relationship between a structurally future justice, a justice *à-venir*, always coming but never arriving (perhaps like a meteoroid that is coming toward Earth but will burn out in entering the atmosphere, so in another sense is never coming even as it is coming), and a justice demanded today, the coming of the kingdom today, in this very moment—both of which are for Caputo's Derrida necessary for justice? Or again: How do we translate a justice to come into a justice that means something today, into a justice that would not be the justice denied of a justice perpetually delayed, or deferred? This is the first problem, the answer to which, I will argue, creates a second, more difficult one. But first things first.

Caputo's Derrida, it seems to me, attempts to effectuate this translation by tying the justice to be done today to the justice to come—in a praying/acting toward a justice to come. So, in the first instance/instant, in light of the justice always *à-venir*, the messianic now—justice today—is a principled, structural refusal to equate justice with the in/justice of the present day, which as such is principally an emancipatory moment. We read: "in messianic time, the event is always yet to come, struck through and through with non-occurrence, no matter what is presently in place. . . . [*V*]*iens* . . . calls for a step beyond that is structurally impossible to complete" (96). The messianic today, in binding itself today—or, better, in being bound—to the messianic future, is unbound from the present, and so is already religion without religion. And then, in a second but same instance/instant, the justice of today is translated as a preparation, which is a waiting, for the justice *à-venir*. Thus we read: "To prepare oneself for this coming (*venue*) of the other is what can be called deconstruction" (114), and, as anyone who was awake during the 1990s knows, "deconstruction is justice," ergo, "To prepare oneself for the coming of the other" . . . "is justice." Indeed, the good or bad logic of this syllogism aside, deconstruction, which is justice, which is "a movement toward the future," is "given up to its waiting for the other and for the event" (131), is "open," is a "waiting for the event as justice" (135). "There is a way," we are told, "of waiting for the future that is going on right now, that begins here and now, and places an urgent demand upon us at this moment" (80). So, the messianic moment, justice today, is a moment, just a moment, of the justice to come, a being open to and a waiting for a messianic justice *à-venir*, that wins its meaning as just in relation to this future in a manner not structurally dissimilar to that of the Heidegger of *Being and Time*, wherein *Dasein* wins its moment of authenticity by being toward its death that is always *à-venir*, even if for Caputo's Derrida it is the promise of a justice to come, rather than the inevitability of death, that opens up the possibility of doing justice, rather than of authenticity, in the moment. Not being toward death, but dreaming/ acting toward a future justice, is the possibility, the measure, of justice today.

But—and we begin to introduce here the second problem—this today, the today in which justice, in being open to the justice to come, is to be done, is not the present of ordinary time, but a messianic moment whose relationship to ordinary time is only negative. We read:

> This now, the Messiah's now, belongs to messianic time and is not the now of ordinary time; the messianic now does not maintain the *maintenant* of *temps ordinaire* but breaks it up, breaks it open, and opens it to what is coming, which is the very structure of messianic time.
>
> (80)

If one is awaiting justice, one had better hope that one is not hungry and thirsty in ordinary time, in lived time. In light of justice in the messianic today (which, rather like the messianic future, is never present), one would seem better off hungering and thirsting after righteousness than after food and drink (though one might not fare too well here with righteousness either). That is, while the putting out of joint of ordinary time by the messianic moment might well create a space in the present structures of injustice (and for Caputo's Derrida they are always unjust) for concrete acts of justice, this space itself feeds no one. Caputo's Derrida confirms this, repeating: "Just saying *viens* is not enough." So an openness to the future, against earlier appearances, while a moment of justice, is just a moment of justice, and not justice itself. In addition, within the space of the opening to the future, in the messianic moment, virtue is required— that is, bread and cold water for the beggars, the poor, the widows, orphans and strangers, concrete justice, today, in the present time, in the ordinary lived time of hunger and thirst.

That is, if hunger and thirst happen in ordinary, lived time, and not in messianic time (where nothing happens[2]), then the important question for justice is not (as in our first problem) how to relate, to translate, a structurally future justice to justice in a messianic today (which, we have shown, are related by Caputo's Derrida by translating the messianic today as an openness to the future), but (and this is the second problem) how to relate, or translate, messianic justice to ordinary time. That is: How do we translate, or follow out the translation, of an openness to the future (and the messianic moment as so open) into concrete acts of justice in lived time? I would argue that Caputo's Derrida is silent here, not about the formal necessity of the relation—that is a border that must be crossed—but about the actual process of such translation.[3]

This is, moreover, no small problem, for while each of these times, the ordinary and the messianic, are necessary to justice, insofar as each is required to make justice just, each also makes justice impossible. In the one case, justice dies the death of presence (or we die the death of its presence— witness St. Thomas), and in the other justice dies the death of absence (or never has a life in life in the first place). Put another way: is justice the provenance of a concrete today or of a messianic future? If it takes place in ordinary time, if there is justice, it cannot—according to this schema—be just, and there is, consequently, no justice. If it belongs to the messianic future, it does not take place (since the Messiah, always coming, never arrives), and there is, therefore, no justice here either. Justice is then im/possible, suspended between the possible and the impossible, suspended between the ordinary present and the messianic future.

What is the future of justice?

I would like, for just a moment, to examine this im/possibility of justice, and this by asking about the temporality of messianic time and about its relationship to ordinary time, the times between which justice—not only the justice of openness to the future but justice as bread and cold water; that is, not only as *viens* but as *bienvenue*—seems to be suspended.

What, then, is messianic time, and what is the meaning of the at least seeming privilege of the future within it? Indeed, if messianic time is to be read as incommensurable with, as not dovetailing with, ordinary time, then any arguments about the messianic future not being "present" must be separated out or distinguished from the argument by definition that the future cannot be present (the not to be gainsaid "Little Orphan Annie" philosophy that "tomorrow is always a day away") as irrelevant to it. The messianic future does not correspond to the ordinary future, as the messianic past and the messianic moment do not correspond to the past and present of ordinary time. Rather, messianic time, including its futurity, has a purely negative relationship to ordinary time, as a disruption or interruption of its ekstases emanating from and cohering in a pure present. But if the relationship of messianic time to ordinary time is purely negative, would not a messianic past (a deep past that never was present), or a messianic now (nonassimilable to the present) do the job of breaking up ordinary time just as efficiently as would a messianic future (as with any "other" to this time under whatever designation)? Could the privileged language of the future with respect to justice be a mere coincidence of the fact that that which is always coming—from whatever temporal direction—to interrupt ordinary time is neatly rendered in French as *à-venir*? And if messianic time is not another time running parallel to ordinary time, but a description of the interruption of ordinary time, must some other meaning for the temporal designations articulated within it (and seemingly on analogy to those of ordinary time) be found? To this I shall return in just a moment.

But first, to continue: if messianic time has its meaning not in being a temporality in its own right but in its relationship to ordinary time as the disruption of the latter, ordinary time also has its meaning, I think, only in relationship to messianic time. For without the interruption of the messianic, ordinary time is not time at all, as Caputo's Derrida recognizes, but would be a static totality without any genuine movement, without temporality. The very distension of time—time as past–present–future—testifies—against the pretensions of the Greeks—to the messianic already internal to time. And if the messianic is the extraordinary, then ordinary time, in implying the messianic insofar as it is time, is not just ordinary either. Rather, in time, every moment is the messianic moment. The messianic—the interruption of ordinary time (which allows time to be time—and so this is an always already), the disjunction between one moment and the next—is not another time, has no time of its own, but is the very temporality of time, of ordinary, lived time.

But this co-implication of messianic and ordinary time (upon which, incidentally, deconstruction depends), deprivileges the messianic, and the messianic future, as the privileged site for justice—and justice can be, must be, brought into time. When it comes to justice, it is not a matter of escaping ordinary time for messianic time. Under the urgent demands of justice there is no time to lose, including ordinary time (which is, moreover, the only time that we have). The messianic time of justice is not another temporality, but a way of living temporality differently, of saying and doing, in this very moment, *viens*, and *bienvenue*, just for a moment, just, for a moment, because in a moment it will be necessary to say them again. Just, for a moment, for a moment in time. I am suggesting, that is, that it is in the moment—defined as the point of intersection of ordinary and messianic time that produces time, as the "ever and again eternal" (as opposed to the "forever and always eternal") of the interruption of the ordinary by the messianic (which are two moments of time)—that we are to find the privileged moment of justice, if it has to have one, and not in the messianic future.

We can perhaps think this suggestion by taking up, in answer to the question posed a moment ago, a discussion of the possible meaning of the temporal ekstases indicated as operative within messianic time (which is, we are claiming, a time without time—and thus without a future)—across the notion of the promise, for the promise is never all at once but is temporally distended, and indeed it is in the discussion of the promise that Caputo's Derrida, more than anywhere else, stays the longest with the "past" modality of messianic time before going futural. For to promise is to find oneself always already in the promise, already promised in a past I did not choose, which means to have no choice but to continue to keep or break a promise (an alliance) already made (for in denying it I will have broken it, even while kept by it; "there will always have been ligar-ture").[4] And to promise, to find oneself in the promise, is to keep promising, to repeat the promise into the *à-venir*, to promise to repeat the promise, no matter what. Likewise, to promise, to be in the promise, in the moment, means to keep the promise even as it is made, to come through, to deliver on the promise such that that which is promised is, for all intents and purposes, already fulfilled, else it be an empty promise, which is no promise at all. It is this moment of the promise, the fulfillment of it, which is just a moment of a broader temporality of promising, but without which I would argue there is no promise (as the fulfillment is constitutive of promising), that seems to me to be given short shrift by Caputo's Derrida.

Let us imagine a promise: when a father promises his son bread, does he give him a stone instead? Now, when the father promises his son bread he has already promised it to him, always already, from before the birth of the son (if he is anything of a father), and his giving his son bread does not acquit him of a promise he must (if he is anything of a father) keep promising. But he does give his son bread, in the moment of his son's hunger. He keeps his promise or it is no promise. The moment of delivery on the promise is its central, though not only, moment.

I sometimes feel that for Caputo's Derrida, keeping the promise is reduced to keeping on promising, rather than delivering on the promise, that justice is a matter of staying open to a justice to come rather than a doing of justice in the moment, coming through on the promise. And while keeping promising is no doubt an indispensable moment of promising, I might, from time to time, rather have a stone than the promise of bread. That is, while I might be quite genuinely moved by my father's passion and repeated promise of *le pain à-venir*, at a certain point I suspect I might get bloody hungry. Now this characterization is more than a little unfair to Caputo's Derrida, for whom the futurity of the promise or of justice is intended precisely to make a space for justice in the instant, at this very moment, but I cannot help thinking in reading the text that this moment of justice (for me the central or essential moment of justice—if justice is a matter of food and drink) is nevertheless taken up into or overshadowed by, becomes a kind of function of, the future justice of which the highest expression is praying and weeping, not feeding and giving to drink.

That is, I wonder whether Caputo's Derrida—in making the moment of justice, today, a kind of function of, as a way of keeping open to, and inspired by, a justice to come—does not inadvertently reduce the moment to a moment of the future justice, and thus contravene his own claim that

> In the messianic time of singularities, historical happenings are idio-syncratic "events" and not "moments" in a larger, teleological or eschato-logical movement. An event is not a moment that can be taken under a more sweeping process, included as an instance or phase that is subordinate to and serves the ends of some deeper purpose.
>
> (138)

Now this kind of reduction is precisely not what Caputo's Derrida wants (rather, he sees the structural futurity of justice as the condition of possibility for any moment of justice), but in tying the moment of justice to a justice to come, I at least wonder whether the singularity of the moment is not subsumed to a kind of sweep, however content-less, whether the momentary act of justice is not degraded by not being justice itself—if (as Caputo often wonders) it has an itself. And of course it is—if that is the standard. But maybe it is time, maybe time demands, that we think justice otherwise than as such a totality (as a total justice, for all singularities, dead, living, and yet to be born) and begin to think justice in the context of the little momentary acts of love, of *bienvenue*, not first as justice for *tout autre à venir* (which is as beautiful a dream as it is impossible) but for the *tout autre* who is *le premier venu*: a cup of cold water, just for a moment, just, for a moment, or *bienvenue*.

That is, I am suggesting here a more humble, less "total" idea of justice (of an absolute justice in an absolute future—neither of which we can ever reach), justice as a momentary act, just for a moment, rather than a "state" in which all the accounts are settled, and everyone is given his or her due; that is, in a democracy *à-venir*, even if it is always *à-venir*. There is a bumper sticker on a car that I pass on my nightly walk to the coffee shop that reads: "Practice random kindness and senseless acts of beauty." Now, while it is certainly a difficult pill to swallow to realize that pretty much the whole of one's philosophy can in fact be summed up on a bumper sticker, I do not think this is a bad place to begin, and begin ever again, when it comes to justice. For justice may better be thought of, rather than as a word that names a cosmic balancing act of just deserts, as "a cup of cold water in the name of the Lord," which, as Levinas reminds us, means the same as "a cup of cold water," whether that cup of cold water be a legislative act that brings some extra measure of hope to welfare mothers, a well-coordinated relief mission, or, interpreted most radically, a cup of cold water.

That is, I wonder whether this total view of justice, that, given its nature as total, needs be, to keep it safe, or to keep us safe from it, "absolutely undetermined," is (to borrow the little bit I've learned from Rorty) not such a good thing to go for, not such a good thing to dream. That is, I wonder whether we wouldn't get further ahead when it comes to justice if we traded in an abstract idea of justice for all (and what could be more abstract than something "completely undetermined" (even if, with the qualifiers "democracy" and "New International," it is determined a little (too much?)), and opted for an idea of justice that focused on cups of cold water for each, in time, one at a time (which is the only number singularities come in), just, for a moment.

Messianic time re-new-ed as *bienvenue*

But if we are to think justice otherwise, more humbly and less totally, as just a momentary event (not subsumed to a justice to come but of itself, as just, open to ever future justices), can we not correlatively think the idea of Messiah differently, not first as a title that the one who will bring justice bears (that would correspond to justice as a state of things to come), but as a verb that names the act of doing justice—messiahing—such that the title adheres to the one who messiahs. Perhaps Jesus is Messiah, Christ, because he, for the space of a moment, and perhaps in an exemplary way, messiahed, did justice.[5] What he did was not just by virtue of his being the Messiah; he is called Messiah by virtue of his doing justice. And that is why I am not entirely dissatisfied with the formulation of Caputo's Derrida, in dialogue with Blanchot, runs like this:

> So when the Messiah says "today," now, he means "Now, if only you heed me, or if you are willing to listen to my voice." The messianic "today" means: if you will begin, now, to respond to the call that the Messiah himself addresses to you, begin to answer the demands he places upon you, if, in other words, you are willing to say *viens* as a response to the Messiah's call, and to call for the Messiah not with hollow words but with virtue.
>
> (80)

Now, I am not entirely satisfied with this formulation insofar as this "today" is made into a messianic today only as a response to a tomorrow of which today is to be the beginning (which, on my reading, degrades the singularity of the today), but I am not entirely dissatisfied either, because here the futurity of justice as a never attained but always aspired to impossible state of things, and/or a perpetual openness to it, is transformed into a justice I must do today, and the Messiah who is bringing this justice with him but who never arrives is transformed into my call to messiah. Here is, on my thinking, the realization of a moment of justice, for just a moment, today: not the *viens*, only, but *bienvenue*, across the space of a cup of cold water, which is just without being justice, and this because it preserves the *viens* of *bien-venue*, the come of wel-come, as one of its moments, without becoming a function or a mere moment of it.

> . . . he spent his whole life
> praying weeping testifying
> teaching preaching partying
> touching healing praising
> casting out demons casting out moneychangers casting out nets
> giving forgiving raising the dead
> sacrificing substituting messiahing

Eighteen ways of doing justice in the concrete, of messiahing today, of having a passion for justice, of impassioning, and being im-Passion-ed. Perhaps that is all the messiah(ing) we need (and quite a concrete messiahing at that), all the justice we can hope for without going total(itarian): just a moment of justice. Maybe it does not matter much if our religion is with or without religion, whether or not our Messiahs are concrete—so long as the hungry are fed, the naked clothed, so long as we messiah in the concrete, so long as we say and do *viens*, and then, *bienvenue*, and *bien-venue* encore, across repeated promises and deliverances of cups of cold water, that need not link up, that need not answer to anything but a momentary thirst. And perhaps Caputo's Derrida would not disagree.

Professor Caputo: *bienvenue . . . bois.*

Notes

1 *The Prayers and Tears of Jacques Derrida* represents the interweaving of a number of voices—Caputo's, Derrida's, Augustine's, Levinas's, Blanchot's, Heidegger's, etc.—that are not so easy to untangle without tearing the fabric of the text. Rather than attempting to do so, I have adopted, by way of shorthand, the principle of naming the textual voice (which is coherent though multiple) by linking the name of the author of the text and that of its principal protagonist. Therefore "Caputo's Derrida" is not always Derrida, and this not only because Caputo's interpretation of Derrida is not Derrida (which goes without saying and is thus not a criticism), but because a lot more is included under this rubric as I am here using it.
2 And this, as we shall see, because messianic time is the happening of happening.
3 This last sentence mimics one from Professor Caputo's as yet unpublished paper entitled *"Adieu."*
4 I am here substituting, suggesting "ligature" (from *ligare*, to bind) in place of Derrida's "literature."
5 This suggestion is made in the context of a certain discourse on postmodern ethics. Theologians will have their own protocols for "messiahship," and my claim is not to be read as an attempt to displace or to dominate that discourse.

2 Dangerous safety, safe danger

The threat of deconstruction to the threat of determinable faith[1]

Ronald A. Kuipers

> We propose to call "religion" the bond that is established between the same and the other without constituting a totality.[2]

Dangerous safety

March 2, 1998 marked the final day that Canadians could contribute to their tax-sheltered Registered Retirement Savings Plans (RRSP) for the preceding fiscal year. During the weeks leading up to this crucial date, big banks and other financial institutions were feverishly busy hustling our investment dollars. They did this by making us anxious about our future security, and by simultaneously promising safety and comfort to those who prudently invested their hard-earned dollars with the particular investment brokerage concerned. During this time, millions of Canadians, myself included, tucked some money away in preparation for just such a "future-present" (how could we resist?), a future-present we hoped would be devoid of any un/pleasant surprises.[3]

At around the same time I also chanced to hear a Canadian woman's most disturbing testimony on CBC radio. Her message traveled in the "other" direction, from security to danger. She began by describing the anxieties she felt surrounding the tax season, that mad annual scramble to ensure our future safety. Quite unexpectedly, she then related her experiences living amid crushing poverty in Vancouver's East End (although she might just as easily have been speaking of Toronto's Regent Park or Jane Finch corridor). She spoke about how her neighborhood had slowly become an area of prolific drug traffic, and now showed the visible human scars that attend this horrific milieu. She, for one, did not have to look far to see the effects of what punk singer Henry Rollins calls "North American city sickness." After putting this terrible world into words quite graphically, she then went on to explain how absurd it seemed to her for us to fret anxiously over our future financial security when we are surrounded by so much misery and danger. She pointed to the irony inherent in the fact that the attempt to protect ourselves through financial investment has only created more anxiety and isolation, while the global economic practices that encourage this activity continue to drive a wedge between the richest and the poorest, a stratification that helps bring about the very suffering from which we pray for protection in the first place. Despite our frantic attempts to vaccinate ourselves, she said, we are none of us immune to such suffering. So her response to the cynical advertising tactics of the powerful financial institutions was to observe wryly that "the promise of safety is about the only thing one should be suspicious of these days."[4]

I immediately made a connection, whether forced or not, between this woman's insight and the difficult themes Professor Caputo leads us to struggle with in his book *The Prayers and Tears of Jacques Derrida: Religion without Religion*. In this book, Caputo tells us that Derrida's message is, much like the Vancouver woman's, a warning to suspect as dangerous any promise of safety whose claim to fulfillment comes too soon. (And is not the promise of the financial institutions a paradigmatic example of such a promise?) Yet despite this warning, and no matter what his critics think, Caputo says, Derrida's deconstruction is at the same time no sneering condemnation of the human longing for safety. Indeed, it so strongly affirms this longing, this hope in the promise, that (dare we say in the name of safety?) it feels duty bound to make us aware of the danger that lurks in this very promise. Indeed, deconstruction understands that part of its responsibility is to be a danger to this promise, or rather, a danger to the way we humans are tempted to think of and inhabit this promise.

Caputo tells his readers that for Derrida, deconstruction is, in its heart of hearts or at the fine outer tip of its soul, an expectation, a longing, a dreamful and tearful prayer for the coming of the impossible, or justice. Deconstruction hopes in the coming of the impossible dream of safety for everyone, faintly echoing (with the volume turned down a little) the promise that "the loud voice from the throne" makes to John in Revelation 21:4: the promise that God will wipe every tear from our eyes (everyone's eyes, not just the eyes of us Euro-Christians), and that Death will be no more, as well as mourning and crying and pain.

This very promise of "no more tears" (which even the advertising industry, in cahoots with Johnson & Johnson's, could not resist commodifying) has the power to make our eyes well up with tears. And if I may be excused a small biographical excursion, I wish here to bear witness to the power this text has had to bring my own father to tears, an event that occurred one time around my family's dinner table, during the Scripture reading with which we habitually ended our evening meal. This outbreak of tears surprised me greatly, for at that time I thought my father to be a man who was overconfidently ensconced within the confines of what Derrida (derisively?[5]) calls *determinable faith*. My father once even told me he couldn't *not* be a Christian because Christianity "answered too many questions," which I interpreted as meaning that he used his religion to ward off all the existential anxieties in his life which nonetheless weighed so obviously upon him.

Until that moment around the dinner table, I thought my father's religious certainties had kept him dangerously safe from such saving tears. Thank God, however, that the determinable shape of his faith did not succeed in immunizing him from the infection of these saving tears. Thank God, too, that the high institutional walls of his orthodox-conservative Christian church are strewn with tears, cracks, and fissures, that they are wearing thin in places, even if he is loath to recognize it, and that his determinable faith can, sometimes in spite of itself, without any preparation and definitely without any *Gelassenheit*, receive the invention of the *tout autre*.[6]

Although I no longer share my father's determinable faith (without, hopefully, having lost *all* faith), something in Caputo's book compels me to attempt here a certain defense of determinable faith. I feel this compulsion, which comes from I know not where, despite the fact that I share many if not all of deconstruction's suspicions concerning positive religion, and, specifically, those concerning the institution of the Christian church. I do not know why Caputo's book has brought out this quasi-defensive posture in me (no one is more surprised about it than I am!), but hopefully this exploration of his book will help me to understand it better.

If I were to attempt an inadequate formulation of my thoughts at this juncture, I would say that I suspect that the determinable faiths are not as determinate as deconstruction often holds them to be. They are frail human institutions, to be sure, and they too often mistake dogmatic certitude for faith. Yet they are also composed of singular individuals who are separate and face each other. This saves them from being monolithic. Although it is fair to say that these institutions can be quite totalitarian in their refusal to expose their dogmatic certainties to risk, and, as Caputo says, that they invariably call in the police to restore order when things get too scrambled (91), they also at the same time and perhaps despite themselves manage to create a place for a bond to be formed between the same and the other, oneself and another, that does not constitute a totality. That is, these communities, while often operating like totalities, can also be "infinities," and when they are, we should celebrate them more than deconstructionists seem willing or able to do.

But this is an inadequate formulation. For I have not yet let deconstruction have its say. First of all, deconstruction has good reasons for being suspicious of determinable faith. Second, deconstruction does not deny that we are all caught up in institutional matrices of one sort or another, or that we all belong to one determinable faith or another. This discourse knows (indeed, wasn't Derrida himself the one who let the secret out?) that there is no place to stand outside of our human texts and institutions, and that the trick is to inhabit them in such a way as not to foreclose upon the singular interruption of the wholly other. Deconstruction recognizes, then, that there is no invention of the *tout autre* apart from these institutions, and so does not entirely fail to recognize their importance and necessity.

Still, deconstruction's relationship with the plurality of determinate communities that make up our "global village" is ambivalent at best. In his attempt to affirm this pluralism and discourage the factious violence that too often erupts between competing groups, Caputo says that Derrida dreams of a "democracy to come," the coming of

> a radically pluralistic polity that resists the terror of an organic, ethnic, spiritual unity, of the natural, native bonds of the nation (*natus, natio*), which grind to dust everything that is not a kin of the ruling kind and genus (*Geschlecht*). He dreams of a nation without nationalist or nativist closure, of a community without identity, of a non-identical community that cannot say I or we, for, after all, the very idea of a community is to fortify (*munis, muneris*) ourselves in common against the other. His work is driven by a sense of the consummate danger of an identitarian community.
>
> (231)

Caputo's exegesis of Derrida here signals Derrida's ambivalent, if not allergic, relationship with determinate, concrete human communities. The operating assumption seems to be that these communities are by their very nature violent, their sense of identity inherently exclusive, and that any such community can understand other groups only as a threat. My main question to Professor Caputo here is how deconstruction can affirm cultural and religious pluralism without at the same time allowing determinate communities to retain a certain sense of unique identity, for after all it is this collocation of differing identities that constitutes such pluralism in the first place. That is, can we affirm this uniqueness while at the same time discouraging the dogmatic exclusivism that encourages the warlike behavior we all dream will cease?

While I do not think such criticisms of identitarian communities miss their mark, in general Caputo's book leaves me with the impression that it has "stacked the deck" against such communities, especially the concrete, positive religions. That is, his descriptions of these institutions, while recognizing their necessity, seem one-sidedly negative. While I agree that determinable faith has much blood to answer for, its institutional structure has also allowed it to work in the world in ways that bring healing and answer the call of the other, important work that would not have been possible without the support that its determinable, institutional apparatus provides. While I find much to affirm in Caputo's book, it nonetheless leaves me wishing for an assessment of determinate faith communities that recognizes not only the damage of which they are no doubt capable, but also the ways they have encouraged us to dream the impossible dream.[7]

Deconstruction's messianicity: affirming faith without determination

Contrary to popular opinion, Caputo argues, deconstruction is not against religion, faith, or even God. He goes so far as to say that deconstruction involves a certain affirmation of what takes place in the discourses and practices, words and deeds, of human religious life. In particular, deconstruction means to affirm those tears that well up when we experience the absence of a world that fits the description of the impossible dream of Revelation 21, a dream world which we nevertheless blindly believe will come (true).

Like most deconstructive affirmations, however, this one has a twist. For, at the same time that it affirms and reaffirms the promise (*viens, oui, oui!*), it also warns us against thinking that the promise has arrived, that it is here, present, among us, even if only future-present (like the tendency to emphasize the "already" in the "already–not yet" schema of New Testament soteriology, or the tendency to have one's future mapped out through prudent financial investment). For, Caputo says,

> the same necessity . . . besets us all, the same *il faut*, which is to pull on our textual pants one leg at a time, to forge slowly and from below certain unities of meaning in which we put our trust, understanding all along the mistrust that co-constitutes that trust, the undecidability that inhabits and makes possible that decision.
>
> (6)

For Caputo, concrete, institutional religions, or what Derrida calls "determinable faiths," are dangerous because they fail to recognize the mistrust that co-constitutes the trust that constitutes their faith (or, as Paul Tillich would say, "the doubt which is implicit in faith"[8]). Determinable faith has the tendency to instill in its adherents a false sense of security, one that makes them complacent in the comfort of their accepted dogmas, and blind to the violence and exclusion such comfort and complacency might effect. According to Caputo,

> determinable faiths—as the history of all the fundamentalisms, Jewish, Islamic, and Christian, instruct us—are uncommonly dangerous to everybody's health, that of their own members as of everyone else, a threat to everyone's safety, not just Palestinians, or Salman Rushdie, or a woman's right to choose, and this precisely because they forget that they are faith and not intuitive knowledge.
>
> (47)

Deconstruction warns us against living as though the limited group with which we identify has a corner or lock on the promise, that we own the truth of the promise. It warns us against considering ourselves to be in possession of secret knowledge about the promise that is withheld from those who happen to disagree with us, those who live differently than we do, those who worship different gods than we do, or simply, those who don't have as much money as we do.[9]

Such warnings concerning determinable faith notwithstanding, Caputo maintains that all of deconstruction's talk about promise and expectancy shows that it is still a discourse which means to affirm a certain (dry, general, abstract) *messianicity*, to affirm a hope in the impossible promise. It does so, however, without thereby wishing to slide into any concrete *messianism*, like the messianisms of determinable faiths, which assure themselves that the promise has been delivered over to them, that they own the promise to the exclusion of all those beyond the boundaries of the chosen group. The latter conviction is extremely dangerous, according to deconstruction, and it is in the name of justice for the other—the widow, the orphan, the stranger, the person with disabilities, the homosexual, the single welfare mom, and the drug addict—that it refuses to affirm determinable faith even while it affirms a certain faith, a faith without determination (because it is necessary to believe).

One could say that the mission of deconstruction, as far as religion is concerned, is not to let faith forget that it is, after all, faith. According to Caputo,

> Derrida differentiates the "determinable" faiths, which are always dangerous, in order to differentiate their triumphalism from faith "itself," the *indeterminate* faith and open-ended hope in what is coming, in the incoming of the *tout autre*, the passion for which is what deconstruction is all about, what deconstruction "is."
>
> (47–48)

According to this take on religion, it is necessary that deconstruction be a danger to the determinable faiths, in order to save us from the danger inherent in their claim to have fulfilled the promise of safety, a fulfillment that, for Caputo and Derrida, always comes too soon.

Caputo reminds us that there is a political impetus behind deconstruction's desire to affirm this religion without religion, the religion of the *sans*:

> Derrida too is trying to offer us a work of thought that thinks the structural possibility of the religious, of a certain radical messianic structure, without the dangerous liaisons of the particular religions, without the dogma, without determinate messianic faiths that divide humanity into warring parties. For Derrida's distinction between the concrete messianisms and the messianic in general is, we cannot forget, a distinction between war and peace.
>
> (195)

It is in the name of peace that deconstruction wishes to think the structural possibility of the religious without getting too close to any particular religion. "For religion," Caputo says, "—the determinate and determinable messianisms, the institutionalized dogmatic—is something to be deconstructed, just as faith, if there is such a thing, cannot be deconstructed" (224). It is in the name of saving faith, and its impossible dream of justice and peace, that, according to Derrida and Caputo, the particular religions must be deconstructed.

It is this fervent desire for justice that explains the ambivalent attitude deconstruction maintains toward concrete institutions and particular communities of more or less determinable faith. I have already signaled my discomfort with what I perceive as a certain one-sidedness in this assessment of determinable faith, one that focuses on its dangers and tends to gloss over its edifying contributions. Before exploring this complex issue, however, I must first explore deconstruction's recognition of the unavoidable necessity of these human institutions.

Dangerous liaisons: the unavoidable risk of society

In *Dynamics of Faith*, Paul Tillich asks two question that are central to my present concerns:

> Can a community of faith—e.g., a church—accept a faith which includes doubt as an intrinsic element and calls the seriousness of doubt an expression of faith? And even if it could allow such an atti-

tude in its ordinary members, how could it permit the same in its leaders?[10]

So far, what we have been hearing from Caputo and Derrida is some pretty serious doubt about whether institutions such as churches are capable of sustaining such doubt. Caputo argues that:

> the Church will only allow this scrambled situation to get so far before it calls the police. The Church can always establish a biblical commission to settle . . . disputes and to keep the identity of everybody on the line clear, and generally to keep everybody in line, or else. The Church will tolerate the anarchy or energy of *écriture* only so long before it puts its institutional, foundationalist foot down.[11]
>
> (91)

Still, according to Tillich,

> the act of faith, like every act in man's spiritual life, is dependent on language and therefore on community. . . . Only as a member of such a community (even if in isolation or expulsion) can man have a content for his ultimate concern. Only in a community of language can man actualize his faith.[12]

For its part, deconstruction has not failed to notice this same necessity. As Caputo argues,

> Everyone privileges something; no one speaks pure chaos; we are all always and already factically situated in some *determinable* faith or another, some *determinable* socio-historico-linguistic world or matrix or another. How could it be otherwise? The danger is only to think that your privileged name cannot be translated, that if someone does not use it, they are against you, like the Pope and his Buddhists, so that when the Pope says, from his balcony, *urbi et orbi*, "my God," he wants the whole city and the whole world to fall in line with him.
>
> (68)

In this passage, Caputo has in my opinion appropriately evoked both the necessity and danger of determinable faith. Elsewhere, he even recognizes that life/death in the absolute desert of deconstructionistic messianicity may be unlivable and that perhaps "messianic hope cannot live apart from the 'determinable faiths'—or even that deconstruction, which is marked by the *gage* or *engagement* of a determinable faith, is something like a certain messianism" (150). Still, I wonder whether we need to deconstruct positive religion in order to rid ourselves of dogmatic exclusivism. For does not the actually existing plurality of determinable faiths already attest to the reality of translative dissemination that deconstruction describes, and thus provide its own opportunity to question this religious exclusivism? Perhaps that is what writers like Derrida and Caputo have been saying all along, that translative dissemination happens and is not performed (by deconstruction, at any rate). Yet their work still leaves me hoping for the possibility that determinate communities can retain a sense of unique identity and still coexist in peace. I hope for a peace, I suppose, that does not require everyone to undergo the arid ascesis of deconstruction's abstract messianicity.

My problem is that deconstruction's recognition of the necessity of determinate institutions is too grudging. It is not enough for us to be wary of the potential dangers of a robust sense of community identity, as Caputo reminds us so effectively in the above passage. No, we must find something inherently violent in the very notion of community itself. For deconstruction, Caputo says, the word "community" connotes:

> a military formation, the wall of protection that the same builds against the other, the way a "people" (the "same") builds a common fortification (*com, munire*) around itself against the other, gathering itself together into One in order to keep safe the uniqueness of its archive. In doing such violence to the other, the One makes itself violent, and tries violently to erase the trace of its own self-differing identity, to make itself One without difference. It guards itself from the other *pour se faire violence*: "because" and "in order to" make/do itself violence.
>
> (271–72)

The dangerous situation Caputo here describes is, of course, always a possibility. But is it a necessity? Could we not think of a community's desire to preserve the uniqueness of its archive *sans* the dogmatic assertiveness that leads to such violence? Would this not also be an affirmation of pluralism, since each group would be able to preserve its own archive without thereby attempting to destroy the other's?

It is this grudging acceptance of institutions as a necessary violence that troubles me about deconstruction. This positioning allows for rather blanket condemnations of determinable faith such as the following:

God rules not in Rome but in the victims of Rome. God rules not in the churches but in the inner cities which the churches abandon as soon as the Sunday contributions fall off. God rules not in respectable upper middle class mostly white suburban families but among the unwed mothers and fatherless children of inner cities whom the churches, perfidiously in league with the right wing, teach us to resent and despise as lazy freeloaders.

(247)

Quite simply, this assessment of determinable faith is a cheap shot at the ambiguous life of institutional religion. One does not have to renounce the determinability of institutionalized religion in order to reject the politics of fundamentalism. Nor is fundamentalism the whole story about the institutional life of religions. I suppose I am frustrated that deconstructionists, who in a certain sense see themselves as defenders of faith, are not willing to go as far in this defense as Barry Allen, a non-religious Canadian philosopher, recently has:

> I read in the newspaper that a coalition of churches in Toronto is (once again) providing sanctuary to 23 illegal aliens whose refugee claims have been denied and who face deportation to a country where they fear for their lives. A spokesperson for the coalition, a Catholic nun, says, "there is a long biblical tradition of sanctuary, in which God is revealed in the dignity of the person. When civil procedures no longer guarantee that the image of God in the person's dignity can be protected, then we have to provide sanctuary."

Allen concludes his observation with the following question: "Who today but the churches would or could pose this non-violent moral counter-power to state administration?"[13] The institutional church's ability to provide refuge is one example of a concrete way in which it answers to the solicitation of the *tout autre*, and it should be recognized as such. Even Emmanuel Levinas remarks that, while Christians during the Second World War did little to resist Nazism, nevertheless, "wherever the black robe was to be seen there was refuge."[14] This is the other side of institutional church life that deconstruction seems unwilling or unable to celebrate and affirm. Yet I do not think that encouraging this side of that life runs the risk of fostering a violent identitarian politics or an exclusive dogmatism.[15]

Uniqueness without exclusivism among communities of the blind

Having articulated my troubles in this way, I would nonetheless like to conclude this chapter by affirming the style of ethical comportment Caputo
urges us to adopt in our communal-institutional life. For Caputo,

> The danger that inheres in the determinate faiths—the "positive"
> religions—which are a little too positive—is that they will confuse seeing
> and believing and forget that the eyes of faith are blind. That is when
> they become intolerant of other faiths: "It is always the other who you
> did not see."
>
> (313)

In the name of justice for this other, deconstruction recommends that we
drop our dogmatic exclusivism, which too often marks the way in which we
find our identity within determinate communities, and admit a certain
blindness. Caputo says:

> To these conflicting visions, Derrida opposes a community, if it is one, of
> the blind, *une communauté aveugle*, of the blind leading the blind. Blind-
> ness makes for good communities, provided we all admit that we do not
> see, that in crucial matters we are all stone blind and without privileged
> access, adrift in the same boat, without a lighthouse to show the other shore.
>
> (313–14)

I have been arguing, but perhaps praying and hoping are better words, that
we can admit such blindness and still have a plurality of identitarian communities, communities whose walls are indeed meant to protect and guard
their archives from foreign invasion, but whose walls can also be used to
shelter and provide sanctuary for strangers in trouble, while simultaneously
allowing for the possibility of inter-library loans between different groups. As
Caputo himself says,

> The uncontestable fact for Derrida is that we are in need of archives: *nous
> sommes en mal d'archive*. The living past cannot rise up from the dead
> and speak to us like dead stones. . . . We must pick our way among the
> remains, wrestle with and conjure the ghosts of the past, ply them with
> patient importunity in order to reconstruct the best story we can.
>
> (273–74)

I could not agree more with this ethical recommendation. Admitting such blindness and lack of direct epistemological access is a crucial part of saving the *viens* which deconstruction so fervently wants to affirm. Although I am not sure whether *deconstruction* delivers these goods, I nonetheless agree that we require "a certain salutary purgation of the positivity of belief, which reminds us all that we do not know what is coming, what is *tout autre*" (150). Deconstruction, itself not far removed from a certain religious faith, does well to remind us that "we do not know what God is, or whether we believe in God or not, or whether what we believe in is God or not, or what we love when we love our God" (150–51).

So with deconstruction I say *Viens*. Thy kingdom come. But with a twist (or, rather, is the kingdom messian*ism* of traditional Christianity itself twisted?): "The kingdom is a community in which the solitude of my accusation, my inescapable identity, the relentless recursivity of my being accused is relieved, lifted up, into a community of those who are forgiven and who forgive one another" (228). It is only when we admit our mutual blindness that we find the humility to forgive one another and let the kingdom come, a kingdom of justice and peace, and no more tears. I can do no better, then, than to agree with Emmanuel Levinas when he says that

> The unity of plurality is peace, and not the coherence of the elements that constitute plurality. Peace therefore cannot be identified with the end of combats that cease for want of combatants, by the defeat of some and the victory of the others, that is, with cemeteries or future universal empires. Peace must be my peace, in a relation that starts from an I and goes to the other, in desire and goodness, where the I both maintains itself and exists without egoism.[16]

Notes

1 Research for this chapter was supported in part by a fellowship from the Social Sciences and Humanities Research Council of Canada, whose support is gratefully acknowledged.

2 Emmanuel Levinas, *Totality and Infinity: An Essay on Exteriority*, Alphonso Lingis, trans. (Pittsburgh: Duquesne University Press, 1969), p. 40.

3 I am still haunted by the TV-commercial image of the man whose remaining life flashes before his eyes, *augenblicklich*, after his wife tells him she is pregnant. Of course, his remaining years are shown to be filled with bliss and happiness as he watches his newborn daughter grow up, go to college, marry, and return home with grandchildren, where he sits in the garage, polishing the brass on the yacht which, presumably, he purchased with his significant RRSP earnings. As the commercial returns us to the present from this idyllic future-present, we hear the wife ask the husband worriedly: "Are we going to be OK?" whereupon he confidently assures her, calling to mind the RRSP to which he has just contributed, "We're going to be just fine."

4 Thank God, by the way, for the Canadian Broadcasting Corporation—commercial-free, institutional-totalitarian, state-sponsored radio!—for airing such an urgent call to responsibility.

5 Please excuse this lame attempt at a pun, but when I run my word processor's spell-checking function, it always asks me if I want to change "Derrida" to "derides," something that initially made me laugh so hard that I have yet to enter "Derrida" into my word processor's dictionary so that the joke can be repeated *ad infinitum*. I still don't know what to make of the program's suggestion to replace Heidegger with "headgear," although I suppose that if you see yourself as a one-man philosophical demolition crew, it would be wise to don a helmet.

6 In fact, one might say that the effect of this invention tends to be more extreme for conservatives such as my father, even if its occurrence more rare, because they often lack the ears to hear the warning, "incoming!," and are thus unable, structurally unable, to duck or find cover.

7 I realize that in this forum we are putting Caputo in the unenviable position of being the locus of a "critical reading," perhaps expecting him to reveal a secret he does not have. But as he himself claims, this artificial arrangement is not without its value, for the troubling of a text, the extent to which it bears and rewards troubling (if indeed I am even capable of getting that far, realizing that *my* troubles might not be all that troubling) is also a mark of its worth. As Caputo himself says, in reference to Derrida's writing: "The worth and the value of . . . texts . . . lies in the 'stimulus' they provide, 'the germ of passion' they plant, the 'passions' they arouse, the controversies and contested readings they impassion and provoke, the sparks that fly up in the clash of contesting interpretations" (110). So I will now let the sparks fly in my exploration of this book that has had no trouble fanning the flames of my hermeneutic passion.

8 *Dynamics of Faith* (New York: Harper & Row, 1957), p.19.

9 Ontario Premier Mike Harris exhibited this latter attitude recently, when he justified his government's cutting of a food stipend for single mothers with the explanation that, while the government would still provide for them, they would no longer be able to squander this public money on beer.

10 *Dynamics of Faith*, p. 23.

11 An example of this is a recent lengthy synodical report of the Christian Reformed Church which settles the issue concerning whether or not it is appropriate to address God with maternal metaphors. The study concludes that God prefers masculine imagery, and that while the desire to speak of God as mother is understandable, official church policy should discourage this way of speaking as ultimately lacking biblical support.

12 *Dynamics of Faith*, p. 24.

13 "Atheism, relativism, enlightenment and truth," *Studies in Religion/Sciences Religieuses* 23 (2) (1994): 171, n. 11.

14 "Judaism and Christianity" in *In the Time of the Nations*, Michael B. Smith, trans. (London: Athlone Press, 1994), p. 162. This piece is a transcription of a conversation between Levinas and Bishop Hemmerle. The full text surrounding the citation reads: "Then comes what you call the Holocaust and what we call the *Shoah*. At that time two things became very clear. First, the fact that all who participated in the *Shoah* had, in their childhood, received a Catholic or Protestant baptism; and they found no interdiction in that! And the second fact, very, very, important: during that period, what you call charity or mercy appeared to me directly. Wherever the black robe was to be seen, there was refuge. There discourse was still possible. A world without recourse is one of despair."

15 On the recent formation of such a sanctuary coalition by various Christian

groups, see Andrew Brouwer, "Living in limbo: Kurdish refugee Sami Durgun's struggle for justice" in *The Catalyst: A Publication of Citizens for Public Justice* 21 (3) (May–June, 1998): 3–4.

16 *Totality and Infinity*, p. 306.

3 "Religion without religion"[1]
Caputo, Derrida, and the violence of particularity[2]

Shane Cudney

> The question is not whether there is a *désir de Dieu*, a passion for God in Jacques Derrida. Who could ever doubt that? . . . the question is, rather, the one put by his North African "compatriot" St. Augustine: "what do I love when I love my God?" Upon the groundless ground of this beautiful and bottomless question . . . Derrida's life and work is an extended commentary.
>
> (xxii)

Introduction: religion without religion

In his most recent book, *The Prayers and Tears of Jacques Derrida*, John Caputo returns to a careful and sensitive—indeed, surprising—rereading of "Derrida's later, more autobiographical pieces" (xxiv–xxv), a rendering that emphasizes that "[w]e will read him [Derrida] less and less well unless we hear the [deeply religious] yes that punctuates and accents the text, the yes to the promise that resonates throughout all his works, a yes first, a yes last, a constant yes. *Oui, oui*" (xxiii). Anticipating the blow that his "academic colleagues" and "secularizing friends" no doubt will suffer from the very idea of linking Derrida with religion, people "for whom the only blasphemy is infidelity to Nietzsche, whom I will have shocked and traumatized by this provocative scene of Derrida weeping at his *prie-Dieu*," Caputo begs their pardon and implores their forgiveness in advance (xxvi).[3]

In a passionate, deconstructive bid to avoid the violence associated with traditional, content-full "religions of the Book" (136), Caputo, following Derrida, proposes an alternative "religion without religion," a posture that, while committed to the general structure of religion, attempts to distance itself from the specific historical exemplifications of that structure. In the same way that a flower defies the rigid dictates of a concrete jungle and finds its way to the surface in an affirmative burst of life, deconstruction is in the business of insinuating itself into the cracks and crevices of the present in a way that "works the provocation of what is to come, . . . against the complacency of the present, against the pleasure the present takes in itself, in order to prevent it from closing in on itself, from collapsing into self-identity" (xx). So strained and bent are the sails of deconstruction "toward what is coming," so deep runs "its posture of expectancy, its passion for the impossible," that it would be "absolutely" impossible for the Messiah to arrive in the flesh (xxiii). This is the "law of the impossible, the 'impossible-rule,'" which means "never to confuse his coming (*venue*) with being present, . . . never to collapse the coming of the just one into the order of what is present or absent" (xxiv).

But what are we to make of this religion without religion, of what Caputo will refer to as a religion of the desert; what are we to do with this region that is haunted by the ghost of a bloodless and bodiless Messiah? What are we to "think" of the attempt to relegate religion to the realm of reason alone (154–55), the desire to confine its content within the bounds of a certain abstraction?[4] Is not the attempt to "bracket" all *doxa* a posture that is itself committed to a certain ideal that inevitably harbors determinate features? How is one able to maintain a universal religion without driving a wedge between faith (*pistis*) and faith(s)? Considering that deconstruction emphasizes the retrieval of a full-bodied existence from a tradition that has often sacrificed the particular (body) on the altar of the universal (ideal), these are curious anomalies, to be sure.

In this chapter, I propose that by determining the motive behind what I will argue is a (philosophical) rift between the "messianic" and Abrahamic "messianisms," we will be able to catch a glimpse of the elusive specter that animates the deconstructive gesture, an "in-site" that will allow us to call into question this "desert religion" (155), or, if you will, "'prophetic postmodernism'" (150).[5] In so doing, I will suggest that something new is able to emerge, a radicalized, post-Kierkaardian-type faith, one might say, rooted in the suffering love of God, one that repeats the possibility of religion within the limits of faith, and faith within the limits of religion. This remythologized myth of justice attempts the "impossible:" to honor both the universal structure of religion and the particular, historical instantiations of that structure.

On the "messianic" and "messianisms"

Part III ('The messianic') of *Prayers and Tears* is arguably the heart of Caputo's text, not only because it is here that we feel its prophetico-messianic pulse, but also because it is here that we find Caputo holding Derrida's hand to the fire of religion, a gesture he believes is necessary if deconstruction is to be consistently deconstructive; that is, true to its original ideals, faithful to its "founding vision," if we can say such things.

Because of his increasing concern for those who fall through the cracks and get crushed by the political and religious power structures that be, his hypersensitivity to the violence done in the name of particular "messianisms" of the Marxist, neo-Hegelian, Islamic, or Christian type, Derrida, like Levinas before him, began by the early 1990s to think in terms of a general "messianic" structure, "one that is cut to fit the hand of deconstruction" (117). By 1994, however, Caputo observes that between the two editions of "The force of law"[6] Derrida had sharpened the edges of deconstruction on the whetstone of Marxism, which produced a messianic structure that took on the form of a more conventional universal, one that seemed more distant from the nitty-gritty of particularity. With a raised eyebrow, yet with a religious reverence, Jack the "bookkeeper" has taken it upon himself to follow Jack the "ragpicker"[7] with an outstretched hand, waiting to catch him lest he fall into the ditch of old philosophical debates that deconstruction is supposed to gingerly avoid. In this "game of Jacks" (xxiv), one might irreverently say that Jack is watching out for Jack's *derrière.*

In the final pages of *Specters of Marx,*[8] Derrida elaborates on the distinction between the messianic and messianisms by posing the following question in a certain straightforward kind of way that seems to turn, as Caputo suggests, on the classical distinction between form and content, between the universal and the particular, "between a 'universal' structure and the concrete realization or embodiment of that structure, between ... 'a structure of experience' and a 'religion'" (135). Derrida formulates the question as follows: "If the messianic appeal belongs properly to a universal structure ... how is one to think it with the figures of Abraham[ic] messianism?"[9] But, on Derrida's own terms, this is a less than adequate formulation.[10] Indeed, are we really to believe that Derrida has finally come home to roost? Has he not spent his entire life attempting to deprive us of the familiar creature comforts of home? Yet, given this present formulation, Derrida does seem to pose two possibilities: either the messianic structure precedes the concrete messianism as an "originary condition," or the concrete messianisms come before the messianic structure as its origin. "Does Abrahamic messianism serve as the source or origin from which we derive an abstract concept of the messianic? Or is the messianic a condition of possibility that antedates the concrete messianisms which are but exemplifications of it?" (135).

What is important to emphasize, especially for the purpose of our discussion, is that these questions bear not only on the relationship between faith, religion and philosophy, but also on the nature of the pre-theoretical commitments that undergird and infuse all of our theoretical endeavors. And while there are distinct religio-prophetic overtones in Derrida's use of this distinction, the very attempt to keep religion(s) at bay—a gap that Caputo will creatively try to negotiate (139–43)—betrays a certain alliance with the Western tradition that needs to be teased out and questioned. By attempting to suspend the content that faith itself entails, is it possible that Derrida (and Caputo) paradoxically conflate religion and faith? And could it be that the very move that paves the way for his structural religion is one that harbors a motive similar to that which gave rise to the traditional distinction between faith and philosophy? We will return to these questions below.

So, the aforementioned Derridean dilemma, Caputo observes, leads us back to a similar Heideggerian (Marburgian) formulation:

> Can there be an "atheological heritage" of the biblical messianisms? Can one strip the biblical messianisms down to an atheological core? Can one, by a work of "desertification" and denuding, by a deconstructive ascesis, remove a biblical surface from a messianic structure?
>
> (135)

In other words, the question is whether Derrida's quasi-atheistic messianic is the condition for biblical messianisms,[11] or an aftereffect, a distillation derived from particular religious accounts, in which case, "[t]he messianic in general would be a conceptual ghost, a specter of philosophy, a poor abstraction, whose cash value is drawn from the accounts of the religions of the Book" (136).

In Derrida's own (English) words, he emphasizes the difficulty that surrounds his "religion without religion", a problem that he promises to return to, but constantly defers.

> The problem remains . . . whether the religions, say, for instance, the religions of the Book, are but specific examples of this general structure of messianicity. There is the general structure of messianicity, as a structure of experience, and on this groundless ground there have been revelations, a history which one calls Judaism or Christianity and so on. That is one possibility, and then you would have a Heideggerian gesture, in style. You would have to go back from these religions to the fundamental ontological conditions of possibilities of religion, to describe the structure of messianicity on the ground of groundless ground on which religions have been made possible.
>
> That is one hypothesis. The other hypothesis—and I confess that I hesitate between these two possibilities—is that the events of revelation . . . have been absolute events, irreducible events which have unveiled this messianicity. We would not know what messianicity is without messianism, without these events which were Abraham, Moses, and Jesus Christ,

and so on. In that case singular events would have unveiled or revealed these universal possibilities and it is only on that condition that we can describe messianicity.[12]

Although Derrida insists that there exists a certain complementarity between these two possibilities, and that he oscillates between them, I suggest that he unwittingly favors one of his sons because it is "impossible" not to, given, that is, my reading of the assumption that underlies the formulation. On the surface, at least, what allows Derrida to linger on the threshold between these two spaces, in the manner he believes he can, is the notion that religious faith and philosophy are quite distinct from one another. Because the philosopher can only say so much, eventually philosophy pushes against the limits of its horizon, beyond which only faith and angels dare to tread. Indeed, whoever or whatever is calling must remain anonymous, and this anonymity is the horizon of faith. The undecidability that surrounds the above distinction between which Derrida oscillates exists primarily because we are dealing here with philosophical knowledge which by definition excludes religious faith. Even though Derrida and Caputo insist that a religious-like trust undergirds and precedes our theorizing, their language betrays a certain "commitment" to, or shall we say faith in, a rather traditional distinction. The assumption that gives shape to this posture I will deal with in the final section of this chapter.

While Caputo is rightly concerned about the drift of deconstruction, and has plotted his own course, adjusting his sail accordingly, my hunch is that because he too sees determinate religions through the lens of a religious (overarching?) structure, he is unable to pull away from Derrida's wake.

On the disjunction between the "messianic" and "messianisms"

Not completely content, then, with swabbing the deck of the good ship "messianic" which purportedly leads to justice, a justice that is always to come, Caputo has, in the spirit of *Radical Hermeneutics*,[13] launched out for himself in order to situate himself on the side of the deconstructive strait that is closest to Kierkegaard. Inspired by the spirit of deconstruction and religious faith, Caputo has cause to question Derrida's recent formulation of the messianic and the implicit "either/or" assumptions which are beginning to leak from it. In an effort to rescue deconstruction from being drawn into "old debates" that would pull it into the whirlpool of some sort of Jewish or even Judeo-Christian philosophy, Caputo insists that these "two standpoints complement rather than compete with each other and it is not a matter of choosing between them" (137). As I have already implied, it is because decon-struction "constitutes a certain anti-essentialism or nominalism" that Caputo is worried that Derrida's formulation of the question problematizes the whole discussion by framing it

> within an assured set of distinctions ... which is the whole point of deconstruction to disturb. For deconstruction ... ought not to be drawn into any debates about whether facts precede essences or essences precede facts, or whether each precedes the other but in different orders and in different ways.
>
> (138)

According to Caputo, if we pay close attention to Derrida's "absolute events" (138), we will see that he means something that is not a specific instance of something more general. "In the messianic time of singularities, historical happenings are idiosyncratic 'events' and not 'moments' in a larger, teleological or eschatological movement" (138). Moreover, given the "Babel-ianism of deconstruction and its delimitation of the traditional idea of trans-lation ... Derrida can hardly put himself in the position of saying that the 'messianic' represents the overarching, universal, metalanguage into which the various concrete messianisms can be translated" (138). The matter does get muddled, however, when Derrida goes so far as to say that he is in search of "a universalizable culture of singularities,"[14] "where every other is wholly other." In this case, one must ask with Caputo: What kind of universality does he have in mind here? Indeed, how can he avoid employing a good old-fashioned universal in all of this? The question of how one is to "describe the status of this indeterminability, this indeterminable messianic ... which can-not be a true or conventional or garden variety universal" (138–39) is the challenge.

Faced with the seeming incommensurability of these competing possi-bilities, Caputo pulls the notion of "formal indication" from his erstwhile Heideggerian hat in order to remedy the situation. This notion, he tells us, unlike the traditional philosophical concept which attempts to encompass and comprehend its object, is purportedly a nonobjectifying indicator,

> a projective sketch that traces out in advance certain salient features of an entity or region of entities. ... The formal indication is not a universal that "contains" "particulars" "underneath" it, but a sign ... pointing to a region where it itself cannot enter.
>
> (138–39)

Caputo is convinced that because the "formal indication" is akin to the factical (immanent) region, it has no transcendental compulsion to control and contain the particulars in a universal meta-net. Understanding the factical requires, then, a certain *Einstellung*, a comportment which leaves philosophy to its own devices, while a detached, philosophically and religiously stripped, ethically sensitive questioning attitude breaks through, in Heidegger's case, into the "prephilosophical" "'revolutionary' experiences" of "the New Testament and the Nichomachean Ethics" (138–39).

Heidegger employed his notion of formal indication, based as it is on the fundamental distrust—indeed, violence—of philosophical discourse, in the business of incessantly questioning traditional categories of thought. Thus, he attempted to forge, as Caputo says,

> a quasi-conceptuality, formed of "formal indications" which are related to the singularity of existence, to factical life, as imperfect sketches or anticipatory foreshadowings of a prior and irreducible excess, an excess that can only be "engaged" or entered into existentially, not grasped conceptually.
>
> (140)

Because the particular is not taken as an inferior chip off the universal block, because "the singular is not a fall (*casus*) from universality whose feet are soaked by the particularity of matter or potency" (140), Caputo sees this Heideggerian gesture as one that might moisten Derrida's parched lips enough to bring him out of a state of heat exhaustion which has induced these very spooky and disturbing hallucinations.

On this account, the messianic would be a more benevolent, modest universal, one that has no pretensions, no illusions of grandeur. However, says Caputo, there is a certain price one pays in traveling the low road of facticity. For if Derrida were to steadfastly follow this less trodden, more difficult path, he would have to concede that the messianic is historically conditioned, which means that he would have to admit—indeed, "confess"—that it harbors "determinable features" (142), which in turn levels the ground to the extent that his "religion without religion" would be ushered into the realm of competing messianisms. "So rather than taking Derrida's messianic as in any way overarching the three historical messianisms of the religions of the Book," Caputo thinks it is more helpful to see it as "one more messianism but with a deconstructive twist" (142). "After all," insists Caputo,

> the Derridean messianic does have certain determinable features, some of which . . . it has borrowed from the prophetic tradition, and some of

which are Derrida's own invention. For Derrida's messianic is through and through an ethico-political idea, having to do all the way down with justice and a democracy to come, and organized under the idea of the "new International." Having begun, like everyone else, and just as he himself predicts, where one is . . . Derrida's messianic has emerged under determinate historical conditions and takes a determinate form.

(142)

On the motive for the disjunction between the "messianic" and "messianisms"

In all of this, Caputo has rightly and inventively attempted to undo the dilemma that deconstruction seems to have worked itself into. That Caputo has, it seems paradoxically, opened some breathing room between the two "spaces" with the help of Heidegger's formal indication, there is little doubt. The question is: Is this necessarily a better way to keep the future from being closed off? Is this enough of a departure from Derrida to make a difference? Must we conclude that to minimize the inevitable violence of particular messianisms, one must "formalize" or bracket out religion? Although in *Prayers and Tears* Caputo presents us with a demythologized Heidegger who has received deconstructive "treatments," what concerns me about this alternative are the assumptions that undergird the idea that there exists some "non-objectifying," "atheistic," "quasi," or "certain" kind of language, a way of thinking or poeticizing that is able to pull away from and, in effect, detach (or, at the very least, distance) itself from the violence of discourse.

While Caputo's version of the messianic is no doubt a more humble, modest universal, I maintain that because it drinks from the same philosophical cistern as Derrida, it does not—indeed, cannot—sufficiently loosen the ties that presently bind deconstruction. So even though Caputo has kept the philosophical dust from settling (something he does quite well), it seems to me that his "neutered" universal, this demasculinized, gelded, more subdued Heideggerianism still cannot genuinely connect with or penetrate the surface of concrete religions, even if it can sing a little higher. Stripped of its aggressive, violent tendencies, the problem is that this docile, more manageable messianic is also stripped of certain very human, gonadian features, which also strikes me as violent.

Although Caputo assures us that on his accounting the singular is not "a fall (*casus*) from universality" (140), I suggest that the singular is a fall within particularity.[15] This means (à la Heidegger) that because every philosophical move, every decision, is structurally finite, they are seen as "'cuts,'" incisions which necessarily amputate and exclude.[16] Indeed, for this reason, the very gesture of philosophy is one of violence. With Derrida, Caputo has all along maintained that the origin is always already fissured from the beginning, that at the origin of language, prior to empirical violence, there is the "arche-violence" of "arche-writing" with its "harsh law of spacing" as "an originary accessory and an essential accident."[17] As such, that which is constitutive to human be-ing is considered structurally violent. Thus, to be human is to be caught in a web of necessary violence. This construal, I suggest, is precisely what binds deconstruction, and what links Caputo and Derrida to one another and to the tradition they rightly seek to deconstruct.

On the surface, at least, the rather obvious reason for the quasi-ascetic, linguistic acrobatics and inventions that surround the production of Derrida's (and Caputo's) "religion without religion" is the violence that determinate "content-full" faiths inevitably inflict in the name of the Law, Truth, and Messiahs. No doubt religions of the Book have a disturbing legacy of violence, and for this reason both Derrida and Caputo consider it imperative to develop a general structure of justice that highlights a desert-like, ascetic detachment from the historical expressions of such a structure. Derrida believes this is necessary, for

> [a]s soon as you reduce the messianic structure to messianism, then you are reducing the universality and this has important political consequences. Then you are accrediting one tradition among others and a notion of an elected people, of a given literal language, a given fundamentalism.[18]

The question of structural violence leads us back another step to the question of trust (that is, (religious) faith (*pistis*), construed here in the broadest possible sense), to the assumption that undergirds and gives shape to the motive to develop a general structure of religion. If the general messianic, on Derrida's account, is the condition for specific messianisms, is it not also true that his belief in this structure presupposes a certain trust, a certain faith in the primordiality of the heterogenous, desert-like "placeless displacing place" (154) called *khôra*, whose sister is the messianic, the place where an a-personal justice from nowhere resides?[19] And if discourse remains grounded in faith, as Derrida himself confesses in *Memoirs of the Blind*,[20] is it not possible to think otherwise than of *khôra* as the condition for im/possibility? And might not this other birth-space produce different offspring?

In an attempt to escape the strictures of ousiology, which inevitably harbours secrets, Derrida, in his article "How not to speak,"[21] which Caputo highlights, has us trek to the far side of negativity, where he explores the analogy and the disanalogy of the *khôra* with the God of negative theology, a place where we are taken to the very limits of language—and beyond. Here Derrida paints a picture of the tension in Plato between what he calls the "two movements or two tropics of negativity,"[22] the "two opposing ways in which philosophical thought finds itself up against its limits . . . two things equally unsayable but for quite opposite reasons."[23] While the first movement presses toward that high hyperousiological point above the clouds which inspires awe in both Neoplatonists and negative theologians alike, the second movement slips under the border of being, below phenomenality, beyond the reach of "all anthropo-theological schemes, all history, all revelation, all truth."[24] This no-place called *khôra* "is neither form (idea), nor sensible thing, but the place (lieu) in which the demiurge impresses or cuts images of the intelligible paradigms, the place which was already there," a "pre-originary origin from nowhere" (35).

Like the owl 'Old Brown' in Beatrix Potter's classic, who has a penchant for honey which lies beyond his means to reach, Derrida takes a keen interest in *khôra* precisely because of its ability to "resist any analogizing or participatory schema, to remain adrift and lost."[25] "*Khôra* is neither present nor absent, active nor passive, the Good nor evil, living nor nonliving." It is "[n]either theomorphic nor anthropomorphic;" rather, it is "atheological and nonhuman" (35–36). Indeed, *khôra* must have no recourse to "meaning," "essence," or "identity." Otherwise, in the language of the gift, it becomes implicated in the economy of exchange, where it would take on the appearance of the giver of all good gifts, a giver that no doubt will eventually come to collect. This re-inscription into the same goes against the "impossible-rule" because "the *khôra* is *tout autre*, very" (36). In order, then, to avoid the violence that lurks behind every tree in a "tit for tat," "dog eat dog" jungle economy, Derrida prefers to speak of the aridity of the desert, a haunted place where messianic spirits love to hide.

But (seriously) what are we to make of the nonhistorical, historical names of *khôra* and her sibling the messianic? How are we to "think" of this placeless place that cannot be "assimilated into philosophy" or religion, this place that historical "things do not in any way stain or mark," that "belongs to a time out of mind, out of memory," out of sight?[26] Through this lens, one can certainly see why Derrida and Caputo cannot say whether *khôra* gives or does not give, why one must ask: "What do I love when I love my God, God or *khôra*? How are we to decide? Do we have to choose?" (37). As I suggested earlier, what this produces is the notion that philosophy can say only so much. Because the philosopher can say only so much, philosophy itself eventually pushes against the limits of its horizon, a point at which philosophy is a little lost for words and finds itself beginning to stutter as it looks for the exit sign.

As far back as *Radical Hermeneutics*,[27] Caputo articulated this same sentiment when he emphasized that one cannot say whether Nietzsche (the tragic) or Kierkegaard (the religious) is right because philosophy is not in the business of making this kind of decision. Not surprisingly, this same distinction is re-peated in *Against Ethics*, where Caputo once again is backed into a philosophical corner when he finds himself unable to say who or what it is that calls, *il* or *il y a*.[28] Things happen, Caputo says, "[t]hey happen 'because' (*weil*) they happen. . . . There is no 'why.' . . . What happens is what there is (*es gibt*). That is all."[29] In Caputo's latest work, the distinction re-peats itself once again in the form of "religion without religion," a messianic without messianisms. Faith in or "passion for the impossible," as he calls it, must keep the messianic in the realm of the *viens*, for once we pull justice into the realm of the possible, it is given over to distortion and violence, a place where "moth and rust doth corrupt."

On my reading, the way Caputo slices the pie (something we all do, of course, if we want a piece) is reminiscent of a Thomistic gesture which dictates that faith remain extrinsic to philosophy. If it is true that humanity is insatiably religious, if we are fundamentally creatures of faith, whose profound experience of both the brokenness and the goodness of life find us hoping and praying, spiralling and re-peating forward, it is difficult to imagine faith being absent from or extrinsic to any mode of being-in-the-world. Indeed, it is hard to imagine a "call" without a "gift," a "yes" without the strings that a symbiotic relationship necessarily entails.

It seems to me that even though Caputo and Derrida posit a "gift," a religio-ethical "yes" which comes before all of life and language, this "yes" is in danger of being nullified, swallowed up by a Barthian-like "no" which is posited against any and all determinate commitments. If it is true that this *ankhôral* "no" is synonymous with Derrida's fractured pre-originary origin, whence come love and the possibility of justice? And if justice is always to come, always "impossible," how is it that evil and violence are not conflated with goodness and thereby put on equal footing? What else can we make of the kind of violence that "always crosses the distance of the other," a violence that permeates and "violates the space of the other"? Is not this kind of "radical evil" the stuff on which deconstruction's "desert, *khôral, ankhôral* religion stands or falls" (158)?

It seems clear that what we are left with here is a justice that is relegated to the realm of chance, and manifests itself only as a random flash-in-the-pan event that immediately burns up upon entering our atmosphere. What kind of justice is this? Must the beautiful thought of justice turn immediately ugly upon its arrival? Might there be another "possibility," another way to navigate the deconstructive strait between the messianic and messianism, another way to prevent the future from being closed off?

While Derrida and Caputo believe that their structural religion is the cleanest dirty way to keep the future open, what bothers me is the same thing that troubles me as a parent: more often than not, I find myself in the frustrating position of saying to my kids the very things that my father said to me, things that I vowed I would never say. Somehow, in some insidious way, they ooze out, betraying a familial bond that runs deeper than we would sometimes like to think. In deconstruction's zeal to purge philosophy of its violence, I hear other voices, a cacophony of past and present voices, one of which it seems to me sanctions a neo-Scholastic bifurcation that, in its deconstructive expression, relegates religious faith to a place that excludes it as a mode of knowing. Though, admittedly, faith knowing cannot be reduced to philosophical knowing, I do suggest that faith permeates every mode of human experience. Whether we are witnessing a beautiful sunset, smelling cowslips in the field, or reflecting on Kierkegaard's *Concept of Anxiety*, are we not always already surrendering to the experience of the world, which is the very condition of knowing the world?

Conclusion: religion within faith

While I have no doubt that an affirmative—indeed, religio-ethical—"yes" marks the texts of both philosophers, it seems to me that this bite-sized "yes" inevitably gets swallowed up in the "heterodidactics between life and death."[30] If this is the case, might it be possible to enlarge this "yes"? Is it possible that this affirmative "yes" can be rethought of as an (inter)personal, life-giving "yes"? And could we say that this "yes" is synonymous with love, a love that is the oxygen that is the very condition for the possibility of all our particular faith(s), whatever they might be?

This shift in emphasis would highlight the reality that, because we live in a world of both connection and disconnection, it is not a matter of oscillating back and forth in a volatile, quasi-neutral space between two absolutes, attempting to escape the tyranny of two despots, being spooked (*Es spukt*)[31] by the "ghost of full presence."[32] The focus, instead, would become more persistently ethical, becoming a question not of how one is to escape violence, but of how one is to respond to the call of love. Indeed, in this economy, the call of love is at once a "gift" that compels us to respond, and a "call" that can be ignored, refused, and abused.

Moreover, this shift would radicalize the notion of undecidability by highlighting the reality that human beings are inherently religious. As we are creatures of faith who are always already caught in the grip of precariously held beliefs, it makes good ethical sense to bring our particular faiths to the fore and confess them (in "fear and trembling"). It is here, in plain view, that we "myth-makers" will be better able to keep our stories, and their potential for violence, in check.

Although Caputo remains religiously committed to his *ankhôral* religion of withdrawal, which implicates him in Derrida's dilemma, this is not an altogether bad thing on my reading. For by conceding that Derrida's absolute desert is unlivable, and that the messianic hope cannot live apart from the determinable faiths, Caputo's analysis not only allows for a certain content, but also admits of a certain genealogy and geography (142) which helps bring the messianic closer to the messianisms. For despite his protestations to the contrary, Derrida's "religion" has very determinable features, which include an affinity for a particular form of democracy and a very specific brand of prophetic justice (142). Indeed, deconstruction itself was forged "at the end of the totalitarianisms of the left and the right, of fascism and Stalinism" (142).

If this is the case, if we allow Caputo to have his way with Derrida, if we admit content into Derrida's messianic structure (will he forgive us?), then the ground will level out to the extent that not only will the messianic become a pharmacological site—and therefore be subject to deconstruction—but concrete messianisms, by the same token, will not be able to be written off as essentially poisonous. This, as I have already hinted, highlights the crucial difference between "necessary" violence and "historical" violence. Allowing for the ubiquity of violence rather than the necessity of violence opens "a political space which can grapple with both the possibility of peace and violence—that is, a political structure that confronts violence as violence precisely against a horizon of possible peace and justice."[33] So instead of having determinate religions be the whipping boy of the messianic, the messianic itself is also ushered into the "beautiful fray" as another messianism among messianisms. In this way, we could release religion to be understood as "a fundamentally deconstructive gesture," yet also a pharmacological site where there exists the possibility "of both poison and cure, violence and peace, exclusion and healing."[34] In other words, if Derrida cannot have his cake and eat it too, if it is impossible to maintain his desert religion, and if we also confess that all discourse begins in faith, then instead of dismissing out of hand the viability of determinate religions in the call for justice, we will be free to bring our particular faiths to the fore in order to cultivate a religio-ethical vigilance that has an ear bent toward the other.

Was not this kind of vigilance demonstrated, for example, by a certain Galilean who by his own account was both prophet and priest, both human and divine, whose kingdom is both "now" and "not yet," and whose "particular" words and work are "universal" in intent and scope?

Notes

1 John D. Caputo, *The Prayers and Tears of Jacques Derrida: Religion without Religion* (Bloomington: Indiana University Press, 1997).

2 It is important at the outset to emphasize that for the deconstructionist, the very gesture of philosophy is one of violence. Because the impulse of the Western philosophical/theological tradition has been one largely focused on a search for an unmovable centerpiece for its house of being, it is believed that this impulse, this spirit, has all along sacrificed difference on the altar of sameness. Indeed, the discovery of the mathematical—that most Greek of all Greek discoveries, which itself stands as a paradigm for philosophical thought—at the same time was a violent rupture that has given birth to many and varied dualisms which the deconstructionist is particularly sensitive to and suspicious of. As the reason—that is, Logos—for what appears, this intelligible, mathematical essence became the veritable apex of reality itself. As such, the Logos becomes first in the order of being, a throne from which this unmediated absolute rules absolutely. In this way, because the Logos cannot help but think totality, reason inevitably "dictates that what is is and what isn't isn't, and that what is, whatever it be, is more truly than what simply appears to be which, strictly speaking, is not at all, or, at the very least, is not really real." See Gary B. Madison, *The Hermeneutics of Postmodernity: Figures and Themes* (Bloomington: Indiana University Press, 1988), p. 129. This way of thinking—that is, Logos as *causa sui*—is traced along the path of development where it finds its full formulation in the modernity of Descartes, Spinoza, Leibniz, and Hegel. Since the time Descartes set out to establish the ego as a point of absolute certainty, being has been characterized by what Spinoza termed *conatus essendi*: "Everything, in so far as it is in itself, endeavors to persist in its own being." See Benedict de Spinoza, *Ethics* in *The Chief Works of Benedict de Spinoza*, R. Elwes, trans. (New York: Dover Publications, 1955), p. 136. Since for Spinoza, God's power is synonymous with his essence, and all things are modes of God, the will-to-power, notes Levinas, becomes the linchpin of modern ontologies. See Emmanuel Levinas, *Totality and Infinity: An Essay on Exteriority*, A. Lingis, trans. (Pittsburgh: Duquesne University Press, 1969), p. 46. On this reading, what has developed over a long history is a process whereby reason has become an instrument of terror, a tool of oppression and domination used by an ego or a society of egos to suppress what is other or different. Jacques Derrida terms this totalizing "motif of homogeneity the theological motif par excellence." See Jacques Derrida, *Positions*, A. Bass, trans. (Chicago: University of Chicago Press, 1981), p. 228. Although this chapter reflects a deep affinity for and respect for the work of Caputo and Derrida, it struggles to think otherwise on this very crucial point of necessary violence. See pp. 41–42, 46 below.

3 By strategically positioning a "formidable" circle of "secularist hermeneutic guards around the text," Caputo, after Kevin Hart, *The Trespass of the Sign* (New York: Cambridge University Press, 1989), pp. 42–47, argues that it is typical of Derrida's commentators to want "to make deconstruction safe for secularism." What deconstruction is concerned with, however, is discourse that is totalizing. "Theology has hardly cornered the market on totalization. If there is any totalizing going on here . . . it is among the secularist commentators on Derrida who would forbid the contamination or 'infestation' of good secular academic goods such as deconstruction with God." Caputo, *Prayers and Tears*, pp. 18–19.

4 Jacques Derrida, "Faith and knowledge: the two sources of 'religion' at the limits of reason alone," in *Religion*, Jacques Derrida and Gianni Vattimo, eds. (Stanford, CA: Stanford University Press, 1998), p. 8.

5 Although this is Cornell West's expression, Caputo thinks it is a good "spectral

image" for the convergence between the "deconstructive resources of religion" and the "religious resources of deconstruction." See also John D. Caputo, *Demythologizing Heidegger: Studies in Philosophy of Religion* (Bloomington: Indiana University Press, 1993), p. 201. Even though Caputo himself reservedly uses the term "postmodernism," he rightly considers that it has become an over-used and much abused word, one that has "been ground into senselessness by opportunistic overuse"; Caputo, *Prayers and Tears*, p. 119. However, as a heuristic term, it does help to describe a growing sense of suspicion and dis-ease in Western culture. From pop culture to politics, it is becoming increasingly evident that the Enlightenment myth of progress is fast losing its ability to inspire enthusiasm and generate faith among its advocates, the spirit of which the term "postmodern" nicely captures.

6 Jacques Derrida, "The force of law: the 'mystical foundation of authority,'" M. Quaintance, trans., in *Deconstruction and the Possibility of Justice*, D. Cornell *et al.*, eds. (New York: Routledge, 1992). See also *Force de loi: "Fondement mystique de l'autorité"* (Paris: Galilée, 1994).
7 John D. Caputo, *Against Ethics: Contributions to a Poetics of Obligation with Constant Reference to Deconstruction* (Bloomington: Indiana University Press, 1993), p. 21.
8 Jacques Derrida, *Specters of Marx: The State of Debt, the Work of Mourning, and the New International*, P. Kamuf, trans. (New York: Routledge, 1994), p. 167.
9 Ibid.
10 Derrida, "The force of law," p. 25.
11 Derrida, "Faith and knowledge," p. 16.
12 Jacques Derrida, "Deconstruction and tradition: the Villanova roundtable with Jacques Derrida," in *Deconstruction in a Nutshell: A Conversation with Jacques Derrida*, J. D. Caputo, ed. (New York: Fordham University Press, 1997), pp. 23f.
13 John D. Caputo, *Radical Hermeneutics: Repetition, Deconstruction, and the Hermeneutic Project* (Bloomington: Indiana University Press, 1987). Although Caputo has come full circle (almost) since *Radical Hermeneutics*, in my opinion his religious strategizing has changed very little. Although he has since given up the attempt to cross-pollinate Derrida's metaphorics of play and frivolity with Heidegger's metaphorics of stillness and meditation (by injecting a "mystical element" into the abyss of withdrawal), he still has his religious camp set up on the side of the deconstructive mean that is closest to Kierkegaard. See chapter 7, "Cold hermeneutics: Heidegger/Derrida," pp. 187–206. My modest attempt in this chapter is to merely hint at the contours of a philosophy (ethics, politics, or whatever the discipline) that is as inescapably religious as it is philosophical.
14 Derrida, "Faith and knowledge," p. 18.
15 What I mean here—and this is an important point—is that whereas the postmodern critique is concerned to deconstruct the modern assumption that particularity is an inferior chip off the universal block (in other words, a "fall from universality"), I contend that the valorization of the messianic represents the flipside of the same economy, a shift that repeats a postlapsarian fall into necessary violence. In this way, violence resurfaces again in a different guise—this time as a "fall within particularity."
16 Caputo, *Demythologizing Heidegger*, p. 196.
17 Jacques Derrida, *Of Grammatology*, G. C. Spivak, trans. (Baltimore: Johns Hopkins University Press, 1976), pp. 112, 200.
18 Derrida, "Deconstruction and tradition," p. 23.
19 On the significance of this quasi-neutral, arid-like, *khôra* space that precedes and engulfs our "yes" and "no," see Jacques Derrida, *"Khôra"* and *"Sauf le nom,"* in *On the Name*, T. Dutoit, ed. (Stanford, CA: Stanford University Press, 1995).

20 Jacques Derrida, *Memoirs of the Blind: The Self-Portrait and Other Ruins*, P.-A. Brault and M. Naas, trans. (Chicago: University of Chicago Press, 1993), pp. 29f.
21 Jacques Derrida, "How not to speak: denials," in *Derrida and Negative Theology*, H. Coward and T. Foshay, eds. (Albany, NY: SUNY Press, 1992).
22 Ibid., p. 101.
23 Caputo, *Deconstruction in a Nutshell*, p. 93.
24 Derrida, *On the Name*, p. 124.
25 Caputo, *Deconstruction in a Nutshell*, p. 94.
26 Ibid., pp. 94f.
27 Caputo, *Radical Hermeneutics*, pp. 278–88.
28 Caputo, *Against Ethics*, pp. 245–47.
29 Caputo, *Against Ethics*, p. 223.
30 Derrida, *Specters of Marx*, p. xviii.
31 Ibid., p. 172.
32 I owe this phrase to James H. Olthuis, "A hermeneutics of suffering love," in *The Very Idea of Radical Hermeneutics*, R. Martinez, ed. (Atlantic Highlands, NJ: Humanities Press, 1997), p. 160.
33 James K. A. Smith, "Determined violence: Derrida's structural religion," *Journal of Religion* 78 (April 1998): 211.
34 Ibid.

4 Is deconstruction an Augustinian science?

Augustine, Derrida, and Caputo on the commitments of philosophy[1]

James K. A. Smith

Said Reason: "God, to whom we have committed ourselves [*cui nos committimus*], will doubtless lend his aid and deliver us from these difficulties. Only let us believe [*modo credamus*] and ask him with the greatest devotion."

(Augustine, *Soliloquies*, 2.6.9)

Suspicions

Jacques Derrida has left many in tears, including his mother, who, like St. Monica, wept over her wandering and wayward "son of these tears"[2] who has broken the covenant and would now, by his own (*cir*)confession, "quite rightly pass for an atheist."[3] And now the prodigal son stands as a father to a most transgressive movement whose filial bonds to Nietzsche haunt its most suspicious and rigorous questioning and criticism such that deconstruction, if we are to believe William Bennett or Allan Bloom, is reason to weep and lament, ushering in the "end" of metaphysics, the closing of the book, the loss of the self, and the death of God. Derrida's incessant questioning marks a suspicion, it is assumed, that negates every commitment in a Dionysian celebration of *différance*; as such, deconstruction would signal the collapse of commitments and function as the nemesis to faith. Deconstruction would see through the façade and ruthlessly expose any grounding or primordial trust as inevitably a construction and myth, as a bluff. Derrida would be yet another "master of suspicion" pledged to questioning every commitment, committed only to questions and questioning.

Or so the story goes. "Do you believe this? [*Vous croyez?*]"[4] Are we to believe this? Are we to believe that deconstruction is intent on eliminating belief, that its probing criticism upsets every trust? Are we to give credence (*credere*) to this tale of deconstruction's dismantling of commitment? Is this reading of Derrida and deconstruction beyond question, or should we perhaps be suspicious of such a reading, which would have Derrida committed to distrust? Could it in fact be the case that Derrida, and even deconstruction, have a certain faith, a certain commitment to commitment? Is there not a specter of this trust—this secret—that haunts deconstruction? Could it be that deconstruction, far from questioning every commitment, is in fact a celebration of commitments which revels in prayer and praise? Could deconstruction be an Augustinian science, which both acknowledges and even confesses that one must believe in order to understand? "You better believe it [*il faut croire*]" (MB, 32).

Derrida's formalization of Augustine

In this chapter, I want to suggest and argue that deconstruction, rather than being characterized by a spirit of suspicion, is concerned with the primordial trust that sets questioning in motion, and thus is itself always already committed. That is to say, what we locate in Derrida's "critique" of reason is a fundamentally Augustinian structure which points to the commitments (trust, faith) that precede knowledge—the pledges that precede philosophy. With Augustine, Derrida would confess that "Unless one believes, one will not understand."[5] "I don't *know*," Derrida responds, "one has to *believe*" (MB, 129, emphasis added). Despite rumors and caricatures streaming from English departments around the world, deconstruction does not side with any secularism—or even liberalism, for that matter. Instead, Derrida insists that a fundamental faith or trust must precede knowledge; on his account, the very structure of knowledge—and thus philosophy—points to a faith or trust which makes knowledge possible. "This is to take a fundamentally Augustinian, religious, and biblical position," Caputo comments, "for on this point Augustine himself is just being a good student of the biblical and prophetic tradition rather than of Plotinus" (PT, 311). Rather than proceeding without presuppositions, previous commitments are the very condition of possibility for knowing.

However, though arguing that this is a fundamentally Augustinian structure, we must also recognize that it is also a formalization of Augustine; that is, the primordial faith that precedes knowledge as its condition of possibility is not, for Derrida, a content-full, determinate religion.[6] For Augustine, the faith that issues in knowledge is ultimately very particular and contentfull: faith in Christ the interior Teacher.

Regarding each of the things we understand, however, we don't consult a speaker who makes sounds outside us, but the Truth that presides within over the mind itself, though perhaps words prompt us to consult Him. What is more, He Who is consulted, He Who is said to dwell in the inner man, does teach: Christ—that is, the unchangeable power and everlasting wisdom of God, which every rational soul does consult, but is disclosed to anyone to the extent that he can apprehend it, according to his good or evil will.[7]

Thus for Augustine, this structure is also wedded to a particular content: the faith that precedes knowledge is precisely a commitment to the Origin and Creator, who is also the inner Teacher, the One who was "in the beginning" and "enlightens every person" (John 1:1, 4–5). In *De vera religione*, Augustine emphasizes that knowledge is possible only insofar as our diseased eyes (of the mind) are healed; and it is precisely faith that is the condition of possibility for healing, which is the condition of possibility of knowledge (*De vera religione*, 3.3–4). This is why, for Augustine, "philosophy, i.e., the pursuit of wisdom, cannot be quite divorced from religion" (5.8).

In Derrida, however, this Augustinian structure is divorced from its determinate content: the faith that precedes knowledge is merely structural, a commitment to something—like one's language—which makes knowledge, philosophy, and science possible. While the structure is "universal" (which must be qualified, based on deconstruction), the content or "object" of commitment is contingent.[8]

Derrida's pledge: of spirit

Deconstruction, then, is doubly committed: it is committed, before criticism, by a certain trust and affirmation, but it is also committed to pointing out these commitments which precede every discourse or theoretical framework, suggesting that thinking entrusts itself to something Other than itself—to the guidance of the Spirit, or let us say *l'esprit*. Thus the site of this commitment to commitment, this pneumatic discourse, may be located in Derrida's little treatise on spirits: *ruah*, *pneuma*, *esprit*, and, especially, *Geist*. Derrida's *Of Spirit* is a discourse on both "spirit" and "avoiding," or, more specifically, *Geist* und *vermeiden*, and how Heidegger (unsuccessfully) attempted to avoid this spirit in his work and life. A life and work haunted by ghosts—is this Heidegger or Derrida? Of course, within Heidegger's *Gesamtausgabe* there lurk a number of disturbing specters: spirits that disturb this corpus but also arise from this corpus to disturb us.[9] Derrida's goal in his little spirit-filled treatise is to reveal that, despite all of his protests and attempts, Heidegger failed to avoid this tormenting *Geist*:

Geist is always haunted by its *Geist*: a spirit, or in other words, in French [and English] as in German, a phantom, always surprises by returning to be the other's ventriloquist. Metaphysics always returns, I mean in the sense of a *revenant* [ghost], and *Geist* is the most fatal figure of this *revenance* [returning, haunting]. . . . Is this not what Heidegger will never finally be able to avoid (*vermeiden*), the unavoidable itself—spirit's double, *Geist* as the *Geist* of *Geist*, spirit as the spirit of the spirit which always comes with its double?[10]

But again we may ask: is there not also a spirit, let us say *l'esprit*, which Derrida cannot avoid, which is the unavoidable? Is there not a specter lurking behind and underneath Derrida's corpus, his body (of writings), his writing body?

We need not consult the witch of Endor to conjure up this spirit, for it is sighted in a startling way later in the text, when Derrida considers the origins of language as promise, a passage hovering between commentary and autobiography.[11]

It remains to find out whether this *Versprechen* [promise] is not the prom-ise which, opening every speaking, makes possible the very question and therefore precedes it without belonging to it: the dissymmetry of an affirmation, of a yes before all opposition of yes and no. . . . Language always, before any question, and in the very question, comes down to the promise. This would also be a promise of spirit.

(OS, 94)

Following on the heels of this passage is an extended note (which, not with-out significance, he offers as a pledge)—an attempt to understand this uninvited visitation of (the) spirit. Here the spirit of promise—of the "pledge"—returns, as that which must precede any question. Thus before any hermeneutics of suspicion (which is, at heart, a hermeneutics of radical questioning), one must place one's trust in the promises of language.

Language is already there, in advance at the moment at which any ques-tion can arise about it. In this it exceeds the question. This advance is, before any contract, a sort of promise of originary allegiance to which we must have in some sense already acquiesced, already said yes, given a pledge, whatever may be the negativity or problematicity of the discourse which may follow.

(OS, 129)

This pledge, he goes on to say, is a "commitment" to what is given in the promise itself. Questioning—the heart and soul of suspicion—does not have the last word, precisely because it does not have the first word, because it is itself grounded in trusting a promise (OS, 130). This pledge happens "before" the question, even before language, in time immemorial: "before the word, there is this sometimes wordless word which we name the 'yes.' A sort of pre-originary pledge which precedes any other engagement in language or action" (OS, 130).

As Derrida notes, then, there is a trust that is more primordial than suspicion, precisely because, Augustine (though not Derrida) would suggest (and he is quite committed to this), goodness is more primordial than evil. The state of affairs composed of deception and false consciousness is an accidental way of being, not an essential one. The *pharmakon*[12] is not original nor constitutive, but rather a contingency resulting from the brokenness of a fallen world. But before this fall, and now in spite of this fall, there is a primordial "yes:" a "wordless word," a living Logos who was "in the beginning," who tabernacles with us in flesh, and whose spirit resides within us (John 1:1–18). It is this wordless Word, this Who, that we name "yes:" "For the Son of God, Christ Jesus, who was preached among you by us—by me and Silvanus and Timothy—was not yes and no, but is yes in Him. For as many as may be the promises of God, in Him they are yes" (II Cor. 1:19–20). That is why parole, Derrida urges, "must first pray, address itself to us: put in us its trust, its confidence, depend on us, and even have already done it" (OS, 134). And this pledge, he continues, this "already", is essential because it reaches back to a moment of already-having-trusted, an older event, part of a past that never returns, and never "was."

In this regard, the fundamental movement of deconstruction is a celebration of commitments, pointing out the pledges and promises that ground discourse—and the academy. Thus the university, any university, is founded on faith: before the work of scholarship happens all scholars say a little prayer, whisper their pledge, commit and entrust themselves to language. The university, we might suggest, is quite religious, even if it has not been founded by priests; and it is this grounding commitment that deconstruction is sworn to celebrate.

Confessions of the blind: Derrida's memoirs

We could say this otherwise, as Derrida does in *Memoirs of the Blind*, his running commentary on the exhibition he hosted at the Louvre. Here his hypothesis is that drawing proceeds from a certain structural blindness, begins where it cannot see and hence, where one cannot "know."[13] As the Western tradition has come to understand, to know is to have an "idea" (*eidos*), hence to "see" (*oida*) (MB, 12). On the basis of this occidental privileging of sight, one who is blind cannot know. But Derrida, along with the New Testament, wants to problematize this, suggesting that knowing or seeing is predicated upon a certain blindness, upon what one does not see; knowing, as such, would proceed from a commitment to that which is beyond seeing, the "unbeseen" as absolute invisibility, to which one is entrusted.[14] In this blind economy of faith, to see is in a sense not to see, such that Jesus' opponents are blind precisely because they claim to see (John 9:40–41). On the other hand, those who are blind nevertheless see, walking by faith, not by sight (MB, 18). To see is not to believe, whereas blindness is a kind of faith such that one must rely on others for direction, often walking with outstretched arms, as in prayer (MB, 1, 4, 6). "Look at Coypel's blind men," Derrida suggests as an example. "They all hold their hands out in front of them, their gesture oscillating in the void between prehending, apprehending, praying, and imploring" (MB, 5).

The movement of modern thought and technology is precisely to probe beyond the limits of sight "with instruments—anoptic or blind—that sound out, that allow one to know [*savoir*] there where one no longer sees [*voir*]" (MB, 32). To expand one's vision is to eliminate faith, to undo the commitment that blindness necessitates; but because of the structural invisibility of the absolutely other than sight, the probes can never sound deep enough, can never plumb the depths of blindness, or faith. Derrida sees this structure outlined in the healing of Tobit's blindness by his son [12–14], behind whom stands an angel as the condition for the possibility of Tobit's healing, who also announces a commandment: "acknowledge God [*rendez grâce à Dieu*]" (MB, 29). The story is a chain of acknowledgments: Tobit thanking his son, who points to the angel Raphael, who in turn indicates that Tobit's debt is to God. His healing is a gift for which he must render thanks, in writing (Tobit 12:20): "in order to give thanks [*rendre grâce*], the memory of the event must be inscribed. The debt must be repaid with words on parchment" (MB, 29).

Thus the healing, and more precisely the story of the healing, begins by and from a debt: "What guides the graphic point, the quill, pencil, or scalpel is the respectful observance of a commandment, the acknowledgements before knowledge, the gratitude of the receiving before seeing, the blessing before knowledge" (MB, 29–30). The angel, then, indicates the place of faith, of acknowledgment, of commitment, and trust; in works such as Bianchi's [13], the angel stands boldly in the center. The debt is acknowledged. But in Rembrandt's rendering [15], for example, the angel is withdrawn, marginalized, and the human actors are now engaged in what appears to be simple surgery, such that the sketch was originally but mistakenly referred to by the title *Surgeon Bandaging a Wounded Man*—a recovery of sight by knowledge, by more seeing. Thus we may locate a movement of a certain "secularity" with the move to a modern era—an exclusion of the angel and a denial of one's debts. And this denial represents, in sum, a denial of commitment—an Enlightenment claim to neutrality and objectivity, freed from prejudice, which is just the kind of prejudice that deconstruction is determined to expose.

Such a (modern) construal, on Derrida's accounting, fails to give credit to the role of faith (*credo*), to the commitments that make such seeing possible. Writing, drawing, speaking are all indebted, committed, owe credit to that which is originarily other, such that

> at the origin of the *graphein* there is debt or gift rather than representational fidelity. More precisely, the fidelity of faith matters more than the representation, whose movement fidelity commands and thus precedes. And faith, in the moment proper to it, is blind.
>
> (MB, 30)

To translate this into a rather classical idiom, Derrida is offering another way to think of the relationship between faith and reason; however, he would see any disjunction or opposition between the two as untenable, precisely because reason is grounded, structurally, in commitments, trust, a pledge. Before knowledge there is acknowledgment; before seeing there is blindness; before questioning there is a commitment; before knowing there is faith.[15]

While blindness is the condition for the possibility of faith, there is also a sense in which faith is blinded because it sees too much, blinded by bedazzlement, "the very bedazzlement that, for example, knocks Paul to the ground on the road to Damascus" (MB, 112) [67, 68]. And if faith is linked to blindness, it is also associated with madness; or, as Derrida remarks, the "clairvoyance of the all-too-evident is Paul's madness" (MB, 117). Paul is mad, Festus asserted (Acts 26:24), or, as we sometimes say, he should be "committed" (to a psychiatric institution, as it were). He is one who should be committed because of his mad commitments—because of his faith. Thus deconstruction, if it is a celebration of commitments, is also a celebration of a certain madness—the madness of faith.[16] Further, deconstruction is committed to pointing out the place of this madness within and before the academic community (the madness of reason), as that which is the very condition for its possibility—which often enough makes people (like Richard Rorty, or Charles Scott) a little mad.

Questions

Having sketched the Augustinian structure of Derrida's account of the relationship between faith and philosophy, which Caputo has also suggested (PT, 311, 328), I shall conclude with just two questions for Professor Caputo in this regard.

First, while suggesting that we find an Augustinian moment in Derrida's understanding of the commitments of philosophy, I wonder whether Caputo does not continue to read this through something of a Thomistic lens, which might undercut the radicality of Derrida's account. When commenting on this aspect of Derrida's thought, we will often find Caputo taking recourse to a Kantian maxim, from the second preface to the first critique: "I have found it necessary to deny knowledge, in order to make room for faith" (e.g. at PT, 312, 328). But is this an Augustinian maxim? For Kant, of course, faith marks the limits of reason, that boundary beyond which philosophy (and "knowledge") cannot venture, the final frontier where philosophy cannot tread. This, it seems to me, preserves the scholastic, and specifically Thomistic, understanding of the relationship between faith and philosophy: faith goes beyond philosophy, speaks where philosophy is lost for words. Faith, in a sense, picks up where philosophy left off. (The Kantian maxim is not even quite Thomist, since Kant seems to posit a discontinuity between faith and reason, whereas Aquinas emphasizes their continuity. Both, however, retain some notion of the *autonomy* of theoretical thought.[17])

But for Augustine, faith is not the boundary or limit of philosophy, but rather the fountain out of which philosophy springs. Faith is not "beyond" philosophy, but "before" philosophy—the condition of possibility of philosophy and knowledge. Rather than faith picking up where philosophy left off, Augustine emphasizes that philosophy would be speechless without the first word of faith—what Derrida describes as "this sometimes wordless word which we name the 'yes'" (OS, 130). Although he describes this Derridean structure as "more Augustinian and Franciscan than Thomistic and Dominican" (PT, 328), it seems to me that Caputo continues to read this through a Thomistic, or at least Kantian, lens which undoes the radicality of the Augustinian position.

Second, if Derrida is right about the relationship between faith and philosophy—and if this is an Augustinian rather than Thomistic structure—then it also seems that Prof. Caputo would need to revise a distinction that has run through his work from *Radical Hermeneutics*[18] to the present. I refer to his distinction between what he describes as the (Kierkegaardian) "religious" and (Nietzschean) "tragic" responses to suffering (RH, ch. 10). Undecidability, he remarks, prevents the privileging of either. But it seems that, ironically, Caputo privileges the Nietzschean by describing the religious response as a "construal," a hermeneusis based on faith which "has looked down the dark well of suffering and found there a loving power which takes the side of suffering" (RH, 279). More recently he says:

> Faith is a matter of a radical hermeneutic, an art of construing shadows, in the midst of what is happening. Faith is neither magic nor an infused knowledge that lifts one above the flux or above the limits of mortality. Faith, on my view, is above all the hermeneia that Someone looks back at us from the abyss, that the spell of anonymity is broken by a Someone who stands with those who suffer, which is why the Exodus and the Crucifixion are central religious symbols. Faith, does not, however, extinguish the abyss but constitutes a certain reading of the abyss, a hermeneutics of the abyss.[19]

Faith is only a construal which is enveloped and haunted by undecidability; Abraham is haunted by Zarathustra's laughter. The construal of the religious response is simply a faith-full way to cope with the cold reality of the flux by construing it as something warm.

But does not this characterization already deny undecidability? Is not his characterization of the flux as "cold" already a privileging of Nietzsche? Is not the tragic also a construal, a faith-full hermeneusis which is also exposed to undecidability? It seems that in this (rather Thomistic) distinction, Nietzsche speaks as a philosopher; Kierkegaard, on the other hand, goes beyond philosophy, making an affirmation of faith which one cannot admit "philosophically." However, though Abraham certainly hears the echo of Zarathustra's laughter, I wonder if Zarathustra ever lies awake at night wondering if Abraham is right. Is that not a more insistent understanding of undecidability? If Augustine and Derrida are right about the commitments of philosophy, then does not Nietzsche have his faith, too? Caputo seems to put the burden of proof upon the religious response, which must answer to Nietzsche. But does not Nietzsche also have some explaining to do? Both the religious and the tragic responses are construals: interpretations of factical life grounded in faith-full commitments. Caputo continually insists on the frigidity of the world while seeing the necessity of a religious response; but this privileging of the tragic interpretation seems to convey that Nietzsche knows what the world is really like (which is a very realist notion). Only a hermeneutic that recognizes the creational nature of faith can truly recognize the all-the-way-downness of undecidability. That, it seems to me, reflects a more Augustinian understanding of the commitments of philosophy—an understanding that Derrida also affirms.

This is Derrida's promise: to announce the promise that precedes us, the commitment that is older than us, the "yes" to which we always already have acquiesced. That is deconstruction's prayer and in-vocation, echoing the prayer of reason in Augustine's *Soliloquies* (2.6.9); as such, it might seem appropriate to close with a prayer, but Derrida's (and Augustine's) request is precisely that we recognize that it is with prayer that we begin (*Sols.*, 1.1–6).

Notes

1 Research for this essay was supported in part by a fellowship from the Social Sciences and Humanities Research Council of Canada, whose support is gratefully acknowledged. Earlier versions of the chapter were presented at the Twenty-second International Conference on Patristic, Medieval, and Renaissance Studies, 1997, and the Eastern International Region of the American Academy of Religion, 1996. Numbers in square brackets refer to selections from the sketches and drawings chosen by Derrida for an exhibition at the Louvre in 1990–91, of which he was the guest curator. The pieces and Derrida's commentary constitute *Memoirs of the Blind*.

2 *Confessions*, 3.12.21, where Monica's tears are in fact prayers which do not go unheard. Tears, including Augustine's tears, are important for Derrida's analyses in *Memoirs of the Blind*. For a close analysis, see also Kim Paffenroth, "Tears of grief and joy: *Confessions* Book 9: Chronological sequence and structure," *Augustinian Studies* 28 (1997): 141–54.

3 Jacques Derrida, "Circumfession: fifty-nine periods and periphrases," in Geoffrey Bennington and Jacques Derrida, *Jacques Derrida* (Chicago: University of Chicago Press, 1993), p. 155. For a commentary on Derrida's "religion without religion," see John D. Caputo, *The Prayers and Tears of Jacques Derrida: Religion Without Religion* (Bloomington: Indiana University Press, 1997), pp. 308–29 (abbreviated in the text as PT). For a critique of Derrida's "formal" or "structural" religion "without content," see James K. A. Smith, "Determined violence: Derrida's structural religion," *Journal of Religion* 78 (April 1998): 197–212. For a discussion of Augustine's *Confessions* and Derrida's *Circumfessions*, see Robert Dodaro, OSA, "Loose canons: Derrida and Augustine on Their Selves," *God, The Gift and Postmodernism*, John D. Caputo and Michael J. Scanlon (Bloomington: Indiana University Press, 1999).

4 Jacques Derrida, *Memoirs of the Blind: The Self-Portrait and Other Ruins*, Pascale-Anne Brault and Michael Naas, trans. (Chicago: University of Chicago Press, 1993), p. 1. Henceforth abbreviated in the text as MB.

5 See, for example, *De Magistro* (CSEL 77), 11.37.

6 Derrida speaks of a "religion without religion," a "structural religion," or a "religion without dogma" to describe this result of a process whereby religious structures are evacuated of any determinate, historical content in order to disclose a structural "logic." For a critique of this project, see Smith, "Determined violence."

7 De universis autem, quae intelligimus, non loquentum, qui personat foris, sed intus ipsi menti praesidentem consulimus veritatem, verbis fortasse ut consulamus admoniti. Ille autem, qui consulitur, docet, qui in interiore homine habitare dictus est Christus, id est incommutabilis dei atque sempiterna sapientia. Quam quidem omnis rationalis anima consulit, sed tantum cuique panditur, quantum capere propter propriam sive malam sive bonam voluntam potest; et si quando fallitur,

non fit vitio consultae veritatis, ut neque huius, quae foris est, lucis vitium est, quod corporei oculi saepe falluntur, quam lucem de rebus visibilibus consuli fatemur, ut eas nobis, quantum cernere valemus, ostendat. *De Magistro*, 11.38, in Augustine, *Against the Academicians and The Teacher*, Peter King, trans., (Indianapolis: Hackett, 1995), p. 139.

8 Thus elsewhere I have linked Derrida's discourse with Kuhn's notion of "paradigms," which are also fundamental commitments to frameworks that are contingent. For a discussion, see James K. A. Smith, "The art of Christian atheism: faith and philosophy in early Heidegger," *Faith and Philosophy* 14 (1997): 71–81; and James K. A. Smith and Shane R. Cudney, "Postmodern freedom and the growth of fundamentalism: was the Grand Inquisitor right?" *Studies in Religion/Sciences Religieuses* 25 (1996): 41–44. I think the same kind of "structural" commitment is glimpsed in Calvin's notion of the *sensus divinitatis*, and its development in Dooyeweerd; for both Calvin and Dooyeweerd, it is not the case that all human persons believe in God, but rather that humans are essentially religious, they need to believe in something. This structural belief can, however, take an apostate direction. For an especially helpful discussion, see Herman Dooyeweerd, *In the Twilight of Western Thought: Studies in the Pretended Autonomy of Theoretical Thought*, James K. A. Smith, ed., *Collected Works*, B/4 (Lewiston: Edwin Mellen Press, 1998), ch. 2, "The concentric character of the self." Cited as TWT.

9 Not least of which is the spirit of Augustine, particularly as glimpsed in the publication of Heidegger's lecture course from the summer semester of 1921, published as "Augustinus und der Neuplatonismus," Claudius Strube, ed., in *Phänomenologie des religiösen Lebens*, Gesamtausgabe, Bd. 60 (Frankfurt: Klostermann, 1995).

10 Jacques Derrida, *Of Spirit: Heidegger and the Question*, Geoffrey Bennington and Rachel Bowlby, trans. (Chicago: University of Chicago Press, 1989), pp. 40f. Cited as OS.

11 Thus, what Derrida observes regarding Heidegger's relation to Trakl could also be said of Derrida's relation to Heidegger: "statements like those I have just cited and translated . . . are obviously statements of Heidegger. Not his own, productions of the subject Martin Heidegger, but statements to which he subscribes apparently without the slightest reluctance. On the one hand, he opposes them to everything which he is in the process of opposing, and which forms a sufficiently determining context. On the other hand, he supports them in a discourse of which the least one can say is that it does not bear even the trace of a reservation. It would thus be completely irrelevant to reduce these statements in ontological form to 'commentaries.' Nothing is more foreign to Heidegger than 'commentary' in its ordinary sense" (OS, 85).

12 Derrida plays with the term *pharmakon* (from Plato's *Gorgias*) in order to show that language—like the meaning of *pharmakon* itself—can be both "poison" and "cure," and is both always already. There is a violence that is equiprimordial with goodness. See Jacques Derrida, "Plato's pharmacy," in *Dissemination*, Barbara Johnson, trans. (Chicago: University of Chicago Press, 1981).

13 As Augustine notes: "what I understand I also believe, but not everything I believe do I also understand. Again, everything I understand I know; but not everything I believe I know," *De Magistro*, 11.37 (trans. modified). Compare also *Soliloquies*, 1.3.8, and *De Vera Religione*, 25.46.

14 Derrida describes this unseen as the "unbeseen" and the "absolutely invisible" in order to emphasize that it is that which is radically heterogeneous to sight, which can never be seen. "To be the other of the visible, absolute invisibility must neither take place elsewhere nor constitute another visible" (MB, 51). Structurally it is the invisible, the *tout autre* (wholly other) of sight.

15 On this question, I am arguing (as does Caputo (PT, 328)) that Derrida would side with Augustine and the Franciscan tradition over against the Thomistic tradition from Thomas to Gilson. For a discussion, see my essay "The art of Christian atheism," pp. 76–79, and 81 n.26.
16 This would also be seen in Derrida's meditation on Kierkegaard's Abraham in *The Gift of Death*, David Wills, trans. (Chicago: University of Chicago Press, 1995).
17 For a discussion of these matters, see TWT.
18 John D. Caputo, *Radical Hermeneutics: Repetition, Deconstruction, and the Hermeneutic Project* (Bloomington: Indiana University Press, 1987). Cited in the text as RH.
19 John D. Caputo, *Against Ethics: Contributions to a Poetics of Obligation with Constant Reference to Deconstruction* (Bloomington: Indiana University Press, 1993), p. 245.

5   Prayers of confession and tears of contrition

John Caputo and a radically "Baptist" hermeneutic of repentance

B. Keith Putt

I begin with a "Catholic" reference, since that is John Caputo's religious tradition. Specifically, I begin with Simon's confession of Jesus as the Christ, the Son of God. After blessing Simon and affirming the truthfulness of his confession, Jesus renames him *Petros*, Peter, the "rock" upon which he will build the church. He then gives Peter privileged authority by giving him the "keys of the kingdom of heaven" (Matt. 16:19). Jesus characterizes these keys as instruments of binding and loosening, both on earth and in heaven, with which Peter, Pope "Rocky" I, can lock and unlock, imprison and liberate, close and disclose. Obviously, Jesus speaks symbolically here and uses an analogy in order to communicate a different order of truth. Yet symbolic language always invites a more playful, disseminative hermeneutic, what Derrida would call a poetic interpretation in contradistinction to a rabbinic one.[1] If we adopt such a poetic perspective, can we tease out a supplementary meaning to Jesus' keynote address? In other words, what if we were to understand these "kingdom" keys not in a mechanical sense but in a musical one? What if Jesus were giving Peter different tonalities in which to sing the refrain of redemption, different scales by which to attune the church's confession to the kerygma's content? Could we, then, play with the polysemy of the word "key" and ask about the tones, the key signatures, to be adopted by those who seek to lift their voices and sing the new songs of Zion?

Leonard Sweet, in his book *Quantum Spirituality*, does indeed raise the issue of which key signature should characterize the music of the kingdom. With a nod toward Bach, he distinguishes two: the B minor chord in which John the Baptist sings his wilderness lament and the G major chord in which Jesus sings the *"gloria in excelsis deo."*[2] The key of B minor perfectly expresses the funereal suffering of the repentant sinner who feels the sting of guilt, while G major produces a joyful noise that motivates an exuberant dance. One might say that the B minor chord conveys the singer's feeling of being bound by sin and death, of being locked inside a prison of his own making. The G major chord, however, is an anthem of liberation, of having the bonds of sin loosened, the dulcet tones of one who has been released into "bliss and blessedness."[3] Such are Sweet's two keys of the kingdom, the two tonalities in which John's *Dies Irae* and Christ's *Hallelujah Chorus* modulate.

Forging forgiveness as gift

I reference Sweet's musical distinction between John the Baptist and Jesus specifically because it coheres with a similar differentiation that Caputo makes between their respective interpretations of repentance. Caputo's contrast between John and Jesus comes to expression from two complementary perspectives: (1) an investigation into the proper definition of *metanoia*, and (2) the relationship between the pure gift and forgiveness. The first perspective may be identified in two texts that expound Caputo's Christian philosophy of the kingdom of God. In "Metanoetics: elements of a postmodern Christian philosophy" and "Reason, history, and a little madness: towards a hermeneutics of the kingdom," he explicitly and implicitly distinguishes John's "Baptist" definition of *metanoia* from Jesus' kingdom definition.[4] The former, according to Caputo, defines the term as "repentance"—a dirgeful, gloomy word meaning to "feel pain again." Baptist repentance focuses on a phrenology that reduces *metanoia* to a consciousness of guilt and shame, which should, in turn, lead to self-deprecating cries of *"mea culpa."* Caputo claims, in a Levinasian vocabulary, that "Baptist" repentance centers on *"le dit,"* on the "said" that rehearses the particular content of the offense and, in doing so, allows the past event to continue to contaminate the present.

Jesus' metanoetic imperative demands a completely different response. He comes proclaiming *metanoia* as a cardiology, specifically as a "change of heart" that calls for forgiveness. This change of heart on the part of an offender obligates the one offended to respond with an amnesia that denies the efficacy of vengeance and absolves both parties from the alienation of the past. For Jesus, *metanoia* should be an instance of *"le dire,"* of a "saying" that abdicates the power of the past and reestablishes the presence of relationship. With changed hearts and forgotten pasts, citizens in God's kingdom can enjoy each day as a gift from the Father, a gift that allows for celebration and the voicing of a *"felix sine culpa."*[5] According to Caputo, "Jesus changes John's prophetic tune of *metanoia*; he wants us to retune, to undergo a change of tuning, of *nous* or *Stimmung.*"[6] Jesus' metanoetic song puts us in a good mood, in a light-hearted mood, perfect for eating, drinking, and dancing; it intentionally prohibits us from being moody and depressed, weighed down by a heavy heart.

In the kingdom of God, *metanoia* results in relational and temporal extravagance. Relationships are no longer predicated on resentment and revenge, and time is no longer constrained by the lingering effects of the past. Caputo expresses this metanoetic character as a different type of economy, specifically a "mad economy" that does not depend upon sane investments and assured returns but upon ledgers that are wiped clean and books that no longer need to be balanced. In raising this economic analogy, he adopts his second perspective on the distinction between John and Jesus. In "Instants, secrets, and singularities: dealing death in Kierkegaard and Derrida"[7] and in *The Prayers and Tears of Jacques Derrida: Religion without Religion*, Caputo reprises his separation of the Baptist and Jesus vis-à-vis repentance. In these texts, he claims that the Baptist version of repentance occupies the epicenter of an economic circle of exchange—the quid pro quo reciprocity of debt and repayment. Here repentance demands some sort of satisfaction, some balancing of spiritual and/or social books in a rational economy predicated upon a calculus of the "zero sum." Caputo hears John's voice crying in the wilderness, articulating a prophetic economy of guilt and retribution, of condemnation and indictment, and of sorrow and remorse. Although he directs his words of judgment at the legalism of hypocritical Pharisees, the Baptist offers only the alternative of another law, a law of duty and debt, of fear and retribution, and not a new "logic" of grace. Caputo finds John's kerygma to be a message of grief and pain, a message revealing a deity of wrath who keeps precise ledgers noting every debit and every credit and who expects all accounts to be reconciled. John's proclamation of this cycle of exchange, however, perverts the mad economics of the kingdom prescribed by Jesus, because the kingdom operates on the notion of gift, which breaks this cycle of exchange by specifically denying the need for balanced books, retired mortgages, or the egalitarianism of retribution. Jesus does not call for feelings of pain and penitential actions that redress imbalances. Instead, he demands changed hearts and gifts of forgiveness, which in themselves make no demands but simply liberate the other from all economic responsibilities.

In addressing the issues of repentance and forgiveness as gift, Caputo explicates the implications of Derrida's quasi-transcendental philosophy of the pure gift as the "grounds" for the possibility and impossibility of breaking with the circular economics of an expenditure with return.[8] A reciprocal economy of exchange continually promotes a structure of similarity by demanding a closed circle within which one should receive the equal of what one contributes. This kinetics of the circle depends upon the polar dynamic of debit and credit. As one receives or takes something within the cycle, one, in essence, takes on a debt, which demands to be repaid. The cycle operates successfully only as long as this equality of disbursement and reimbursement continues; consequently, any instance of lack or of extravagance introduces the alterity of inequality into the process and threatens to shut it down. Consequently, the balanced economy of self-gathering accounts disallows the realization of any pure gift. The pure gift cannot traffic with the *do ut des* of the sane economy of exchange, because a pure gift should not be contaminated by the necessity of indebtedness, nor should it result in any self-reflexive movement. The pure gift requires anonymity with reference to each of its constituents; that is, in a pure gift the giver is not known, the gifted is not known, and the gift is not known. As a result, the giver receives nothing, and the gifted feels no necessity for response. This anonymity of the pure gift demands extravagance, which, as stated above, cannot be contained within the structures of an economy of exchange. As a result, the pure gift cuts into the circle of exchange, rupturing its reciprocity of equality.

Caputo illustrates Derrida's quasi-economy of the pure gift in three ways. First, he references *The Gift of Death*, Derrida's interpretation of Kierkegaard's interpretation of the sacrifice of Isaac. Abraham offers Isaac to God without any concern for return, without any thought that investing his son's life will bring him any greater rewards. Instead, Abraham prepares to give to Isaac the gift of death and in so doing to give that gift through Isaac in an act of pure sacrifice to God. Such a gift disintegrates the circle of reciprocity and reveals an expenditure without return (201). Such an expenditure sacrifices duty and obligation and converts Abraham's sacrifice of economy into an economy of sacrifice (213). Second, Caputo references Mark 12:41–44, a passage that narrates a widow's extravagant gift. The widow—who had little, barely enough, in reality not enough—gives all she has to the temple. Like Abraham's sacrifice, her gift shatters any sane economy and expresses the madness of an inconceivable and unprogrammable excess. The widow does not give legalistically out of duty or instrumentally out of self-interest. She gives, instead, without a why, giving only for the sake of giving and, in doing so, not only gives "more" than all the others but, unlike all the others, gives the paradigmatic gift (176–77).

Third, Caputo insists that "the question of the gift or giving is inseparable from that of forgiving" (178). The word itself reveals the interconnection between gift and forgiveness: "for-*giving*" and its synonym "par-*don*," "by [a] gift." Forgiveness, then, is donative, a giving that should not be perverted into some type of reciprocal exchange predicated upon duty or equal return. Forgiveness as gift naturally reprises for Caputo his postmodern Christian hermeneutic of the madness of Jesus' kingdom economy, an economy that Jesus often communicates through significant parables, such as the parable of the prodigal son. Whereas John the Baptist, with his sane economy of guilt and revenge, could not, in good conscience, tell that parable, Jesus would and, indeed, does. The story of a father who refuses to relate to his sinful son according to balanced books, economies of exchange, or resentment and retribution, but who desires only to forget the past and restore his son through various gifts of forgiveness, reveals Jesus' understanding of the Heavenly Father and the type of extravagant grace and acceptance that he desires within his kingdom. Not only are revenge and repayment not required in the kingdom of God, but they are also inconsistent with its metanoetic ethic and temporality. God requires changed hearts willing to give away what is due them, willing to release the offending other from obligation, willing to dismiss the past and be bound only by the law of love, which is the law of the gift.[9] God proscribes *ressentiment* or condemnation and prescribes compassion, forgiveness, and mercy—all of which must be expressed lavishly. When the other sins against you and says her heart has changed, you are to forgive her and release her from any obligation or debt. Even were she to do so seven times a day, or seven times seven times a day, or seven times seventy times a day, the metanoetics of the kingdom requires that you forgive her and give away your rights to retribution (cf. Luke 17:4). In God's kingdom, the proper confession of the sinner is, "My heart has changed; I have turned around." In God's kingdom, the proper confession of the one sinned against is "I forgive you; forget it—it never happened; I expect no return."

Caputo does indeed have strong etymological support for his translation of *metanoia* as a "change of heart (mind)" and not technically as "repentance," if by "repentance" one means remorse or regret. Traditionally, those terms better translate the Greek word *metamelosthai*; however, the two ideas can and often do come together, since a change of heart (mind) can result in or from an affective state of regret.[10] Such a relationship becomes quite significant if one understands *metanoia* as "after" (*meta*) "thinking" (*noia*) or "thinking otherwise," a type of thinking or rethinking that may well ensue from one's recognition that an earlier form of thinking and acting was inappropriate or sinful. "After thinking" would then be a redirection of thinking and action, specifically a "turning" or "conversion" to a new heart and/or mind. At this point, *metanoia* has general resemblance to the Hebrew word *teshuvah*, which derives from a word meaning "to return," religiously a (re)turning from disobedience to obedience, an aversion to sin and an adversion to God.[11] The Greek equivalents are *epistrophē* and *epistrepsomai*, both of which mean "to turn" or "to convert." *Epistrophē* and *metanoia* can indeed complement each other, as in the verse from Luke referenced above:

"If [the other] trespass against you seven times in a day, and seven times in a day turn [*épistrephō*] again to you, saying, I repent [*metanoéō*]: you shall forgive [the other]."[12]

Notwithstanding the etymological evidence for interpreting *metanoia* as something other than "repentance" proper, one need not necessarily abandon or attenuate the "Baptist" notion of regret and sorrow as Caputo threatens to do. The old Texas Baptist B. H. Carroll, the founder and first president of Southwestern Baptist Theological Seminary, agrees that *metanoia* should not be reduced to repentance in the sense of regret or sorrow; however, he contends that neither should it exclude these affective responses. He insists that if one examines the broader biblical revelation, one will certainly discover that there can be no genuine change of heart or mind if there is not, concomitant with that change, some sense of sorrow and contrition, what the Apostle Paul calls the "godly sorrow" that leads to repentance.[13] "Godly sorrow" expresses a genuine sense of responsibility, the affirmation on the part of the sinner (the victimizer) that he or she has truly committed a wrong against God or some other individual (the victim). Why would any victimizer turn to a victim and confess a change of heart if the victimizer did not first feel the pangs of responsibility and the sorrow of having wounded another? Why would a victim, even one dedicated to a Caputoan/Christian "pardonology," diminish that feeling of responsibility and manifest a functional contempt for the other's self-interpretation? If one reduces forgiveness to "forget it; it was nothing," one may actually depreciate the other's and one's own self-respect by apparently condoning the victimization. Ostensibly, however, the only way to circumvent such a reduction of forgiveness to what Aurel Kolnai terms "condonation"[14] would be to reintroduce an economic cycle of duty and obligation, that is, to return to a Baptist sense of repentance, which Caputo assiduously wants to circumvent. But can Caputo indisputably totalize his intended abandonment of some type of economy? Can one understand *metanoia* as not including an obligatory reciprocity of responsibility and remorse? Is there actually a ghost of a chance that an economy of repentance can be avoided so that sinners are allowed to "take a walk"?[15]

Throughout Caputo's brilliant and provocative Derridean/Christian hermeneutic of the kingdom of God, of mad economics, of metanoetics, of forgiveness, and of the pure gift, one should be able to discern a specter that continually haunts the discussion—the specter of the "quasi," the spirit of the "almost." Caputo affirms that the idea of the pure gift is a quasi-transcendental concept that not only grounds the structure of giving—its possibility—but also grounds the structure of nongiving; that is, its impossibility (170). One might say, therefore, that there is a pure gift—almost. That "almost" results in a contamination of the "pure" gift in that there can never truly be a pure gift, a gift without some residual economy operating alongside it. At best, the idea of "pure" gift acts as a supplement to economy, which in its Derridean dissemination means both an addendum to *and* a replacement of economy. Consequently, one must avoid the fallacy of bifurcation and never think disjunctively that *either* the pure gift obtains *or* that the closed circle of an economy of exchange obtains. One must spread one's Hegelian eagle wings and fly to the dialectic. Now I am aware, of course, that the dialectical "both/and" is one of the pet notions of metaphysical, logocentric thinkers. Yet I am also aware that the polarity fits this particular situation perfectly. Nor am I alone in thinking so. I quote a fellow "Hegelian:" "Learn *both* to give *and* to exchange; learn to see that each depends upon, invades, and interweaves with the other."[16] So writes John Caputo as he sums up in a nutshell the relationship between gift and economy! He confesses that gift and economy constantly move in a *pas de deux*, with economy leading round and round in a circle of exchange and the gift always taking surprising steps toward a more improvisational movement. As a result, there is never, ever any pure economy or pure gift, but there is the tension between the two that keeps the circle of exchange loose, open for the aleatoric, and accommodating alterity.[17]

Of course, if gift and economy do correlate, then forgiveness and *metanoia* cannot themselves necessarily avoid economic miscegenation. Issues of debt, return, and obligation do arise even within the milieu of a postmodern Christian philosophy of the kingdom. I suggest that these issues must continue to hold significance, for, if they do not, then Caputo's interpretation of forgiveness might threaten to deteriorate into a passive acceptance of sin and oppression. Now I do not accuse Caputo of promoting that deterioration. On the contrary, I hope to show that his radical hermeneutics offers strategies for avoiding it; however, I do believe that Caputo's abhorrence of a "pure" economy of retribution and resentment leads him to use a rhetoric that appears to advocate just such a dismissive attitude toward sinful and unethical behavior. "Forget it; it was nothing" may be taken as an expression of a tolerant attitude toward sin and offense. In other words, I fear that his approach might lead to confusing the *pardoning* of sin with the *condoning* of sin.

One way of avoiding the confusion of pardoning with condoning is to rethink the relationship between John and Jesus with reference to repentance and *metanoia*. Perhaps Caputo himself comes close to committing the fallacy of bifurcation and fails to realize that one need not choose between a "Baptist" and a "kingdom" explanation of repentance. There may well be two keys to the kingdom: one that locks the offender in the reality of disobedience toward God and disregard for the other, and another that liberates from the judgment that disobedience truly deserves. What if repentance and forgiveness compose a symphony in the kingdom of God, a symphony with two movements—the first in B minor, a movement of grief and remorse, and the second in G major, a movement celebrating liberation and reconciliation? What if the two motifs of grace and judgment are interwoven into the texture of the piece in such a way that the dissonance of guilt supplies a counterpoint to the harmony of absolution? It would be far better, within the broader parameters of Caputo's forging of forgiveness as a *quasi*-pure gift, to critique the economy of exchange and direct a hermeneutic of suspicion against every circle of retribution and every attempt at perverting forgiveness into a debt, but without threatening to disparage—that is, to cheapen—the experience of suffering inflicted and clemency given.

The debt of obligation and the gift of death

In all honesty, I wonder whether Caputo's reaction to the Baptist view of repentance does not reveal something of a residual Catholic understanding of the penitential process. Or as a mutual friend, Merold Westphal, once opined, perhaps Caputo continues to be haunted by the nuns! Such a Catholic contamination of the Baptist view would certainly explain his reaction against what, in many ways, is indeed a penitential protocol predicated upon a closed circle of exchange—a definite expenditure with return. Thomas Aquinas exemplifies just such a protocol. He clearly delineates a fourfold procedure for attaining forgiveness. First, the mind, which in sin turns against God and the good, must be reordered so as to rethink the disobedience and grieve over the profanation of divine grace. This rethinking obviously is *metanoia* or contrition. Yet *metanoia* does not preclude the necessity for some type of punishment; consequently, Aquinas prescribes that confession must be made to one of God's ministers; that is, a priest. The priest, in turn, may remit some of the temporal punishment for the debt of sin; however, he may also require the penitent to make reparation, to pay back the debt he has incurred in sinning. This economic transaction is satisfaction, engaging in prescribed acts that result in meeting one's contractual obligations. Afterwards, the process may conclude with the affirmation of absolution, although again, there is no guarantee that residual punishment is not still required.[18] Undoubtedly, for Caputo, the vexing moment in this process is step three, satisfaction. No other station along the itinerary toward absolution so belies the gift character of forgiveness. No matter how much Aquinas may extol the gift dimension of divine grace, his insistence on repaying the debt through acts of satisfaction subverts any genuine sense of receiving forgiveness as gift.[19] In this stratagem, one functionally earns forgiveness through a purely economic process. The sinner is the debtor, God is the one owed, and the priest becomes the collection agent.

If John the Baptist is actually John the Catholic, then I join Caputo in his denunciation of repentance and welcome his substituting for it the donative dynamic of metanoetic forgiveness. I am not convinced, however, that he has appropriately heard John's wilderness voice. John the Baptist's role in the kingdom of God is as herald, as the one who comes before to announce the coming Messiah. John's ministry aims at preparing hearts and minds for the liberating good news brought by Jesus—the news that the cycle of debt and retribution has been broken by the gracious acts of God. Yet this message is good news only for those who are trapped in the economic cycle of resentment and will be heard only by those who believe that they need to hear it. Consequently, only those who rethink their position before God, who affirm that they need the gift, who realize that they cannot gain heaven economically, will await the Messiah's advent. In other words, only those who accept responsibility for their sin, who mourn over their transgressions, who insist on empirically confirming the sincerity of their changed hearts, and who confess their inability to merit redemption will change their hearts and seek divine benefaction. In confirming the seriousness of their sin, they in turn enhance the mystery of the divine endowments of forgiveness and reconciliation.

Actually, a genuine rapprochement between *metanoia* as gift and as economy might not be completely alien to Caputo's thought. Within the broader structures of Caputo's radical hermeneutics, one can argue for a more dialectical interpretation of repentance that synthesizes John and Jesus. I wish to reference two of these areas in something of a tentative thought experiment. First, in Caputo's kingdom hermeneutic, he emphasizes the significance of the other, the singular enfleshed individual who is a *tout autre* over against the ipseity of my own self. Although the kingdom of God invites all people to live within its borders, it uniquely concerns itself with those fleshly others who have been victimized, the widows and the orphans, those whom Lyotard calls *les juifs*. These others who have been afflicted by physical, emotional, and/or spiritual disasters cry out for response, for someone to hear their laments and acknowledge their worth as human beings. Caputo insists that in the kingdom, the call of the suffering other addresses me and obligates me, binding (*ligare*) me toward (*ob*) the other, demanding my response, my *me voici*—"here I am."[20] I have a responsibility toward the other, the widows and the orphans, those laid low, those who have lost face, who have been silenced, who have been excluded, excised, excommunicated, X'd out by the ruling authorities. Consequently, Caputo's critique of the circle of exchange cannot be interpreted as a complete dismissal of a protocol of reciprocity, since I do exist in a *Mitwelt* within which I have certain responsibilities toward the suffering other.

Yet if obligation happens and I recognize a responsibility for and to the other, how exactly am I to respond to the call of injured flesh? On the one hand, I could engage in theological and philosophical ruminations and seek to create or discover a system of ethics that would ground my obligatory actions. Of course, while I am waiting to determine the universal ethical grounds upon which I must stand in order to adjudicate moral situations and from which I must deliberate my appropriate responses, the fleshly other remains condemned to her or his abyss of suffering. Consequently, this perspective may seduce me to inactivity, to an ethical paralysis brought on by my inability to close the system. On the other hand, I could reach out to the other therapeutically and respond to a heteronomy outside myself, to the other law, to the law (*nomos*) of the other (*heteros*), and just accept my obligation to respond. Caputo adopts this second perspective and calls it a "responsible postmodernism."[21] He warns that I should not seek the safety of systems or the security of certainty before I act on behalf of the other. I do not know why obligations happen; they just do. I cannot always identify the source of the call of obligation. Is it Being? Is it the conscience? Is it God? I do not know for sure. I only know that there are obligations—*Il y a, es gibt* obligation. Obligations just happen.[22]

Or do they? Always? Or are there instances in which I know precisely why the enfleshed individual calls out in pain and why he or she calls out in pain *to me*? The call may well come in the accusative case because it is a call of accusation, condemning *me* for oppressing, wounding, and exploiting the other. Through physical and/or emotional violence, through stinging words, and/or through neglect and a dismissive attitude, I may be the one guilty of violating the other, of transforming the other into *le juif*. In denying any transcendental theoretical grounds for obligation, Caputo writes of the "somewhat mute pointing of my finger (*indicare*) to indicate what is happening (*arrive*)."[23] When I have wronged another, my mute finger points back at me, indicating that *I* am the victimizer, that it is *I* who have created an economic situation and made myself accountable to the other on account of my offensive actions. I do indeed now owe the other my response to the call of obligation, since I am liable for the offense. I can no longer claim some Nietzschean innocence of becoming, some heteromorphic play of cosmic forces. On the contrary, I have an obligation to feel the pain of contrition, to confess "yes, I am guilty," and to beg the other for forgiveness—which the other does not owe me—because I have become the victimizer.

I am suggesting that one can comprehend Caputo's stand against ethics as offering a possible reconsideration of repentance as a proper voicing of the *me voici.* Furthermore, I am suggesting that such an understanding prohibits forgiveness from deteriorating into condonation expressly because a responsibly postmodern confession of sin should be predicated upon a sincere concession to the personal worth of the victim. Jeffrie Murphy, in his work on retribution, mercy, and forgiveness, argues against condonation from the perspective of the self-worth of the victim. He acknowledges that in contemporary philosophy of criminal law, passions such as anger and revenge are oftentimes considered to be less than civilized and even non-Christian. He calls such sensations "retributive emotions" and contends that these emotions actually express a sense of resentment, which in turn manifests an intrinsic feeling of self-respect.[24] In other words, I am in a position to forgive precisely because I believe that I do not deserve injustice and that I suffer innocently at the victimizer's hand. The victimization degrades me and insults me, which results in an awareness of losing face and in resentment.[25] Utilizing Joseph Butler's definition of forgiveness as the "forswearing of resentment," Murphy contends that my forgiving another should not be confused with excusing, justifying, or showing mercy. Instead, forgiveness should focus on overcoming the feelings that I have toward the one who has wounded me, but not in such a way as to sacrifice my self-esteem or pervert morality; that is, forgiveness should be the overcoming of resentment for proper reasons, among which are the following: the victimizer repents; his motives were good; or he has suffered enough for his action.

The significance of self-esteem in the context of repentance and forgiveness comes to expression through a number of different cultural idioms. For example, David Park, a Korean Christian, indicts the traditional ecclesiastical concern with sin as being too absorbed with the sinner and not with the victim of sin. He attempts to rectify that imbalance by referencing the Korean concept of *han*, which refers to the "abysmal experience of pain" that derives from the individual's being injured by sinful acts.[26] *Han* may come to expression actively or passively as frustrated hope, as letting go, as resentful bitterness, as self-denigration, as resignation, or as self-hatred.[27] Regardless of how it comes to expression, however, *han* always indicates that a person implicitly worthy of respect has been injured and that that person's feelings should not be minimized by any semblance of condonation. Obviously, *han* references the same consideration of self-esteem that Murphy broaches from his more Western perspective. Again, the issue of forgiveness must account for the negative emotions and moral rights that a victim possesses. Principally because I do have the "right" to feel retributive emotions and can morally exercise my right to respond retributively to the victimization am I in a position to change those emotions, give up my rights for revenge, and forgive the victimizer, especially when the victimizer acknowledges feelings of self-resentment over the wrongful acts and confesses to a change of heart over what they have done. But at no point in the process of repentance and forgiveness should the reality of the wrong be denied, at no point should the worth of the wounded other be disparaged by a cavalier repudiation of the severity of the wrong, and at no point should the gift of forgiveness be so disdained as to accept it as "giving" permission for the wrong to be repeated.

What I am arguing here with reference to the worth of individuals might be understood as a commentary on Caputo's "antinomy of obligation—holding both a forgetful forgiveness and the 'dangerous memory of suffering.'"[28] This Caputoan antinomy reinforces what I have already stated quite clearly, that is, that I do not think Caputo goes so far as to collapse forgiveness into con-donation. Yet I continue to feel a bit uncomfortable with some of his more radical statements in opposition to any economic character to the dynamic of forgiveness. For example, if I do understand repentance and forgiveness from within a Caputoan poetics of obligation, can I sincerely accept his claim that my *metanoia* should be merely a verbal expression acknowledging that my heart has changed and requesting that the victim give me forgiveness? Is that always enough? Or should there not be at times the need for some type of "satisfaction," some empirical, tangible expression of my remorse? I am not referring to an economics of restitution, to the need for securing some oper-ant currency with which to retire my debt and purchase forgiveness, but to Jesus' own injunction to "bring forth fruit in keeping with repentance" (Matt. 3:8). If I may be permitted a bit of heresy in an essay on a noted Continental philosopher and allowed to reference an Analytical theme, I might interpret Jesus' statement as avowing that repentance is *not* a performative, that I do not accomplish repentance in the simple act of speaking the words. No mat-ter how often or loudly I claim that my heart has changed, I may well be giving false testimony by dissimulating my true intention behind hypocritical confessions. Repentance, therefore, needs some confirmation, some orthopraxic manifestation of sincerity.

Now I do concede that actions might be just as hypocritical as words. Both verbal and tangible expressions of repentance ultimately are confessions that must be given credence; that is, accepted on faith. I certainly agree with Caputo when he admits that I must encounter the other with an initial faith, giving the other credit based not on "demonstrative certainty" but on the evanescence of testimony.[29] Even actions ostensibly evidencing the fidelity of my intentions may well be counterfeit; however, acts of contrition may well serve as corroborating pragmatic confirmation that my change of heart has been genuine. So I am not bribing the other into forgiving but am simply *giving* evidence to the other of my purity of heart. The biblical narrative of

Zaccheus (Luke 19:1–8) illustrates my point well. After Zaccheus encounters Christ and has his heart changed, he decides to give half of his fortune to the poor and to compensate those he has defrauded by returning to them four times what he took. He does this not by command or out of guilt but as a voluntary metanoetic expression of his repentance, a repentance that eventuates in an extravagance of donation and return, not merely in some parsimonious repayment of a debt. Zaccheus hears the call of obligation; he responds with his *me voici*; and he gives concrete confirmation of his *metanoia* and his contrition. He instantiates Caputo's declaration that the "yield of giving is more giving" (227).

The second aspect of my thought experiment references Caputo's dependence upon Derrida's notion of the "gift of death," a dependence that invites another comparison with a Baptist account of repentance. This comparison's attraction stems from the significance that the "gift of death" has for shattering the economic circle of exchange and for establishing the quasi-transcendentality of the pure gift. Caputo correctly identifies the meaning of repentance as "to feel pain again," a meaning that he takes to be confined to an economy of retribution. The word "repent" certainly does derive from the root *paen*, yielding the cognate "pain." Yet the root actually means "almost," carrying the idea that suffering or pain is "almost" death.[30] Consequently, one could say that if I have caused someone pain—that is, victimized another in some way—then I have given them death almost (*donner la mort . . . presque*).[31] The call of obligation from the other whom I have caused pain accuses me of my sin and demands my repentance, the repetition of pain, but this time the feeling of pain again myself. Under these circumstances, one could interpret repentance as "giving again the 'gift of death . . . almost.'" In this second gift, however, I would be giving death to myself, the "self" who inflicted the disaster on the flesh of the other. Feeling the pain of remorse expresses my dissatisfaction with myself as victimizer. I no longer desire, then, to be that old self. Consequently, I rethink myself and my actions; I resolve to become another person, to change my mind and my heart. I wish death upon the old self, to have it crucified, not as a sacrifice but as an execution, as "giving death . . . almost." But is this not in actuality what Jesus—and Caputo—mean by *metanoia*? My old thoughts are dead; my old heart no longer beats; I have become a new person. Consequently, my "giving death . . . almost" to myself—my quasi-death—forms the basis of my metanoetic metamorphosis.

Understanding *metanoia* as a quasi-death, as a "giving death . . . almost" to the "old" self, allows for the paradox of forgiveness to become less paradoxical. The paradox of forgiveness concerns the issue of whether forgiveness need actually be given to a genuinely repentant person. If a person does have a change of heart, renounces the old self that committed the offense, and becomes a new person intent on avoiding such behavior in the future, does the victim any longer have a legitimate context within which to grant forgiveness? Why does this "new" self need the gift of forgiveness if she or he is not the self that committed the wrong? Does repentance not make forgiveness pointless?[32] If one understands *metanoia* as a quasi-death, one can answer this last question negatively. Forgiveness is certainly *not* pointless, since the new self is not a total repudiation of the old. Repentance is "giving death . . . *almost*" to the old person, not giving death completely. The new self maintains a continuity with the old and, in doing so, retains responsibility for the previous victimizing act. Were it not for this continuity, the only forgiveness allowable would be the forgiveness of the *un*repentant victimizer, the one who refused to die to the old self—a situation that would be untenable both to Jesus and to Caputo.

Yet just as *metanoia* results from a "giving death . . . almost" on the part of the victimizer, it also motivates a "giving death . . . almost" on the part of the victim. The victim has every right to demand retribution and is under no obligation to donate forgiveness. In my sin against the other, I have established the validity of an economics of revenge, so that the afflicted other may indeed demand whatever pound of flesh I should repay for having injured her or his flesh. The *metanoia* prescribed by Jesus, however, induces the victim to "give death . . . almost" to the "self" that possesses the entitlement to feel resentment. The letting go, the forgetting, and the gift of pardon come from a new "self," one that has had a change of heart, that has been itself freed from the constraints of the claustrophobic enclosure of the quid pro quo. The "giving death . . . almost" to the resentful self allows for the gift of forgiveness, which thereby becomes a *donner la vie*—a giving life back to an estranged relationship, a realization of a reconciliation that is no longer a reconciling of accounts but of hearts and minds.

Were I to express my point theologically, I would say that forgiveness of sin should never be established on the ruins of God's holiness; that is, God's self-esteem and worth as the Creator. Sin is always an affront to God and a wounding of the divine heart. I say this on the basis of my comprehension of a theology of the cross. My own Christian understanding of Jesus' death and resurrection, which I admit differs from Caputo's, leads me to recognize that judgment and grace do not mutually exclude each other. L. Gregory Jones says it best: "If the cross provides the judgment of God's grace, the resurrection provides the grace of that judgment."[33] In other words, God gives forgiveness to all human beings, yet without any intimation that their sins are insignificant. God forgets sins, separates the sinner from the sin as far as East is from West, but again does not do so in such a way that the amnesty and the amnesia are misconstrued. The cross event constantly reminds us that God's grace may be free and genuinely unearned, but it is not cheap. Consequently, the avoidance of any semblance of condonation in Christian forgiveness is crucial.

Conclusion

One may now ask: "Is Caputo correct when he claims that the 'kingdom of God does not turn on pain and repentance . . . ?'" (223).[34] The answer most consistent with this essay is "Well, yes and no." The kingdom of God does indeed "turn on" pain in the sense of coming out against it, attacking it, desiring to defeat it. Jesus reveals that God wishes to redeem, to restore, and to forgive through an incomprehensible grace that binds the divine and the human together in a community of giving. Yet this grace in no way minimizes the gravity of sin that pulls people away from God and from each other and that demands to be addressed and not merely avoided. God's pardoning is not condoning; it disallows turning a blind eye and/or a deaf ear to the serious repercussions of sin. Consequently, the kingdom does turn on the pain of repentance, of giving death to the old self that rebels against God and inflicts injury on the other. It turns on a turning and a returning, on the turning of contrition and confession, on *teshuvah* and *epistropheē*, on the returning to God and to the enfleshed singular individual who has suffered at the hands of the victimizer. It turns on the turning over of a new leaf, on the turning out of an old heart, on the turning toward the other with a response of *me voici, je regrette d'avoir fait cela*.

Ironically, through it all, I believe that Caputo comes quite close to being more Baptist than he might admit, not only in that his thought allows for the two movements of the symphony of salvation—John's B minor dirge and Jesus' G major anthem—but also on the implicit critique he directs at the arrogance and self-righteousness of a salvation by works instead of by grace. Baptists have always centered salvation in the divine gift of Jesus Christ, denying any soteriology that attempts to make redemption a reward or a wage that God pays to those who earn God's favor. Baptists only accept an economy of exchange that reveals the wages of sin, that if God dealt with us in a purely mercantile fashion, we would receive the wages of our sin, which is, of course, death—not death . . . almost. Baptists may embrace, therefore, Caputo's malediction pronounced against the economy of retribution and the circle of exchange and read it as a gloss on Ephesians 2:8–9, a passage dearly loved by Baptists: "For by grace have you been saved through faith; and that not of yourselves, it is the gift of God; not of works, that no one should boast." So on behalf of Baptists everywhere, I extend to Professor

Caputo the call *Viens! Viens!* "Come! Come!" and embrace a Baptist understanding of repentance. Let us hear your *me voici* and your *oui, oui*.[35] We await *l'invention de l'autre catholique*—the incoming of the Catholic other![36] Or if I may paraphrase a prophetic call—with apologies to Pope Rocky I and his Pentecostal sermon in Acts 2:38—I admonish Caputo to "Repent and be a Baptist for the forgiveness of sins and you shall receive the gift of the Holy Spirit!"

Notes

1 Jacques Derrida, "Edmund Jabès and the question of the book," in *Writing and Difference*, Alan Bass, trans. (Chicago: University of Chicago Press, 1978), p. 67.
2 Leonard Sweet, *Quantum Spirituality: A Postmodern Apologetic* (Dayton, OH: Whaleprints, 1994), pp. 84–91.
3 Ibid., p. 87.
4 John D. Caputo, "Metanoetics: elements of a postmodern Christian philosophy," unpublished manuscript; John D. Caputo, "Reason, history and a little madness: towards a hermeneutics of the kingdom," *Proceedings of the American Catholic Philosophical Association* 68 (1994): 27–44. Caputo has revised the latter article as "Reason, history, and a little madness: towards an ethics of the kingdom," in Richard Kearney and Mark Dooley, eds., *Questioning Ethics: Contemporary Debates in Philosophy* (New York: Routledge, 1999), pp. 84–104.
5 Caputo uses "Felix Sineculpa" as the proper name for one of the "Lyrical-philosophical discourse" authors in *Against Ethics*. This *nom de guerre* represents the heteromorphic, Nietzschean perspective of an "irresponsible" postmodernism, one that embraces the "innocence of becoming" beyond any distinction between good and evil (*Against Ethics: Contributions to a Poetics of Obligation with Constant Reference to Deconstruction* (Bloomington: Indiana University Press, 1993), p. 134). With reference to his radical hermeneutics of repentance, the phrase should be taken in its literal Latin meaning of "happy without guilt" and not as a reference to any version of an irresponsible postmodernism. Cf. also note 26 below.
6 Caputo, "Metanoetics," p. 11.
7 John D. Caputo, "'Instants, secrets, and singularities: dealing death in Kierkegaard and Derrida", in *Kierkegaard in Post/Modernity,* Martin J. Matuŏtík and Merold Westphal, eds. (Bloomington: Indiana University Press, 1995), pp. 232–37.
8 Derrida's more explicit treatments of the notion of gift may be found in *Given Time, I: Counterfeit Money*, Peggy Kamuf, trans. (Chicago: University of Chicago Press, 1991) and *The Gift of Death*, David Wills, trans. (Chicago: University of Chicago Press, 1995). The topic, however, is so significant to his philosophy that it arises constantly throughout his work. Cf. *Specters of Marx: The State of the Debt, the Work of Mourning, and the New International*, Peggy Kamuf, trans. (New York: Routledge, 1994), pp. 22–28; *Points . . . Interviews, 1974–94*, Peggy Kamuf, et al., trans. (Stanford, CA: Stanford University Press, 1995), pp. 97, 209; and "The Villanova round table: a conversation with Jacques Derrida," in John D. Caputo, *Deconstruction in a Nutshell: A Conversation with Jacques Derrida* (New York: Fordham University Press, 1997), pp. 18–19.
9 For a creative "postmodern" interpretation of this parable as it relates to an economy of gift, see Jean-Luc Marion, *God without Being*, Thomas Carlson, trans. (Chicago: University of Chicago Press, 1991), pp. 95–101.

10 *Theological Dictionary of the New Testament*, Gerhard Friedrich, ed., Geoffrey W. Bromiley, trans. (Grand Rapids, MI: William B. Eerdmans, 1971), IV:626.
11 Jacob Neusner, "Repentance in Judaism," in *Repentance: A Comparative Perspective*, Amitai Etzioni and David E. Carney, eds. (Lanham, MD: Rowman & Littlefield, 1997), p. 61; cf. also Harold O. J. Brown, "Godly sorrow, sorrow of the world: some Christian thoughts on repentance," ibid., p. 35.
12 *Theological Dictionary of the New Testament*, VII:726.
13 B. H. Carroll, *The Bible Doctrine of Repentance* (Louisville, KY: Baptist Book Concern, 1897), pp. 43f.
14 Aurel Kolnai, "Forgiveness," *Proceedings of the Aristotelian Society* (1973–74), p. 96.
15 John D. Caputo, "The end of ethics." Forthcoming in *Blackwell Guide to Ethics*, p. 27.
16 *Deconstruction in a Nutshell*, p. 146.
17 Ibid., p. 147.
18 Thomas Aquinas, *Summa Contra Gentiles*, IV, 72.
19 Thomas Aquinas, *Summa Theologia*, 3a. 88. 2.
20 *Against Ethics*, pp. 10–11; *Prayers and Tears*, p. 199; "Instants, secrets, and singularities," p. 220.
21 Caputo first makes an explicit distinction between a "responsible" and an "irresponsible" postmodernism in "Sacred anarchy: fragments of a postmodern ethics," an unpublished paper presented to the "Deconstruction and Catholic Theology" symposium at Conception Seminary, February 1990, p. 9. This same polarity comes to expression under the rubrics of "heteronomism" and "heteromorphism" in *Against Ethics*, pp. 43–68.
22 *Against Ethics*, pp. 6–8, 24, 85.
23 Ibid., p. 24.
24 Jeffrie Murphy, "Forgiveness and resentment," in *Forgiveness and Mercy*, Jeffrie G. Murphy and Jean Hampton, eds. (New York: Cambridge University Press, 1988), p. 16.
25 Ibid., p. 28.
26 David Park, *The Wounded Heart of God* (Nashville, TN: Abingdon Press, 1993), p. 15.
27 Ibid., pp. 31, 33.
28 *Against Ethics*, p. 118.
29 *Deconstruction in a Nutshell*, pp. 167f.
30 Joseph T. Shipley, *The Origins of English Words: A Discursive Dictionary of Indo-European Roots* (Baltimore: Johns Hopkins University Press, 1984), p. 287.
31 *Donner la mort* is the original title of Derrida's *The Gift of Death*.
32 Kolnai, pp. 98f.
33 Gregory Jones, *Embodying Forgiveness: A Theological Analysis* (Grand Rapids, MI: William B. Eerdmans, 1995), p. 124. Cf. also Cornelius Plantinga, Jr., *Not the Way It's Supposed to Be* (Grand Rapids, MI: William B. Eerdmans, 1995), p. 199.
34 Cf. "Instants, secrets, and singularities," p. 233.
35 Caputo claims that deconstruction focuses on the "to come," passionately anticipating the unknown that has not yet arrived. The call of deconstruction then is twofold: Come, *viens* and Yes, *oui*. Together these themes identify the messianic character of Derrida's passion for the impossible. They reveal the affirmative nature of his philosophy and are counterfactual to every misinterpretation of deconstruction as negative and nihilistic. Cf. *Prayers and Tears*, pp. 56–57; *Deconstruction in a Nutshell*, p. 179.
36 "Invention of the other" (*l'invention de l'autre*) should be read in its etymological sense of "*in-venire*," the in-coming of the other. This phrase coheres thematically

with *viens*, *oui*, the messianic, and the affirmative nature of deconstruction. Cf. *Deconstruction in a Nutshell*, p. 42 and Jacques Derrida, "Psyche: inventions of the other" in *Reading De Man Reading*, Lindsey Waters and Wlad Godzich, eds. (Minneapolis: University of Minnesota Press, 1989), p. 56.

6　Caputo's Derrida

David Goicoechea

Jack Caputo's reading of Derrida's philosophy of religion is well organized, thorough and clear. He selects six essential traits of religion for his
table of contents and crafts his text around them. His choice of (1) the
apophatic, (2) the apocalyptic, (3) the Messiah, (4) the gift, (5) circumcision, and (6) confession is simple and yet profound. We might wonder if
there could be a better way of dividing up the religious phenomenon for
the sake of analysis. His organization around these six points is simple and
yet he is able to be very thorough. By treating the prayers and tears of
Derrida, Caputo is most of all able to keep the passion in religion. He is
able to put Derrida in good company with the divine madness of Plato's
Phaedrus, the wonder of Aristotle and Descartes, the enthusiasm of those
God-intoxicated philosophers Spinoza and Nietzsche. By abiding very close
to Derrida's reverent and yet playful exploration of those three great secret
things, sex, death, and religion, Caputo keeps alive the passion for the
mysterium tremendum. And yet, in spite of his wandering in the unlimited
realm of religious depths, heights, surfaces and horizons, Caputo brings out
Derrida's meticulous precision as a philosopher. Derrida's third logic of
mixed opposites is clearly differentiated from the old logic of exclusive
opposites and the modern logic of implicational opposites. The meaning
and force of prayers and tears as they relate to the six essential traits of
religion are clearly distinguished from what prayers and tears would be in
the Platonic Aristotelian logic of noncontradiction or the Hegelian logic of
contradiction.

The precision of Derrida's philosophizing is indicated in Caputo's subtitle:
Religion without Religion. The task is to show in what way the variety of
interpretations of the religious ideal each claim how we should do with and
without prayers, with and without tears, with and without the apocalyptic,
the Messiah, the gift, circumcision and confession. Just as traditional and
modern philosophy arrived at precision concerning the "with" and the

"without" through demonstration, definition, distinction, and dialectics, so Derrida gets this precision with his undecidability, dissemination, *différance*, and deconstruction. Caputo clarifies the essential phenomena of faith by means of these philosophical categories of Derrida's reasoning. He clearly shows how the dissemination of ethics and religion can foster an ethics and religion of dissemination.

However, as I read Caputo, it seems to me that his reading of Nietzsche, Heidegger, and Levinas is not quite Derrida's reading. Furthermore, my reading of Kierkegaard differs from both Derrida's and Caputo's. They both seem to agree with Kierkegaard completely. However, it seems to me that the "with" and the "without" of Derrida and of Caputo differ from the "without" of Kierkegaard in a way that will have implications for their understanding of the gift, the Messiah, prayer, etc. It all has to do with just how to read undecidability. I will argue that Derrida thinks with more undecidability than does Caputo. Derrida is always undecidable about the "with" and the "without." Caputo puts more emphasis on the "without." But Derrida's is not quite the well-balanced "with" and "without" of Kierkegaard; for Derrida emphasizes only the first movement of the leap's pure giving and not also the second movement of the leap's receiving of the gift. In order to show how in the very material that Caputo provides there needs to be a slightly other understanding of the "with" and the "without," I will reflect upon Caputo's treatment of: (1) undecidability, Kierkegaard, and the giving of the gift; (2) dissemination, Nietzsche, and guidance in the desert; (3) *différance*, Heidegger, and the origin of messianicity; and (4) deconstruction, Levinas, and martyrdom.

Undecidability, Kierkegaard, and the giving of the gift

Caputo's focus upon the notion of "religion without religion" indicates an important task for the philosopher of religion. Historical process happens when new forms or traits of religion replace old forms or traits. In what way the replacing remains a repeating is part of the question. Philosophy of religion since Hegel seeks to account for the processes that let there be, for example, Kierkegaard's religiousness B with or without religiousness A. In *The Gift of Death* Derrida concerns himself with what traits of orgiastic religion Platonic philosophy does without and yet in some way retains. He treats the ways in which Christianity seeks to do without Platonism and the ways in which it retains it. Derrida works very hard in showing how certain remains are retained even if much is done without. He writes that Kant, Hegel, Kierkegaard, and many key Continental philosophers "belong to that tradition that consists of proposing a nondogmatic doublet of dogma, a philosophical and metaphysical doublet, in any case, a thinking that repeats the possibility of religion without religion."[1]

Derrida with his philosophy of undecidability does this too. In reflecting upon the leap of undecidability, he universalizes Kierkegaard's treatment of Abraham's leap when he decided to sacrifice Isaac. Derrida seems to think that his interpretation of the leap over the abyss of undecidability is essentially the same as Kierkegaard's. But is it? If we conceptually contrast the meaning of Derrida's image of the hedgehog crossing the highway with the knight of faith living on all three floors of the house at once, the difference will become clear.

Derrida's philosophy of giving works with the distinction and the opposition between giving and taking. His task is to valorize pure giving, which alone lets the gift be a gift. If a gift is given only in the context of an exchange of gifts, then it is not really a gift. There has to be an element of asymmetrical giving without return that will let the giving be morally a giving. Derrida is able to show that even though a taking will accompany every giving, it is possible still to have a pure giving that is distinct from the giving and taking. This impossible pure giving, impossible because there must always be returns, becomes possible because of the principle of dissemination that makes there be unlimited returns.[2] Insofar as she/he gives with the awareness of unlimited returns, the giver gives in oblivion. She/he does not give with only the expectation of some definite returns. She/he can give over the abyss of uncertainty with trust. She/he cannot be certain of any particular good gift in return. Derrida, in valorizing pure giving, shows with his principle of dissemination which makes for undecidability, how it is possible. He explains how ethical or spiritual giving can be.

But Kierkegaard does not treat the give and the take; rather he treats the give and the get and he valorizes both. He does not decide between them and think that the giving is worthy and that the getting is not. Kierkegaard's interpretation of Abraham's leap of faith is different from Derrida's. Derrida valorizes the single-movement leap over the abyss of undecidability; but Kierkegaard valorizes the double-movement leap of faith. Kierkegaard's Abraham is willing to give Isaac up in an act of pure giving which absolutely loves the absolute; but by faith he also believes by virtue of the absurd that he will get Isaac back. By faith he also relatively loves the relative. Derrida does not deny that Abraham might get Isaac back. He does not actively do without that. He makes explicit Kierkegaard's reflection upon getting Isaac back.[3] But he does not valorize the getting as he does the giving. Kierkegaard valorizes the getting back even more than he valorizes the giving up. Pure giving for him is infinite resignation; but getting Isaac back is a matter of faith.

With his disconcerting principle of dissemination Derrida can explain much about the saying from Matthew 6:1–4: "But when thou doest alms, let not thy left hand know what thy right hand doeth; That thine alms may be in secret; and thy Father which seeth in secret shall reward thee openly."[4] He can explain the oblivion of the left hand's not knowing.

This is central to Derrida's philosophy. His hedgehog of "*Che cos è la poesia?*"[5] seeks to cross the highway of the event, the decision, the gift, the promise, the translation, however you want to interpret it. When he is in the middle of the highway he hears the approaching car. He halts, rolling up into a defensive ball in order to ward off the danger with his quills. Simply getting across the road of pure giving or deciding is impossible. It is impossible that the giving be pure. It will always get returns. It is impossible that the decision can ever be calculated with certainty because its outcomes are unlimited. We are always halted by the abyss of undecidability. The three aporias of not enough time, not enough knowledge, and not enough precedents always halt us before the abyss. But it is urgent that we decide or give even if there can be no objective certainty and even if there will be unknown returns. So Derrida's hedgehog does decide with the leap of faith over the abyss. But even with that, he still never gets across the road. He is always on the way with the abyss in front of him. This is what Caputo loves so much: the ongoing task that never loses its passion. If we ever could get across and achieve justice and peace, passionate life would halt. Because the hedgehog halts before the abyss, he can always be on the way and never halted in his passion for justice and peace.

But Kierkegaard's double-movement leap of faith is different from the single-movement leap of Derrida's hedgehog. In *Sickness unto Death,*[6] with an image that is pertinent to his whole philosophy, Kierkegaard has Anti Climacus explain that many people are only aesthetes who live lives of despair in the basement of their spiritual house. However, a person can move out of impulsive immediacy and go up and live on the first floor of ethical reflection or decision. But, as Job's life shows, even the ethical life can become one of despair and sickness unto death. However, the person can then leap up to the second floor through infinite resignation in which he or she becomes resigned to not loving the relative absolutely, but loves only the absolute absolutely. But that could still be a life of despair over the relative values of the finite and temporal. Next, it is possible that while still living on the second floor they can also go back and repeat life in the basement and on the first floor. The second movement of the leap, after leaping up to the second floor, is to leap back by virtue of the absurd into the basement of the aesthetic and the first floor of the ethical. In Kierkegaard's belief, this is an imitation of the God-man who appropriated by his incarnation both the eternal and the temporal at once. Kierkegaard valorizes both the religiousness A of the second floor's pure giving and the recovery of the aesthetic and ethical getting back which is religiousness B.

Derrida is very close to Kierkegaard. He has the same third logic of mixed opposites which takes him beyond Plato's logic of the principle of identity and the principle of noncontradiction. It also takes him beyond the second logic of Hegel's *Aufhebung* through contradiction. Plato's prisoner at the bottom of the cave would leave the lower opposites for the higher opposites. Hegel's person of progress would ascend the staircase of the dialectic by going through the lower opposites to attain the higher. Derrida's hedgehog never leaves behind the so-called lower values of either the cave or the staircase. He stays there always with the lower give and take that makes pure giving impossible. Derrida elaborates the logic of the mixed opposites with the *pharmakon*, the dangerous supplement, the parergon, etc. He has the third logic of the mixed opposites, as does Kierkegaard with his logic of the paradox which valorizes the higher floor of the house and the lower floors at once. Derrida dramatizes the challenge with his abyss of undecidability and shows how the impossible pure giving can take place because the left hand is left in the dark by the oblivion of dissemination. But he is not interested in the reward the Father gives to Abraham by giving Isaac back. He is only interested in glorifying the leap of the universal sacrifice that every decision, even the decision to give, entails. Derrida's ideal has to do with the ethical and religious event that undecidability makes possible. He always remains undecided between opposites, even the opposites of pure giving and the gift that takes. He does not do without either giving or getting, but he valorizes only pure giving, whereas Kierkegaard valorizes primarily the getting back of Isaac. Caputo agrees with Derrida in a wholehearted acceptance of Kierkegaard's madness of the leap; but neither of them keeps alive both sides of the paradox of pure giving and of getting back.

Dissemination, Nietzsche, and guidance in the desert

By focusing upon the prayers and tears of religious persons, Caputo never trivializes religion in the way many philosophers do when they treat only the God of the philosophers and not the God of Abraham, Isaac, and Jacob. Caputo connects the prayers and tears of Derrida with the prayers and tears of Augustine's mother, Monica, when she was praying and crying for her lost and wandering son. She always prayed and was distraught for her child, just as Derrida's mother was for him and just as Derrida has been for his two sons. Caputo shows how Derrida thinks that those with religious passion are always praying with great care for others, just as Jesus looked down upon the people of Jerusalem and prayed: "How often would I have gathered you together as a mother hen gathers her chicks under her wings? But you would not." He explains in detail how Derrida's prayer is that of the Yes, Yes and the Come. Derrida's prayer is always that of the Yes, Yes of praise for the promise of justice and peace that has been given. It always has the petition of seeking that justice and peace with the Come, Come. We, as humans, are wandering nomads, lost in a desert. We are the frightened hedgehog with cars roaring down upon us. In this condition of parents of lost and threatened children we constantly pray for them in fear and trembling.

We are so lost because God is hidden, and this has to do not so much with the apophatic *via negativa* as with the disconcerting principle of dissemination. Whatever sign we find as we wander in the desert only points to another sign. The desert is an endless proliferation of signs that never get back to a transcendental signified that can be the foundation of meaning for us. Husserl's analysis of unlimited further perspectives is elaborated by Derrida as revealing an excess of meanings and forces which make us tremble in our postmodern world. Nietzsche's perspectivism totally supports this Husserlian view. We are wandering in a desert. Our children are as vulnerable and as fragile as the hedgehog. We can only utter the Yes, Yes prayer to the promise of justice and peace. We can only utter the Come, Come prayer that works for justice and peace. We are in a worse than apophatic world. God is not just the greatest presence hidden behind the metaphor of a personal God. We are in an apocalyptic world waiting for a Messiah that can never come. This Messiah that is always coming but can never come is a key factor in Caputo's conception of *Religion without Religion*. Wandering in the desert without a guide, without angels, without the pope, without the sacraments, even in a way without religion, without thanks, without prayer and without the book are all connected for Caputo to our being without the Messiah. Caputo sees this as Derrida's Jewish philosophy of religion.

Caputo interprets Nietzsche as the great philosopher of our postmodern disaster who has made clear for us our loss of the heavenly guide. In his book on religion without religion, Caputo refers to his own treatment of Nietzsche in his book *Against Ethics*. Caputo's Nietzsche is not quite Derrida's Nietzsche, and this gives us a clue as to why Caputo's religion without religion is not quite Derrida's religion without religion. Caputo confesses that Nietzsche's overman is too much for him. Caputo feels compelled to do without much more of Nietzsche than does Derrida. For example, Caputo thinks that a good deal of what Nietzsche calls "slavish socialist, egalitarian, democratic, Jewish, Christian, feminine"[7] is really quite appealing. But so does Nietzsche. The lion in the Zarathustra drama may do without these or mock them. But the child can affirm them. If we were to think about any of these issues in a Derridean way it would become very complicated and a mixture of opposites. Derrida would show how for Nietzsche it was loaded with the excess of dissemination. We could see this if we were to pick any of them such as that of the feminine. Derrida's book *Spurs* is a deconstructive reading of Nietzsche on truth as a woman. Nietzsche is at least as much a proto-feminist as he is a misogynist. In *Thus Spoke Zarathustra*, at the end of Book 2 in a section called "The stillest hour," Zarathustra tells of a woman who guides him away from his pride and arrogance to a humble, childlike attitude in which he can affirm all of existence with a Yes and Amen. This woman guide is like Socrates' daimon who calls Zarathustra away from obstacles to his true vocation. The story of this woman is significant. She guides Zarathustra in the abyss of his desert. In "The second dance song" the woman Life leads Zarathustra along. Zarathustra has the Yes and Amen prayer. He has a guide who is a woman. He always uses the third logic of mixed opposites. In fact, Derrida might begin really working with this third logic first in *Spurs*. In *The Antichrist*, Nietzsche worked out his own model of religion without religion concerning the evangel and the Christ. He believed in the guidance of the gentle and generous evangel. He did without the judging Christ. In Book 4 of *Zarathustra*, Nietzsche does not do without the pope. The *Retired from Service* because God is dead guides Zarathustra and teaches him of love's highest ideal: to love the way a mother does, unconditionally and beyond judgment.

Derrida also does not do without the heavenly guide. In *Glas*, when he writes of the Hebrews being in the desert, he recalls the pillar of cloud that guided them by day and the pillar of fire that guided them by night. He even hints that the two columns of *Glas*, the column of castration and the column of dissemination, might be such guides.[8] As Caputo points out in *Memories of the Blind*, two scouts go out before the blind that the blind might be guided (318).

Caputo thinks that Nietzsche does without religious guidance. He thinks that Derrida does without it. He seems to think that he has to do without it. However, he has his own version of the guide, for, as he tells us in *Against Ethics*, he keeps a painting on his mantel. It is a gift some anonymous person sent him of Dionysus with the soul of a Rabbi.[9] This ideal guides Caputo's prayers and tears. It guides his thinking and believing. Caputo's religious life is guided by the rabbi, who tells of a Messiah who is always coming and never here. His religious life is guided by Nietzsche's Dionysus, who laughs and cries in the desert of disaster, or without the guiding star, as Caputo thinks. However, Caputo's Dionysian rabbi is not quite Derrida's hedgehog, nor Kierkegaard's knight of faith living on all floors of the house at once, nor Nietzsche's prisoner dancing in his chains. Caputo seems willing to do without his rabbi becoming the gentle and generous evangel. Caputo seems to do without Jesus even though he wants to keep the Messiah or Christ who has not come. But Derrida retains more undecidability. In *Glas* he writes of Hegel's Jesus, who says he must depart that the Holy Spirit might come.[10] In Derrida's philosophy the anointed one can be as present as he is absent and, in fact, he is more present because he is more absent. Kierkegaard, Nietzsche, and Derrida do not do without the guidance of Jesus, who teaches that every other is wholly other, a teaching that always guides. They do not do without the oblivion of Jesus' guidance when he says that when we give with our right hand the left hand should not know it. Caputo seems willing to do without the guidance of Jesus, the angels, the Book, the pope, etc. Maybe some of Kierkegaard's pseudonyms do that. But Kierkegaard does not. The incarnate God-man always guides Kierkegaard, whose task it is to appropriate that very paradox of both the eternal and the temporal.

Caputo writes:

> Derrida has only *écriture*, no Book, which was also his argument with Jabès, no guiding light or guiding star, and he is more than a little worried by those religious which, having been given a Book, always use them to spell war not peace.
>
> (307)

From Derrida's point of view, surely this has to be a one-sided exaggeration that forgets the notion of undecidability which arises out of the insight into the disconcerting principle of dissemination. Of course, the Bible will get unlimited and contradictory readings. It is disseminated into infinite readings. But to decide that those readings spell war and not peace is a reading that does not appreciate undecidability. Caputo makes this sort of claim throughout his book (See pp. 195 and 204 of *Prayers and Tears*, for example). Rather than do without the Bible as a guide, Derrida sees the Christian Bible even as guiding us into a responsibility beyond that of the orgiastic and the Platonic. Derrida appreciates guidance toward justice and peace. Peace is part of the apocalyptic promise. Caputo is right about a guiding light. Derrida's guidance has more to do with being led in the dark without a light. Caputo is right about Derrida's great vigilance in regard to war and injustice. This is the strong point of the undecidability of religion without religion. But Derrida's, like Nietzsche's, is not a religion without all guidance.

Différance, **Heidegger, and the origin of messianicity**

When Derrida uses the term "religion without religion" in *The Gift of Death* he has a definite meaning. Kierkegaard, Nietzsche, Heidegger, Levinas, Patocka, and others have a religion without religion[11] because they universalize or generalize a religious dogma into a nondogmatic doublet. They, in short, translate a religious theme and network of themes into a philosophical language. But Caputo uses this term "religion without religion" in different ways. For him it has to do with religion without a heavenly guide, without angels, without the pope, without the Book, without religious fundamentalism, etc. Caputo wants to do without almost anything except the prayers and tears connected with justice for the suffering. It has been my point that Derrida does not do without these religious elements. He keeps them as he complicates them. The principle of dissemination does not do without God, the person, the Book, history, guides, etc. It only sets them within an unlimited relational process. However, Caputo does focus strongly on the primary meaning of Derrida's religion without religion.

To my knowledge, Caputo disagrees with Derrida only on one issue, and that has to do with the relation between the universal notion of messianicity and the particular historical messianisms such as Abraham's, Moses', Jesus' and Marx's. On p. 136 of *Prayers and Tears*, Caputo cites Derrida as writing:

> The problem remains—and this is really a problem for me, an enigma— whether the religions, say, for instance, the religions of the Book, are but specific examples of this general structure, of messianicity. There is the general structure of messianicity, as a structure of experience, and on this groundless ground there have been revelations, a history which one calls Judaism or Christianity and so on. That is one possibility, and then you would have a Heideggerian gesture, in style. You would have to go back from these religions to the fundamental ontological conditions of possibilities of religions, to describe the structure of messianicity on the ground of a groundless ground on which religions have been made possible.
>
> This is one hypothesis. The other hypothesis—and I confess that I hesitate between these two possibilities—is that the events of revelation, the biblical traditions, the Jewish, Christian, and Islamic traditions, have been absolute events, irreducible events which have unveiled this messianicity. We would not know what messianicity is without messianism, without these events which were Abraham, Moses and Jesus Christ and so on. In that case, singular events would have unveiled or revealed these

universal possibilities and it is only on that condition that we can describe messianicity. Between the two possibilities I must confess I oscillate and I think some other scheme has to be constructed to understand the two at the same time.

(136)

Caputo wrestles valiantly with these two opposites and concludes:

Were it the case, and I think it must be, that the historical messianisms are to be treated as irreducible singularities, and were that point adhered to in a sufficiently steadfast way, then it would be impossible to say that the messianic in general is a universal, essential structure under which the historical messianisms may be subsumed, for that is exactly what is excluded by treating an event as a singularity as opposed to a particular subsumable under a universal.

(136)

This decision, which Caputo makes by clearly taking one side and which Derrida still understands as involving undecidability, has to do with the difference between the Heideggerian ontological difference and the Derridean *différance*. In his ontology, Heidegger still retains a metaphysics of presence by seeing Being as the presence or the third that allows thinking within the hermeneutical circle. It is essential to Heidegger to distinguish Being from the being of things, humans and God. Being is identity for Heidegger, and presence even though it is nothingness. Derrida, given his principle of dissemination, sees *différance* as the trace which is prior to identity in persons, places, things and the absolute. The trace of presence or *différance* as distance and deferral are essential to the *arche* and the *telos*. Dissemination reveals that *différance* is the reason for deconstruction. Insofar as he retains the *arche* trace, or what throughout *Prayers and Tears* is called the quasi-transcendental, Derrida is still making a trace of the Heideggerian gesture. But the quasi-transcendental for him is *différance* itself, and it is not the Heideggerian Being as presence which is free from difference.

Given the difference between the Heideggerian ontological difference and the Derridean *différance*, Derrida treats the *Ereignis* or the event of the new in a different way than Heidegger. "*Che cos è la poesia?*" is Derrida's redoing of *The Origin of a Work of Art*. Derrida is universalizing the Heideggerian event, just as he universalizes the Kierkegaardian reading of Abraham's mad leap. Derrida is saying that in every decision, every event of pure giving, every promise, there is the coming to be of the wholly new in the mad and impossible leap. Derrida's reading of the messianic and Caputo's reading of that are, according to Derrida's account, new moments of inspired revelation. Reading the messianic as the coming of justice is of course very old. Elijah and Amos were already doing that. But strictly speaking, the messianic did not begin with Abraham or Moses. It began with David. The Davidic covenant theology of the promise of the Messiah was the context for the writing of the Abraham promise stories. Moses' election theology was united with the Davidic messianic theology by the Deuteronomists. The messianic theme and the apocalyptic movement which continued it had to do with mercy and a humble walk with God as well as justice. Derrida and Caputo do not stress the mercy, which is perhaps most central to the messianic. So Derrida complicates the *Ereignis* and the moments of revelation by contaminating the borders between the canon and the readings. With Kierkegaard in *The Fragments*, he argues that any believer during the last 1840 years has been able to make the leap of faith only with the help of a revelation here and now. So in his treatment of the *Ereignis*, Derrida retains a trace of the Heideggerian gesture. The role that Being plays for Heidegger in the event is played for Derrida by the quasi-transcendental trace.

But it would seem that early in *Prayers and Tears*, Caputo retains the Heideggerian gesture too. In a section called "Derrida and Levinas on the Impossible," he discusses Derrida's defense of Husserl and Heidegger against Levinas. Levinas argues that when the suffering other claims me morally, he or she does that as a radical other who is not just actuating potencies within me. But Caputo argues that Derrida shows how there must be a lot of preparation in advance or the *tout autre* will never be able to claim me. Caputo argues that "if you remove the anteriorities that Husserl and Heidegger put in place" (21) then it will really be impossible, let's say, for the hedgehog to respond to a call from the other to cross the road. "If we have not adequately prepared ourselves in advance for the shock of alterity, the alter, instead of shocking us, will just pass us by without a ripple" (22). Could not the Heideggerian ground of groundless ground which Derrida does not choose against be this *praeparatio evangelica* as Husserl and Heidegger account for it? Caputo appreciates Heidegger very much, especially as can be seen in his book *Radical Hermeneutics*. He sees the postmodern line running from Kierkegaard through Heidegger to Derrida. But he has many reproaches against Heidegger's denial of faith and against his implied political position. Caputo thinks that Heidegger does without too much of religion, for he does without prayers and tears. However, as we see concerning the question of the relation between the singular event and the condition for it, Caputo is more deconstructive of Heidegger than Derrida. Caputo does not seem to think that there is any need for Heidegger's ontological difference to live on in the *différance* of Derrida. If Caputo took seriously his own defense of Derrida's defense of Heidegger against Levinas, would he not have to retain a trace of the ontological difference or the Heideggerian gesture?

Deconstruction, Levinas, and martyrdom

Caputo does not take exception explicitly to Derrida concerning Levinas the way he does, however slightly, concerning Heidegger. But Caputo's approach to Levinas is quite different from Derrida's nonetheless. Caputo's philosophy does without more of Levinas's religion than does Derrida's, and Caputo's religion does without more of Levinas's philosophy than does Derrida's. This can be seen if we focus on Caputo's approach toward Levinas's theory of martyrdom and toward Levinas's approach to Plato, Descartes and Greek–modern-German philosophy in general.

> To pray is not only to say "Yes, Yes" and "Come" to justice but it also is to open one's mouth and say "Yes." To pray is to open one's mouth and say "Come." Let the Other come. Let something Other, something In-Coming, come.
>
> (298)

Derrida's prayer is Levinasian in saying "Yes" "Come" to the other as well as to justice for the other. Derrida in his article "Violence and metaphysics" took exception to Levinas, as we have seen, by defending Husserl and Heidegger and claiming that the radical other cannot come to us unless we have been prepared. But Caputo is more negative toward Levinas than is Derrida. Levinas argues that in Plato's *epekeina tes ousias* and in the *heteron* of the *Sophist* there is already a Platonic preparation for the radical other. However, Caputo writes:

> About that, I think, Levinas is fundamentally mistaken, surprisingly far too philosophical, far too Greek, and—he will hate this—far too Heideggerian. Levinas seems to me to swing wildly between extremes. After protesting too much on behalf of the *tout autre*, Levinas concedes too much to philosophy, as if Plato's *epekeina tes ousias* or the form of the *heteron* in the *Sophist* had anything to do with the widows and orphans and strangers of prophetic faith.
>
> (25)

I want to argue that Derrida philosophically and religiously appreciates what Caputo calls the philosophic extreme and the religious extreme. First I will argue that Levinas practices a deconstruction that is entirely compatible with

Derrida's and then I will show that Levinas's notion of martyrdom is in line with Derrida's.

In Levinas's philosophical model there are two places for philosophy as distinct from the elemental moral response. First, Levinas focuses upon Plato's *epekeina tes ousias* and *heteron* and Plotinus's One, which is otherwise than Being and Descartes's Infinite and Husserl's transcendence in immanence, and uses these notions as *praeparatio evangelica* for his own notion of the radical other. Just as Derrida uses the *pharmakon* as a Platonic notion against Platonism and the dangerous supplement as a Rousseauian notion against Rousseauism, so Levinas is moving away from rather than into the Platonic, Plotinian, Cartesian, and Husserlian totalities by highlighting the universal other or singular in these philosophies. Just as Caputo argues for the Husserlian and Heideggerian preparation for receiving the radical other, which is a lived groundless ground for receiving the messianic singularity, so Levinas is able to make a case with his readers by beginning with the legitimate bits of Plato, Plotinus, Descartes, Husserl, and Heidegger with which they are familiar.

Second, Levinas argues that after there is the elemental response of the *me voici* to the calls, demands, and charges of the other, there needs to be, for the sake of distributive justice, the said of philosophy, truth, and justice that comes with my relation to the other other or the third party. This brings Levinas to legitimize the ethical thinking of the tradition, but only after it is correctly located in relation to the primary elemental saying. Caputo reads Kierkegaard and Derrida as being willing to make a sacrifice of ethics (207). Obligation begins to move only when one is paralyzed by the aporia. But he sees Levinas as retaining the ethical. However, as the preface to "The concept of anxiety" makes clear, Kierkegaard not only moves beyond the first ethics of rational universality, but he has a second ethics or a religious ethics which his double-movement leap affirms. Once the first ethics, as he shows in *Works of Love*, of a noble eros or philia is dethroned, it is then allowed its rightful place next to agape. It seems to me that Levinas is like Kierkegaard in retaining a place for philosophical ethics.

According to Caputo, Levinas makes a twofold mistake. Besides being too philosophical, he is too religious; he protests too much on behalf of the *tout autre*. What this means is again well spelled out in *Against Ethics*. There Caputo writes:

> That undeconstructed Levinas has a center, a transcendental signified that organizes and centers things for him, not around the same, to be sure, but around the Other. For all his resistance to totalization, and all his talk of decentering the same, the fact is that things are radically

recentered for him around the Other, which is an infinite and absolute ec-center, a kind of transcendental eccentricity. It is part of my infidel nature that I attribute to this undeconstructed Levinas a transcendental move.

(83–84)

So Caputo thinks that Levinas has failed to be thoroughly a deconstruction-ist. However, Levinas is very clear that phenomenology can follow thematiza-tion up to the point of the approach of the other and can show its reverting into anarchy. After that, the new ethical language of responsibility, persecu-tion, accusation, passivity, etc. must be used to describe the response of the *me voici* to the trace.[12] Just as Derrida's dissemination arises out of Husserl's analysis of infinite *Abschattungen* and the Nietzschean analysis of unlimited perspectives, so does the Levinasian anarchy. And that anarchy is connected with the trace of the other that can never be thematized. Most of all, that other is the human other. Levinas has no more of a transcendental than does Derrida. Derrida has the trace of *différance* as a quasi-transcendental. Levi-nas has the Good that as withdrawal orders the face that orders. Levinas's move beyond phenomenology is the move of deconstruction.

But when Caputo writes that Levinas protests too much on behalf of the *tout autre*, I think he is protesting that Levinas is a bit too religious for him in the sense of having a persecution complex or of overvaluing martyrdom. Caputo is quite careful with the notion of martyrdom. He treats it on pp. 46, 57, 102, 106, 111, and 112 of *Prayers and Tears*. He points out that the Greek word "martyr" is connected with the Latin word "to testify." Thus, attesting, detesting, protesting are all connected with the test of the martyr. So when he says that Levinas protests too much on behalf of the other, he is not referring so much to the prophetic protest on behalf of the poor (Caputo is all for that), but he means that the martyr attests too much to the other as transcen-dental. Caputo's religion is not only without the guide (58, 307, 318), without the pope (55, 68), without the angels (93), but it is also without the martyr, at least to the extent of what he thinks of as the Levinasian exaggeration. Caputo does not want to do without prayers and tears. But he is willing to do without the blood of martyrs. For example, he writes: "I wish to show here, in a kind of quasi-theological addendum to this treatment of negative the-ology, that deconstruction is something like a *fin de siècle* faith, but without the martyrdom and without the nihilism" (57).

I would think that this reference to martyrdom resonates the world of Levinas just as the reference to nihilism resonates the world of Nietzsche. Caputo's image of the Dionysian rabbi is a mix of Nietzsche and Levinas. He thinks that Derrida too is a Dionysian rabbi. So Caputo is a Nietzschean Levinasian, but without the nihilism and without the martyrdom. Caputo thinks that Nietzsche's nihilism means that Nietzscheans are without a heavenly guide. However, I have suggested that Derrida does not do without the guide even though Caputo does. Furthermore, even Nietzsche does not do without the guide. Nietzsche is not simply a nihilist. Nihilism is the great abyss, and Nietzsche transformed it into humankind's highest affirmation with his *amor fati*, which is his dancing in chains. Now, does Derrida do without the Levinasian martyrdom? The image for the later Levinas is the hostage suffering from and for his or her persecutor. This is definitely an image of witnessing and martyrdom that is unpacked with such concepts as responsibility, proximity, asymmetry, passivity, accusation, etc. This is the same sort of martyrdom that lets Socrates be more compelling than Plato, especially for existential postmodernists. Derrida's hedgehog seems close to the martyr. His being halted on the road by the car that could make roadkill of him is connected with Derrida's mourning of the martyr. Derrida may not make quite the case for the truth that suffers as do Levinas and Kierkegaard, but he does not rule it out, any more than he rules out the pillar of fire and the pillar of cloud that led the Hebrews in the desert.

Concluding reflections

So Caputo's book on Derrida's philosophy of religion is excellent. He shows how Derrida's philosophemes such as decidability, dissemination, deconstruction, and *différance* are philosophic translations of such ethical religious themes as responsibility, justice, prayer, tears, the messianic, circumcision of the heart, giving, and the apocalyptic. Derrida, as a very precise and logical thinker in opening his new third logic with its quasi-metaphysics of excess and his new epistemology of embracing uncertainty, gives a new and richer reading to the traditional religious themes. He, like Kierkegaard, Nietzsche, and Levinas, has a religion without religion, a nondogmatic doublet of dogma. Caputo interprets this religion without religion as doing without certain aspects of religion such as the guide, the pope, the angels, the martyr, etc. However, if you just consider *Glas* for example, Derrida does not do without any religious morsel of the code, the creed, the cult, or the canon. With his principle of dissemination he just opens each writing, gift, and promise to unlimited returns, showing the deep meaning of the left hand not knowing what the right hand does. His writings on Hegel and Genet do without nothing of religion. In *Glas* you are invited to reflect more deeply upon the Trinity, the global event of the Last Supper at the Oedipal crossroads and all the joyful, sorrowful, and glorious mysteries. Caputo is wonderful in opening us to the wonders of Derrida's rich religious world. His book invites us to ponder especially what he thinks we might do without.

Notes

1 Jacques Derrida, *The Gift of Death*, David Wills, trans. (Chicago: University of Chicago Press, 1995), p. 49. This passage, from which Caputo takes his subtitle, has the special meaning of a philosophical language that no longer contains the language of religious dogma, but which translates it into another terminology. Caputo often contends, as do the prophets once in a while, that God wants justice, not religion. This is not Derrida's contention or practice. There seems to be something American rather than Derridean about Caputo's doing without many key religious traits.

2 Jacques Derrida, *Given Time: 1. Counterfeit Money*, Peggy Kamuf, trans. (Chicago: University of Chicago Press, 1992), p. 100. This is the best simple passage I know of in which Derrida explains pure giving in terms of dissemination.

3 Derrida, *The Gift of Death*, pp. 95–98.

4 Ibid., p. 108.

5 Jacques Derrida, *A Derrida Reader between the Blinds*, Peggy Kamuf, ed. (New York: Columbia University Press, 1991) "Che cos è la poesia?," p. 233.

6 Soren Kierkegaard, *The Sickness unto Death*, Howard V. Hong and Edna H. Hong, trans. (Princeton, NJ: Princeton University Press, 1980), p. 43.

7 John D. Caputo, *Against Ethics: Contributions to a Poetics of Obligation with constant Reference to Deconstruction* (Bloomington: Indiana University Press, 1993), p. 54.

8 Jacques Derrida, *Glas*, Richard Rond and John Leavey, Jr., trans. (Lincoln: University of Nebraska Press, 1986), pp. 37, 49.

9 Caputo, *Against Ethics*, p. 42.

10 Derrida, *Glas*, p. 87.

11 Derrida, *The Gift of Death*, p. 49.

12 Emmanuel Levinas, *Otherwise Than Being or Beyond Essence*, Alphonso Lingis, trans. (Dordrecht: Kluwer, 1991), p. 121.

7 Between biblical religion and deconstruction
The possibility of repetition

Avron Kulak

In *The Prayers and Tears of Jacques Derrida,* John D. Caputo argues strongly for a fundamental relationship between biblical religion and deconstruction. What, however, is the condition of possibility for there being, in the beginning or always already, anything between religion and deconstruction? How shall we conceive of their "between"?

Caputo's examination of the relationship between religion and deconstruction comprises two fundamental claims whose interconnection will be the subject of this chapter.[1] First, central to *Prayers and Tears* is the claim that "the point of view of Derrida's work as an author is religious—but without religion and without religion's God" (xviii). In thus transferring to Derrida the claim that Kierkegaard makes in reference to his own authorship, Caputo holds that deconstruction—"in the spirit of a certain Kierkegaard"—enters into "a new *alliance,* a new covenant (*convenire*) with the incoming (*invenire*), which 'repeats' the movements of the first covenant," but, this time, "in a religion without religion" (195; xx–xxi). Second, Caputo claims that throughout his book, he has been attempting to resituate deconstruction within a "de-Hellenizing tradition, trying patiently to restring the wires of deconstruction back to another source, and this on the advice of Derrida himself, who has complained that otherwise he will have been read less and less well" (335). As I shall proceed to argue, the two claims that deconstruction is religious without religion and that, as such, it is to be situated within a de-Hellenizing tradition, presuppose a biblical notion of history—a deconstructive notion of temporality. Yet in light of this notion of history, how would it be possible also to hold that "the West itself was born in two famous deaths; the death of Socrates and the death of Jesus" (191)?

What the repetition of the "first" covenant in the "new" covenant expresses for Caputo is that which Derrida elucidates as the "paradox of iterability." For Derrida, "iterability requires the origin to repeat itself originarily, to alter itself so as to have the value of origin" (FL, 1007–1009). Deconstruction at work, he holds, "inscribes iterability in originarity, in unicity and singularity" (1003). Yet when does the work of deconstruction begin? What concept of history does deconstruction presuppose? Since the paradox of what Derrida calls iterability and what Caputo calls repetition already deconstructs any possible binary opposition between the "first" and the "new" covenant, is the first covenant not, in the beginning, already (conceived as) iterable? Caputo further deepens the paradoxical relationship between what is "first" and what is "new" when he claims that a repetition of religion *without* religion incurs a "strange logic" of the "without," one that involves "no simple negation" (xxi). For repetition, he says, citing Derrida's *Circumfession*, is that which is "without continuity but without rupture" (xviii). What, then, are we to make of this strange, iterable logic that, in disclaiming continuity while rejecting rupture, is neither first nor new? Is it neither first nor new because it is undecidably both?

When we follow, in Caputo's text, the thread or theme of iterability, we learn that its logic commits us in advance to a certain risk. Caputo, citing Derrida, points out that since prayer, for example, is inexorably inscribed in the play of traces which opens the same to difference, there is no pure possibility of prayer without the risk of contamination. "Once inscribed," Caputo writes, "prayer exposes itself to repetition, to empty rote or enthusiastic reenactment, to ritualistic ceremony or to a daily rhythm of prayerful life. Those," he says, "are the structurally ingredient possibilities within prayer, within the play of the trace" (41). The iterable trace is exposed, in other words, to the risk of bad faith, to the alternative between faith and idolatry, an alternative that is utterly biblical. Yet as the condition of possibility for the risk of bad faith, iterability also constitutes the condition of fidelity, the condition of faithful response, which, Caputo points out, involves the redoubling of affirmation: every "yes" is committed in advance to a second "yes." Iterability, in thus expressing time as the time of promise and memory, the time of faithful response, demands that we maintain a deconstructive wariness regarding the simple self-assurance that produces the dogmatic slumbers of the "good" conscience. Faith is to be regarded as "a certain loyalty to itself which presupposes its own lack of identity," for there is no promise that does not run the risk that accompanies iterability (64). To say "yes" is, therefore, to bind oneself to the future, to bind oneself to a second "yes" which promises to keep the memory of the first. This, Caputo holds, is what Derrida calls repetition, "the repetition that comes *first*," since the "first yes will not have taken place without the second, without the promise of the second, even as the second is the memory of the first, the yes itself being internally divided into yes, yes" (65).

It is the iterable interval between traces—between the trace of the first yes in the last and the last yes in the first—that exposes address and response, promise and memory, to risk. Prayer, promise, and memory involve, in other words, *différance*, the disruption of the temporal present and of all self-present certitude through what Derrida describes as the joining of temporization and spacing (MP, 8–9). *Différance* affirms that the present contains, within itself, a space that renders it no longer simply present. The temporal is, in light of *différance*, constituted not as a self-identical present but as a relationship, as the time of relationship, the history of promise and memory. Deconstruction renders the temporal historical and the historical covenantal. The self in deconstructive time is a self that, in engaging the other, runs the risk of (not) being other to itself. All that which exists within the *différantial* spacing of the temporal exists only in relation to itself as other; that is, only insofar as it is constituted on the basis of the trace within itself of the other.

Caputo further addresses the paradox of biblical, deconstructive iterability, in light of which we are always already committed in advance to the promise of memory and the memory of promise, in the context of reminding us that religion, for Derrida, is response. "When I am addressed by the other," Caputo writes, "I give the other my word: I am speaking the truth, believe me, have faith and trust in my good faith, 'I promise you the truth.' That structure," Caputo points out,

> is in place even—and especially—when I am lying through my teeth. For then above all I am counting on, relying upon, the trust and faith that sustains and supports the address to the other. If no one ever believed a word I say, I would never be able to lie at all.
>
> (PT, 156–57)

Since the condition of possibility for lying is faith, Caputo thus observes that, for Derrida, it is only insofar as faith is the ether of the relationship to the other as wholly other that we can have the experience of nonrelation—the experience of absolute interruption—between self and other.

We shall later have reason to reinvoke the category of risk and the relationship between faith and lying in which iterability involves us. I want now, however, to engage our second area of concern. It is again in light of iterability—in which deconstructed time, the time of deconstruction, becomes the time of history, the time of promise, the time of covenant—that our first theme, the relationship of religion and deconstruction, begins to converge with our second theme, deconstruction as in the tradition of the de-Hellenization of modernity. In citing both Kierkegaard and Derrida,

Caputo distinguishes between that which he calls the Greek backward repetition of the same and the biblical or deconstructive forward repetition of the new. What we call an "event" can occur, he writes, only when something new happens. "Kierkegaard and Derrida in Kierkegaard's wake," Caputo is clear, invoke in their work precisely "a biblical model of the 'new,'" one that, for Caputo, is opposed to "philosophy's un-motions: Platonic recollection" on the one hand, "and the sham movement of the Hegelian *Aufhebung*" on the other. Thus, he holds, "if time means the eventuation of something new, then the Greeks, as Kierkegaard said, lacked the idea of time." For Caputo,

> Kierkegaard thus has in mind, as does Derrida, a movement that does not remain confined within an economy of the same. . . . Kierkegaard and Derrida describe the movements of the repetition that repeats forward, into something new, the movement of an unrestricted giving without reserve, of the gift, the *qualitative* leap.
>
> (50)

The distinction between the Greek backward repetition of the same and the biblical, deconstructive forward repetition of the new raises a series of questions regarding the very origins of modernity. If there is no event outside the biblical, deconstructive forward repetition of the new, and if, on that basis, we must say, with Kierkegaard, that the Greeks lacked the idea of time, what are we to make of the relationship between modernity and Greek thought? Is there an event in the Greek world? What would be the "event" of a Greek text? If iterability presupposes that in order to constitute an event, what we repeat must, as Caputo says, be repeated with a difference, are Greek texts iterable? "What would a mark [or a text] be," Derrida asks, "that one could not cite? And whose origin could not be lost on the way?" (MP, 321). What, in other words, would a text be that did not run the risk of contamination, the risk of failing to keep the memory of its first "yes" as that which always already will have called for its reduplication? Would Derrida acknowledge that Greek texts are, in the strict sense, not iterable? For if there is no event in the Greek text, there can be no "yes" that is at risk. It is only in light of the biblical repetition forward of the new that the "yes" can become lost; can become, that is, what Kierkegaard calls the demonic and what Nietzsche calls nihilism. It is only in light of the capacity to "repeat" forward that we engage the risk of falling backward. But what we cannot do—the option that is closed to us forever in light of biblical iterability—is, as Caputo shows, not promise, not risk. The option that is closed to us forever in light of biblical iterability is, in other words, the Greek world.

Kierkegaard addresses the relationship between Greek and biblical thought in a brilliant exegesis of the story of the Fall in *The Concept of Anxiety*.[2] He in fact understands the Fall to be precisely the difference between Greek fate and biblical freedom. Fate, in the Greek world, Kierkegaard shows, is the end that moves all, the end of all movement. To be subject to fate, however, is to be ignorant of the end by which you are moved. There is thus no accounting for one's fate, no promise that can be made in light of fate, since, as Kierkegaard notes, fate is precisely the oracular, the negative unity of accident and necessity, in which there is no means by which one can locate the authority of the oracular voice or of divine command (CA, 96–97). Is there, then, a transition from fate to freedom? Kierkegaard insists that "paganism would have perished upon the contradiction that one became guilty"—that one became freely responsible, that one could promise or fall—"by fate. Precisely this," he says, "is the greatest contradiction, and out of this contradiction Christianity breaks forth. Paganism does not comprehend it because it is too light-minded in its determination of the concept of sin. The concepts of sin and guilt posit precisely the single individual as the single individual. There is no question about his relation to the whole world or to all the past. The point is only that he is guilty, and yet," Kierkegaard writes, as he prepares to elaborate the contradictory logic involved in presupposing a transition from fate to freedom, the contradictory logic (out of) which Christianity "breaks forth" as the paradox of freedom, "he is supposed to have become guilty by fate, consequently by all that of which there is no question, and thereby he is supposed to have become something that precisely cancels the concept of fate, and this he is supposed to have become by fate" (CA, 97–98). The Greek world perishes, in other words, on the contradiction that, owing to the structure of fate by which it is constituted, it could not posit as contradiction, let alone freely appropriate or deconstruct as paradox. What, then, is the relationship of the Greek and biblical worlds to modernity understood as the deconstruction of the promise and the promise of deconstruction?[3]

For Kierkegaard, the story of the Fall is, when properly understood, a critique of the very concept of origin which it appears to depict. The problem in comprehending the story as a paradoxical account of origin is, he indicates, the temptation to project upon it the antitheses—particularly the antithesis between original and hereditary sin—in which common understanding is prone to think the leap. In thus opening his exegesis of the Fall with the question of whether the concept of hereditary sin is to be understood as identical with the concept of original sin, Kierkegaard observes that, at times, it has been correctly understood so. Yet when "thought met with difficulties," he writes, an expedient was seized upon. In order to explain at least something, a fantastic presupposition was introduced, the loss of which constituted the fall as the consequence. The advantage gained thereby was that everyone willingly admitted that a condition such as the one described was not found anywhere in the world, but that they forgot that as a result the doubt became a different one, namely, whether such a condition ever had existed, something that was quite necessary in order to lose it. The history of the human race acquired a fantastic beginning. Adam was fantastically placed outside this history.

(CA, 25)

Thus, he adds, "according to traditional concepts, the difference between Adam's first sin and the first sin of every other man is this: Adam's sin conditions sinfulness as a consequence, the other first sin presupposes sinfulness as a state. Were this so," Kierkegaard repeats, "Adam would actually stand outside the race, and the race would not have begun with him but would have had a beginning outside itself, something that is contrary to every concept" (CA, 29–30). In fact, Kierkegaard comments, "no matter how the problem is raised, as soon as Adam's sin is placed fantastically on the outside, everything is confused" (CA, 28).

In insisting that we must avoid the contradiction of placing Adam (not to mention Eve and God) outside history, Kierkegaard begins to indicate that the true import of the story of the Fall is that Adam's story must be our story. The paradox of Adam—the contradiction with which readers of the Fall are confronted—is, Kierkegaard holds, that Adam, a single individual, is both himself and the race. In presenting him as such, the biblical authors present Adam as ourselves. Adam's (hi)story is the (hi)story of the single individual. It is, in other words, precisely the opposition between that which is first or original and that which is second or fallen that is deconstructed by the story of the Fall. "That the *first* sin signifies something different from *a* sin (i.e. a sin like many others), something different from *one* sin (i.e. number 1 in relation to number 2), is," Kierkegaard observes, "quite obvious. The first sin constitutes the nature of the quality. . . . The new quality appears with the first, with the leap, with the suddenness of the enigmatic. If," however, "the first means *one* sin in the numerical sense," then "no history can result from it, and sin will have no history, either in the individual or in the race" (CA, 30). If we place Adam outside history, we too, it appears, are placed outside history. If, in other words, the sin of the single individual has its cause outside that individual's particular history—if Adam and Eve stand in relationship to the sin of subsequent individuals as first cause—then, as merely inherited, sin is no longer the responsibility of the single individual. Sin becomes fate, rather than that concept whereby the single individual freely and responsibly expresses existence as the paradox of history, the paradox of the qualitative leap. Since sin is a concept of responsibility, it is, moreover, precisely in light of biblical principles that the opposition between original and hereditary sin is deconstructed.

The task for the reader of the Fall, Kierkegaard shows, is to recognize that in presenting the story of Adam and Eve, the biblical authors do not intend to present knowledge of good and evil as involving a transition from a prior, ahistorical state of innocence to a posterior, (a)historical state of fallenness. Kierkegaard maintains, in fact, that "the Genesis story presents the only dialectically consistent view. Its whole content," he writes

> is really concentrated in one statement: *Sin came into the world by a sin.* . . . The difficulty for the understanding is precisely the triumph of the explanation and its profound consequence, namely, that sin presupposes itself, that sin comes into the world in such a way that by the fact that it is, it is presupposed.
>
> (CA, 32)

The hermeneutical import of the story of the Fall, we learn from Kierkegaard, is, therefore, that there is nothing outside history, nothing outside sin. The Fall, as the very deconstruction of fallenness, is a non-originary origin, the non-originary origin of the single, responsible individual. Adam's story is our story, the story iterable for each single individual, that story which, according to its very nature, can be repeated only without repetition.

The Fall is deconstruction at work, that which, to recall Derrida, inscribes iterability in the heart of originarity. There is, moreover, as Kierkegaard shows, no transition, no Fall, from the Greek to the biblical world which does not already presuppose the biblical world.[4] It is the biblical world that is, as Caputo reiterates, the impossible, nonoriginary origin of deconstruction. Yet if it is true that deconstruction is utterly biblical and not Greek, and if we now also recall that faith, "once inscribed" in the iterable trace, is the possibility of both disrelation and radical evil, how, then, are we to understand what Caputo describes as the relationship between biblical religion as determinate, and deconstruction as "the structural possibility of the religious unencumbered by the dangerous baggage of particular, determinate religions and their determinate faiths" (PT, 195)? This, for me, is the most complex aspect of Caputo's book. What does Caputo mean by "determinate"?

Caputo is clear that "deconstruction *is* itself faith." Yet, he adds, "it goes against the grain of deconstruction . . . to specify some *determinable* faith, to specify what faith is faith in, to calm the storm or arrest the play in which faith takes shape by proposing a determinate object of faith, some common faith," for deconstruction "has no business in identifying the *tout autre*" (64). In light of the distinction between deconstructive faith and determinable or determinate faith, Caputo holds that Derrida is thus

> trying to offer us a work of thought that thinks the structural possibility of the religious, of a certain radical messianic structure, without the dangerous liaisons of the particular religions, without the dogma, without the determinate messianic faiths that divide humanity into warring parties.
>
> (195)

But is the distinction between faith and determinable faith the same as the distinction between deconstruction and biblical religion? Are Judaism and Christianity, as opposed to deconstruction, merely determinate, messianic faiths? The relationship of deconstruction to religion is, as we have seen Caputo note, without continuity but without rupture. Deconstruction repeats "the structure of religious experience, i.e., of a specifically biblical, covenantal, Abrahamic experience," but without religion and without religion's God (xxi). Yet deconstruction's repetition of religion without religion produces, Caputo says, "a disturbing chiasmic effect" in their relationship. "For if, in deconstruction, one has no assurance about what is an example of what, then how are we to decide," he asks, "whether deconstruction is an example of the religious, or whether the religious is an example of deconstruction?" (114, 196). In "any *repetitio* worthy of its name," he indicates, both are first (114). Further, Caputo observes, since the very distinction between a radical and a determinate messianic faith is, according to Derrida, itself subtle and unstable, the door is open for us to pose the question of whether Derrida's messianic religion without messianism is not another messianism after all. The question of Derrida and religion, Caputo holds, "involves the twin questions, the two ghosts, both of the deconstructive resources of religion . . . and of the religious resources of deconstruction. . . . It may be," Caputo writes, "that the messianic hope cannot live apart from the determinable faiths—or even that deconstruction, which is marked by the *gage* or *engagement* of a determinable faith, is something like a certain messianism" (150).

Deconstruction is something *like* a certain messianism. What, however, is the nature of this "like"? What notion of iterability, what chiasmic effect, is contained therein? Although the relationship between religion and deconstruction produces a disturbing chiasmic effect, owing to which it is impossible to tell which is the repetition of which, Caputo also tells us that, for deconstruction, the messianic cannot "be confined within Abrahamic religion, even though it bears an Abrahamic name" (155). But is it the case that Abrahamic religion can be confined within the Abrahamic name? Caputo recognizes that "we are all always and already factically situated in some *determinable* faith or another, some *determinable* socio-historico-linguistic world or matrix or another. How," he asks, "could it be otherwise? The danger," he says, "is only to think that your privileged name cannot be translated" (68). What, however, is the nature of this situatedness? Is it not precisely Abraham who breaks with his factical situatedness—in order to regain it? Abraham is the single individual who, on the basis of the absolute relationship to the absolute, has, in fact, always already broken with, always already regained, his factical situatedness understood as merely ethical continuity or aesthetic rupture. Is Abraham's story, then, not our story, deconstruction's story, the iterable story *par excellence*, since, whenever it is repeated, it properly situates us in a repetition without repetition, one without continuity but without rupture?[5] Is deconstruction not, therefore, a Jewish science? Much will depend, Caputo says, "on how the very terms *Jewish* and *deconstruction* are to be defined" (279).

Much will also depend on how the term *determinable* is to be defined. Either determinable means historical and, therefore, covenantal and faithful, or determinable means finite and idolatrous. Is biblical religion, as historical—as factically situated—merely finite? Is it not biblical thought that produces the very distinction between the covenantal and the idolatrous, between the determinable and the determinable? It is precisely the biblical category of singularity that, as iterable, exposes faithful testimony to contamination, to risk and to finitization, with horrendous results. One individual (Adam, Abraham), one people chosen (the ancient Hebrews), one Messiah (Jesus)—all of whom are themselves and the race. One God (Yahweh), "who is what He is," Caputo remarks, "and who," nevertheless, or in addition, "separates himself from every name" (66). The very idea of "one," of being the one "chosen" (individual, people, messiah—or God), involves both faithful choice—the iterability, or translatability, of your privileged name—and the risk of idolatrous reduction and exclusion. We cannot divest ourselves of the risk of idolatry which accompanies the category of singularity without divesting ourselves of the iterability of faith. Yet the faithful, iterable content of what it means to be "chosen" is, in Caputo and Derrida's terms, the fact that we are committed in advance, always already, to the paradoxes and risks involved in responding to the other as wholly other.

Nevertheless, our chosenness in advance is to be utterly distinguished from what, in *Fear and Trembling*, Kierkegaard describes as that ethical or universal *telos*, that "chosenness" (in) which we cannot choose and which he aligns with the categories of Greek thought. The true notion of chosenness confers, upon the already factically situated individual, the singular responsibility for bringing faith as iterable into existence, a responsibility that Kierkegaard expresses through the paradox that if faith has always existed, then it has never existed. Faith is that by which we are chosen, but if we have always been chosen (without choosing), then we have never (been) chosen. It is precisely our being chosen that we must constantly bring into existence, constantly re-iterate, as (our) faithful choice (of the other).

The paradox of iterability is, as Caputo demonstrates, that the historical and covenantal is the condition of possibility for the idolatrous and finite. Both lying and the rote repetition of faithless prayer presuppose, as their condition of possibility, truth and the daily rhythm of a faithful life. The determinable, understood as the idolatrous and finite, is not, in itself, iterable. If biblical religion were merely finitely determinable, it would not be iterable. If biblical religion were not iterable, there would be no deconstruction, as Caputo recognizes. Deconstruction would never have existed, because it would always have existed—as the Socratic, Platonic, Hellenistic *eidos*. Like biblical religion, "deconstruction is a certain faith," Caputo remarks. "Indeed," he asks, "what is not? When I speak to you that exchange transpires in the 'magical,' 'miraculous' medium of our mutual faith, a faith," he reminds us, "that of course is never self-identical, that is always already disturbed from within by bad faith" (149). Is deconstruction, then, not subject to being disturbed from within by bad faith, not subject to being determinable? Like biblical critique, deconstruction is the deconstruction of bad faith. Indeed, it is the very condition of possibility for bad faith. But there is no deconstruction without the risk of contamination, or, as Kierkegaard remarks in *Philosophical Fragments*, we return to Socrates. Since, as Caputo and Derrida insist, deconstruction refuses to specify some determinable object of faith, it can do so only on the basis of biblical religion.

The two claims of Caputo with which we began were (1) that the point of view of Derrida's work is religious, but without religion and without religion's God; and (2) that deconstruction is to be situated within a de-Hellenizing tradition. If Caputo is right in his claims—as I believe he is—then what are we to make of Derrida's claim that we live "in the difference between the Jew and the Greek," a difference "which is perhaps the unity of what is called history"? What does Derrida mean when he speaks of the "historical *coupling* of Judaism and Hellenism" (WD, 153)? For Derrida,

"Judeo-Christianity is an extremely complex entity which, in large part, only constituted itself qua Judeo-Christianity by its assimilation into the schemas of Greek philosophy. Hence," he says, "what we know as Christian and Jewish theology today is a cultural ensemble which has already been largely 'Hellenized.'" Yet, he adds,

> one can argue that these original, heterogeneous elements of Judaism and Christianity were never completely eradicated by Western metaphysics. They perdure throughout the centuries, threatening and unsettling the assured "identities" of Western philosophy. So that the surreptitious deconstruction of the Greek *Logos* is at work from the very origin of our Western culture.
>
> (DCCT, 116–17)

In what sense, then, is history or deconstruction the difference between, or the coupling of, the Jew and the Greek, especially since, as we have learned from Kierkegaard, the de-Hellenization of Hellenism is not possible on the basis of Hellenism? Is this what Derrida means in saying that the deconstruction of the Greek Logos is at work from the very *origin* of our Western culture, given that the original elements of Judaism and Christianity were never completely eradicated by Western metaphysics? What, moreover, does he have in mind when he calls this deconstruction "surreptitious"? Derrida, in directly identifying deconstruction with justice in "The force of law," acknowledges that justice is the movement of deconstruction at work in history "before it even presents itself as the discourse that the academy or modern culture labels 'deconstructionism'" (FL, 965). He elsewhere holds, however, that the deconstruction of Greek metaphysics "is not necessarily something which comes to Greek philosophy from the 'outside'"; that is, from the non-Hellenic world. From the very beginnings of Greek philosophy the self-identity of the Logos is already fissured and divided. I think one can discern signs of such fissures of *différance* in every great philosopher," he claims, citing, as an example, Plato's *Republic* (DCCT, 117). Yet as Caputo rightly argues, modernity's notions of justice are not Greek but biblical. Further, as Kierkegaard shows, there is no transition from Platonic *eidos* to biblical justice. What, then, if deconstruction is justice, would the movement of deconstruction at work be in Greek texts? Is deconstruction in fact at work in Greek texts?

We have seen Derrida insist that iterability, deconstruction at work, requires "the origin to repeat itself originarily, to alter itself so as to have the value of origin." Is it not the case, then, that the origin must itself, in the beginning, be conceived precisely as iterable, as iterability? Yet if the Hellenistic *eidos* or concept of origin is not iterable, in what sense can decon-struction be Greek, or even Jewgreek? As Caputo indicates, what the Bible calls idolatry is precisely the unity of Jew and Greek, the reduction of biblical concepts to Hellenistic notions of perfection, the decision "that the Torah had to find a place on the shelves of the Alexandrian library, that you could or even should try to make sense of Yahweh by way of Plato and Aristotle" (PT, 335). Yahweh, as Caputo often points out, is not Being. Yahweh, like deconstruction, is the call for justice, which, as modern, cannot be made sense of by way of Plato and Aristotle. The possibility of repetition between biblical religion and deconstruction, the possibility of religion without determinable religion, exists, therefore, on the basis that Yahweh is conceived, in the beginning and always already, as the principle (no less deconstructive than religious), the iterable origin (no less religious than deconstructive), whereby our privileged names separate themselves from every name—in the name of justice.[6] Deconstruction, the call for justice situated within the de-Hellenizing tradition of modernity, has, as *The Prayers and Tears of Jacques Derrida* shows, a history—an origin—which is biblical.

Notes

1 In this chapter I use the following abbreviations: FL for "The Force of Law: The Mystical Foundation of Authority," tr. Mary Quaintance in *The Cardozo Law Review*, Volume 11, 1990; MP for Jacques Derrida's *Margins of Philosophy*, tr. Alan Bass (Chicago: University of Chicago Press, 1982); GD for Jacques Derrida's *The Gift of Death*, tr. David Wills (Chicago: University of Chicago Press, 1995); CA for Søren Kierkegaard's *The Concept of Anxiety*, tr. Reidar Thomte (Princeton: Princeton University Press, 1980), and DCCT for *Dialogues with Contemporary Continental Thinkers*, ed. Richard Kearney (Manchester: Manchester University Press, 1984). Bracketed page numbers without further specification are references to John D. Caputo's *The Prayers and Tears of Jacques Derrida*.
2 I follow here the more detailed analysis that I provide in "Derrida and Kierkegaard: thinking the Fall," *The European Legacy* 6(1) (2001).
3 The most original (radical) and comprehensive analysis known to me of the rela-tionship of the Greek and biblical worlds to modernity is provided by Brayton Polka in *The Dialectic of Biblical Critique: Interpretation and Existence* (New York: St. Martin's Press, 1986). In engaging the tradition of biblical critique as developed especially by Spinoza, Kant, Hegel, and Kierkegaard, Polka argues (1) that Greek logic, based on what he calls the doctrine of opposites, utterly lacks a conception of either interpretation or existence; and (2) that it is the hermeneutical demand expressed by the golden rule of biblical critique—so interpret the existence of the other as you would have the other interpret your existence—that, in insisting that thought continually re-address the dualisms by which it is haunted, provides the very basis (impetus) of modern philosophy, theology, literature, and art. See also his *Truth and Interpretation: An Essay in Thinking* (New York: St. Martin's Press, 1990).

4 Although I cannot follow more fully here Kierkegaard's distinction between the
   Greek and biblical worlds, I would like to recall, in that regard, two areas high-
   lighted in the fruitful discussion that followed the presentation of my paper at the
   Institute for Christian Studies. (1) The first area of discussion involved Kierkegaard's analysis of Socratic irony in *The Concept of Irony*. Kierkegaard points out
   there that Socratic ignorance—exemplified in the claim made by Socrates in the
   Apology that he is the wisest man in Greece since he, at least, knows that he knows
   nothing—does not hide a higher positive content but is utterly negative and, like
   the Socratic dialectic in general, is designed merely to show that all claims to
   knowledge in the Greek world are empty. See, in *The Concept of Irony*, especially
   pp. 36–37, 89, and 170–173. (2) The second area of discussion involved Kierkegaard's distinction between paganism (the Greek world) and rationalized paganism
   (idolatry, the "repetition" of paganism within Christianity), the latter of which, in
   already presupposing the biblical world, equally presupposes not ignorance of but
   resistance to the golden rule (what Derrida and Caputo articulate as the call for
   justice). In addition, a third area of discussion stemming from the above involved a
   reconsideration of the very concept of modernity, the idea that modernity cannot
   be reduced to the belief in—the quest for or the assertion of—an overarching
   universal. Modernity is rather to be understood as the (biblical) history of justice
   and love, including the risks in which that history involves us (for faith always risks
   idolatry).

5 In *The Gift of Death* Derrida acknowledges that "when we once defined dissemination as 'that which doesn't come back to the father' we might as well have been
   describing the instant of Abraham's *renunciation*" of the life of Isaac (96, my
   emphasis). What does it mean, however, to renounce the life of Isaac? It is worth
   noting Kierkegaard's insistence, in *Fear and Trembling*, that "by faith I do not
   renounce anything; on the contrary, by faith I receive everything" (48–49). Are
   Derrida's and Kierkegaard's readings of the binding of Isaac thus inconsistent with
   one another? For Kierkegaard, faith suspends all "human calculation," all justifica-
   tion of human action in light of an external telos which annuls human singularity
   (and which Kierkegaard identifies with Greek philosophy (35–36; 54–55)). For Derrida, dissemination equally entails a risk which is heterogeneous with the calculable:
   Abraham sees that God gives Isaac back to him, Derrida writes, because Abraham
   "renounced calculation" (GD, 97). Important here is the distinction Derrida makes
   in "The force of law" between calculable law and incalculable justice; that is,
   between judgments of a "calculable or programmable order" and the singular,
   "just, free, and responsible" decision which requires us ever again to "negotiate the
   relation between the calculable and the incalculable" (961, 971). In renouncing
   the life of Isaac, what Abraham thus renounces, for Derrida as for Kierkegaard, is
   the possibility of "receiving" Isaac on any basis that reduces human existence to
   the order of the calculable. To renounce the life of Isaac, to suspend the calculable
   or negotiate the relationship between the calculable and incalculable, is to establish
   the relationship to Isaac in justice, responsibility, and freedom; that is, in fear and
   trembling.

6 That our privileged names must continually separate themselves from every name
   places an enormous demand on justice. For Derrida, the just decision "must rend
   time and defy dialectics," thus remaining "the very dimension of events irreducibly to come" (FL, 967, 969). In belonging to a future that is structurally always
   to come, justice therefore belongs a future that in principle never arrives and,
   indeed, *must* never arrive. How, then, are we to understand this structural *différance*? Like the deconstruction of originary presence entailed in the idea that the
   text is *always already* subject to its auto-deconstruction, the idea of a justice that
   will never arrive is understood by Derrida as the deconstruction of "all presump-

tion of a determinate certitude of a present justice," one that itself "operates on the basis of an infinite idea of justice" (965). Can we not therefore hold in radical continuity the two paradoxes that constitute the deconstruction of presence? If justice never will arrive, it is because it has always already arrived. Yet, as Caputo shows in *Prayers and Tears*, this double paradox, the infinite idea of responsibility upon which deconstruction as justice is based, is the very structure of biblical thought. Similarly, Kierkegaard renders the biblical concept of responsibility—the notion that faith, the infinite, or the eternal come into existence—through the following two paradoxes of origin: as soon as it is, it must always have been; but if it always has been, then it never has been. That the infinite is continually to be brought into existence is the biblical idea shared by Kierkegaard, Derrida, and Caputo.

8 The test of *khôra*

Grâce à Dieu

James H. Olthuis

John D. Caputo's reputation as one of North America's leading Continental philosophers is firmly established by the publication in 1997 of two remarkable volumes: *Deconstruction in a Nutshell: A Conversation with Jacques Derrida*[1] and *The Prayers and Tears of Jacques Derrida: Religion without Religion*. Not only is *Deconstruction in a Nutshell* (DN) a wonderful, nuanced, and extremely lucid introduction to Derrida and deconstruction (I know of none its equal!), *Prayers and Tears* (PT) surveys new territory in its creative exploration of the uncharted borderlands between religion and deconstruction. For anyone searching for an introductory text to the ways and wiles of deconstruction that is neither cursory nor superficial, DN is a dream of a book. It begins with a transcript of an exceptionally straightforward and illuminating conversation with Jacques Derrida at a roundtable held at Villanova University in 1994. In twenty-five short pages, Derrida answers questions about his work—extemporaneously, concisely, and frankly—signaling virtually all his major themes. As if that were not enough, Caputo has provided us with an inestimable service by the "dangerous supplement of a commentary." Incidentally, though not accidentally, this response to Caputo's two books will be a supplement to a supplement, a reading-with which seeks to continue exploring the intersections between deconstruction and religion.

In typical Derridean fashion, Caputo embraces the paradox of putting deconstruction into a nutshell when it is the very mission of deconstruction to crack nutshells open. It is precisely this kind of reversal in thought, the tenuous possibility of this "impossibility," that, rather than wiping out deconstruction, actually generates, nourishes, and impassions it. Caputo eloquently argues that deconstruction, rather than being a kind of an anything-goes-relativism, is "the endless, bottomless affirmation of the absolutely undeconstructible" (DN, 42). Indeed, it is in virtue of the undeconstructible, in the name of the "yes, yes" (*oui, oui*) of justice, that every nutshell is cracked open, deconstructed, to make way for the in-coming of the other. Caputo, then, proceeds to treat six themes as an encouragement to each of us to tackle these "nuts" on our own: the right to philosophy, *khôra* and *différance*, community and hospitality, justice and the gift, the messianic and messianisms, iterability and "yes, yes."

Each of these themes reappears in PT—a "follow-up" to DN—with a "religio-messianic twist" (DN, 47). For many years, argues Caputo, Derrida went about his disseminative mission of deconstructing totalities, disturbing unities, resisting closure, disturbing tranquilities without explicitly divulging, as he now has, that, all along, his motivating passion was openness to the other and the problem of justice. Indeed, in his 1989 *Circumfession*, Derrida goes so far as to claim that he has been "read less and less well over almost twenty years" because his readers knew nothing about his broken covenant with Judaism—"my religion about which nobody understands anything."

This is the immediate impulse that gave rise to PT, an engaging and compelling argument that "deconstruction is a certain negative propheticism . . . whose most vivid and perfect illustration or exemplification (or repetition) is to be found in the biblical, prophetic notion of justice" (196). For Caputo, these two comings—"the prophetic passion to let justice flow" and "the deconstructive passion for the coming of the other" (114)—flow together. In that confluence, "the name of God is a name that calls for the other, that calls from the other, the name the other calls" (113). "In short," he concludes, deconstruction as "the passion for the impossible 'is' . . . the passion for God, the passion of God" (339).

At the same time, and throughout the book, Caputo is quick to note his "little proviso" of "undecidability" (196). Neither he nor Derrida knows "whether deconstruction is an example of the religious, or whether the religious is an example of deconstruction." The "is" trembles in undecidability. "Which comes first? . . . Who cares? Does it matter, so long as we say *viens*, and then, once more, yes, yes, with passion?" (114).

To emphasize and celebrate the connections and slippage between deconstruction and religion, Caputo begins with a discussion of negative theology (the apophatic), moves on to deconstruction's focus on what is coming (the apocalyptic), which in turn leads to his discussion of the messianic, the heart of Derrida's religion and the pivot of this text. After addressing the question of the im/possibility of the gift and the figure of circumcision, he ends with a reading of Derrida's religion, his confession, prayers, and tears. Along the way, he inserts a series of six playful, if slightly impish, "edifying divertissements." The richness of the book and the brilliance of its exposition cannot be captured in a review. What I can do is give voice—more as an exuberant lookout than a dutiful *Extraskriver*—to some of the sightings, hints, and queries that emerged as I followed the twists and turns of deconstruction's journey with religion.

Twists and turns, for when one makes his or her way into the tangled shubbery of "which comes first?" a surprise answer awaits: neither. For, although deconstruction and the religious are "both first, as in any *repetito* worthy of its name" (114), in another way, as repetitions, both are responses—and thus not truly originary. As Derrida explains in *Specters of Marx*, both respond to, and both turn on a "certain experience of the emancipatory promise . . . a messianic . . . an idea of justice" (128). That is why Caputo can declare: "The passion of this promise is the very heart of deconstruction . . . provoking the prayers and tears of Jacques Derrida . . . the religion, the religious aspiration of deconstruction" (xxi).

For Derrida, we always speak "'within *the* promise'" (29). By this archipromise that is older than any of us—"a *yes* more 'ancient,'" before all historical affirmation and negation, which "performs (and pre-forms) us before we perform it" (31)—we are entered into a archi-covenant or alliance. We take up this covenant in an "archi-act of promising," an act of faith that is an "'unconditional, imperative, and immediate'" (64) "yes, yes" to the impossible, the stranger, the other, justice, and God. Since this "archi-yes by which we are promised and engaged is already, as soon as it starts, a *response* to what calls upon and engages us" (65), it is an excessively responsible, risky endeavor. Right from the beginning, my "yes"—a cry of faith shrouded in the mists of undecidability—may be a parody or a rote repetition. Moreover, since built into "yes" is the promise to "keep the memory of the first yes and confirm it, to repeat it" (65), the dangers of such mimicry or programmed repetition with every subsequent "yes" are always already with us.

It is this experience of the promise—what I like to call the covenantal structure of reality—that calls attention to, as Derrida puts it, "the trust" of "a sort of faith . . . 'before' all questioning, thus 'before' all knowledge, all philosophy, etc."[2] In that way, says Caputo, proceeding by faith alone, *sans savoir, sans avoir, sans voir*, "deconstruction itself comes limping along lamely 'after' the name of God, *post-posé*, after the fact" (66). In a sentence, "deconstruction is not the destruction of religion, but its reinvention" (DN 159).

Derrida gives two historical names to this not-historical religion which springs up in "*a certain desert . . .* more than *archi-originary, the most anarchic and anarchivable place possible*"(FK, 16): the messianic and *khôra*. The messianic—nourished by an "invincible desire for justice"—is "the opening to the future or to the coming of the other as the advent of justice" (FK, 17–18).

The test of *khôra*

The second name is *khôra*, the undeconstructible, totally unique—"neither Being nor Nothing, God nor Man, Nature nor History, Matter nor Spirit" (156)—placeless place in which all things take their place, although they do so without the slightest generosity, either divine or human. The most that we can do is call out: "'Who are you, *Khôra?*'" (36). *Khôra* is, for Derrida, "the very spacing of deconstruction," the "surname"[3] (ON, 80, 126) of the desert of *différance. Différance*—itself, "the nameless name of this open-ended, uncontainable, generalizable play of traces" (DN, 105)—is an "absolutely neutral receptacle" (DN, 105).

Although for Caputo "*différance* is *khôra*'s cousin, not God's," together a "couple of bastards" (DN, 97), I confess that I see a more positive connection between God and the *différance–khôra* couple. Derrida raises the question of issue in *Sauf le nom:*

> —Is this place created by God? Is it part of the play? Or else is it God himself? . . . it remains to be known if this . . . place is opened by God, by the name of God . . . or if it is 'older' than the time of creation. . . . It remains to be known (beyond knowing) if the place is opened by appeal . . . or if it remains impassively foreign, like *Khôra*, to everything that takes its place and replaces itself and plays within this place, including what is named God. Let's call this the test of *Khôra*.
>
> (ON, 75–76)

While recognizing the difficulties of making such a judgment (to the point of wondering if it is even possible to do so at all!) because the strange logic of the "with-without, or without-with" (ON, 76) that relates these two "places" to each other, Derrida and Caputo, in the test of *khôra*, show a decided preference for this space as *khôra*, as an anonymous, barren, nontemporal abyss. I want to suggest that describing this "place" as the matrix, the place "opened by God . . . by appeal"—what I call the friendly with-place of creation—seems more true to experience and more phenomenologically sound because of a number of considerations that, within the confines of this chapter, I will only be able briefly to explore—with the hope of stimulating more discussion.

1 Even though Caputo considers *différance* as the very spacing of deconstruction to be an "absolutely neutral receptacle" preceding and precontaining all oppositions inscribed within it, and sees *khôra* as the impassively foreign place–nonplace older than the time of creation, he insists

that "deconstruction is not ultimately neutral" (13). Neutrality is only a "provisional feature." "Beyond neutrality, *différance* is inventive, interventive, and affirmative" (344) because it gives precedence to the *oui, oui*, the archi-promise, justice, the *viens* of ur-affirmation, the gift, the messianic. Here we touch a crucial and knotted cluster of issues: the connection between the *oui, oui* and justice, the connection between justice and the messianic, and the respective connections between *oui, oui*, justice, the messianic and *khôra* with its play of *différance*.

If *différance* and *khôra* enjoy an "armed neutrality . . . even-handedly antagonistic to all claims of existence or nonexistence" (14), how can Caputo consistently read the *oui, oui* not merely as the *oui* that lets things be ("hello, yes, we are speaking, there is language" (256)), but—as the "yes" of justice to the stranger, to God, to justice, to hospitality, to the gift—as the opening of messianic time? Is justice, for Caputo, still a hyperbolic effect of *khôra*'s play of *différance* (as it was in *Against Ethics*) or is justice—as the invincible desire for justice and its undeconstructibility intimate—the very condition of possibility for *khôra* and its play of *différance*?

If *khôra* is "impassively foreign," "older" than the time of creation, if it does not give or promise anything, if nothing positive takes place, how can it in any way invite, evoke, or privilege the undeconstructibility of justice and the invincible desire for justice over a Nietzschean perspective on "just-ice" in which suffering belongs integrally to the cosmic economy? For *khôra* in its impassivity would seem to leave the affirmative character of decon-struction in its passion for the impossible of justice spinning in the winds of chance—the only connection to *khôra* being one of aleatory effect. How, then, do we "know" that justice is undeconstructible, and its desire invincible?

On the other hand, when the place is a matrix, a friendly space opened by appeal, the affirmative character of deconstruction with its normative bent towards justice is no longer simply a matter of aleatory effect. When matrix is the "place" evoked by the *oui, oui* of love and justice, with the process of *différance* as effect, then God and matrix, rather than only having a random, indifferent "bastard" connection, become, as it were, kissing cousins. Then, matrix—even when it is a ruptured womb, or abyssal desert—has not only a yearning but a congeniality for justice. It becomes a "quasi-messianic place, a . . . desert no-where" in which "the flower of a certain Jewish Augustianism" (333) that Caputo cherishes can grow.

With the call to justice as condition for *différance* and *khôra*, *différance* still remains an uncertain, risky play of undecidability with no guaranteed, cer-tainly no programmable, production of justice. The risk of violence is always present, and there always remains an irreducible gap between the call to justice with its opening of the possibility for justice and the reality that this or that is the incarnation of justice. At the same time, one is able to take up a critical stance with respect to any specific action or proposal in the name of the most originary possibility of justice.

Moreover, in this reading of this pre-originary place, the connection among justice, the messianic, and "*khôra*" is not left to aleatory eventfulness, but is a covenantal connection, one without automatic or necessary continuity or fusion, but also without ontic rupture—in striking parallel with Derrida's covenant with Judaism, which is "without continuity but without rupture."

2   For Caputo and Derrida, however, the gap between what is and the justice to come is something other than an empirical or contingent shortfall. Although the whole point of deconstruction is "to inflame our passion for the impossible" (59), justice, for deconstruction, never comes, and can never come—except by the "ghost of a chance-event" (124). That is so because there is an archi-violence which belongs irreducibly, inevitably, and irrevocably to the play of *différance* and the cycles of time and history. That explains why, for example, in his comments on self-portraits in *Memoirs of the Blind*, Derrida insists, as Caputo explains, that "[r]uin ... is the conditioning structure of experience itself, and of memory." "Already from the origin" a self-portrait is structurally inhabited by ruin because of the "inherent spacing and withdrawal that inhabits experience" (322, 321).

But why, I ask, does the inescapability and necessity of language, mediation, conditionality, interpretation, signs, and horizons give us over "structurally" to violence and ruin? Why need this mean that "the violence of language is inscribed in our being"? Why do we construe the inherent distance and absence of language as necessarily a "mis-speaking" and not (by the principle of undecidability) as the structural conditions of experience with the possibility and risk (but not the necessity) of violence? Why? Unless—despite its correct insistence that "pure presence without representation" (19) is an impossible, dangerous myth—deconstruction is itself haunted by the ghost of purity and full presence. Agreed. There is no possession, fusion, pure presence, only risk—the abyss of risk and confusion which tempts us to fixation, possession, and totalization. But the risk of violence is not the same as necessary violence; the risk of totalization is not the same as its inevitability.

This significance of this point is hard to overestimate since it means that, for Caputo and Derrida, any determinate act and any determinate religion are necessarily violent. Caputo talks of the "cycle of violence that drives the concrete messianisms" (337). No wonder they seek a messianic religion of peace without determinate religions, their messianisms, and the inevitability of war. However, since the whole thrust of deconstruction has been to undermine the metaphysics of universals, and since Derrida's messianic is "the very structure of urgency and engagement" (141), it cannot be a Greek universal or a Heideggerian formal indication without content. Faced with this dilemma, Caputo suggests that the Derridean position is "one more messianism . . . with certain determinable features," including the prophetic tradition of justice and an inclination for democracy (142). But if content is admitted into Derrida's messianic structure which is not necessarily violent, that would seem to support the need to make a distinction between the risk (the historical production) of violence and the necessity (the structural production) of violence.

3   Since violence is for Derrida "irreducible" within time and history, within what he calls "the order of meaning (presence, science, knowledge)," justice, along with the messianic and the gift, belong to "the order of the gift"[4] which—although impinging on and beckoning time and history—is always the future-to-come that is "structurally impossible to complete" (96). Indeed, because it remains forever structurally future, Derrida forthrightly talks of his "despairing 'messianism'" with its "curious taste . . . of death."[5]

Again, I must admit, this gives me pause, and for reasons similar to those invoked above. It is true—without a shred of doubt—that historical economies can easily, and often do, become cycles of violence, closing themselves off from justice. The question is whether such violence is inevitable and inescapable—in which case, with Caputo and Derrida, we need to attempt to minimize the violence and recognize that the impossible is always beyond. Or, as I am suggesting, are there possibilities, capacities, and resources within the creational economy that not only act against closure but also invite and evoke acts of justice and love? Even though the impulse to love and justice in history is entangled with a proneness to evil and violence, evil—in view of the "yes more ancient"—can never, I would insist, be equiprimordial with the good.

This way of thinking allows us to recognize in time and history (intentional) acts of loving service—cups of cold water—that incarnate justice genuinely and truly. To say it in traditional theological categories: even though the creation in our experience is a fallen creation in need of re-creation and reconciliation, it is still God's creation, and as such "good." Under the aegis of God's redeeming and transforming grace, creaturely life in the creation is able—in spite of evil—to embody love and justice as flesh and blood signs of God's kingdom, a kingdom that is coming, and which, in Jesus' words, is already among us.

4   There is for Derrida and Caputo another weighty feature which helps explain why justice cannot be done and remains always impossible—except by aleatory accident. In their view, human intentionality is always necessarily self-seeking appropriation: to be a subject is to be aggressive, always a threat to everyone else, inexorably a "capitalist . . . bent on making a profit" (168). No doubt the risk of being a capitalist is always a beguiling temptation, but is it a necessity?

When intersubjectivity is conceived as inexorably a relation of hostile opposition, there is simply no possibility—despite their obligatory and mandated urgency—of intentional acts of love and justice. Coupling irremissibly the intention to give with the interest of return brings with it an element of calculation and violence that annuls any act of gifting. Thus, only by "the aleatory alogic of messianic time, by a certain chance" (100) can events (not acts) of love and justice happen, and this below the plane of human intentionality.

What, however, if there were—thanks to a creational matrix already primed toward the good—the possibility of acts of love and justice hospitably open towards others as an alternative to a tit-for-tat economy of exchange? Derrida himself hints at the possibility of such a nonoppositional economy when he speaks of a "welcoming, hospitable narcissism, one that is much more open to the experience of the other as other."[6] In such an economy of love there is the possibility of gifts—gifts intentionally given and received—that escape the destructive circle of violence.

5   Let me touch on one other area where I feel some bewilderment and where I want to make a suggestion: the faith–knowledge nexus. Both Derrida and Caputo continue to insist on a strong contrast between faith and knowledge, in spite of the fact that it is "the whole point of deconstruction to disturb . . . assured sets of distinctions" (138), and in spite of the fact—and here is my bafflement—that they themselves give ample indication that the borders between faith and knowledge are porous and not clear-cut. Thus, Caputo emphasizes that "the whole point of" deconstruction's analysis of reason is "to show the extent to which reason is woven from the very fabric of faith" (DN, 164). In a similar vein, Derrida not only takes issue with Heidegger's claim that faith has no place in thought by insisting that "the incalculable is at the heart of the calculable" (FK, 65), but also admits that "elementary trust, the 'good faith'" is "never pure . . . of all *calculability*" (FK, 63). Here comes my suggestion: Is it not time that we give up the time-worn, now outworn, contrast between faith and knowledge—and think the connection otherwise?

Along these lines, although I believe—along with Caputo and Derrida—that testimony is not "'reducible, precisely, to verification, to proof or to demonstration, in a word to knowledge'" (112), testimony would be, I suggest, a knowing-otherwise with its own unique kind of concepts. In much the same way that Derrida's concept of iterability (along with *différance* and "several others") has a "strange status . . . it is an aconceptual concept or another kind of concept, heterogeneous to the philosophical concept of the concept,"[7] faith concepts would enjoy a "strange status." Moreover, it strikes me that Caputo—in his discussion of Heidegger's "formal indications"—gives a superb description of faith concepts when he speaks of concepts that can only be engaged existentially, that are not grasped conceptually, but are precursive indicators, pointing at something, at an excess that cannot be contained (140).

Faith concepts would be ingredients in an act of faith which, in Derrida's words, "exceeds through its structure, all intuition and all proof, all knowledge" (FK, 63). As Caputo brings to our attention (107), Derrida testifies that the "structural non-knowing (*non-savoir*)" of faith is a "more ancient, more originary experience, if you will, of the secret . . . an experience that does not make itself available to information" (P, 201). In another context, Derrida points out that we "know something" about the reference of negative theology. "We preunderstand it. . . . We come *after* this knowledge, however minimal and precarious" (ON, 48). Indeed, Derrida's entire discussion is not, it strikes me, so much another version of Kant's "religion within the bounds of reason"—although Derrida himself, admittedly, gives that impression in "Faith and knowledge"—as a postmodern Augustinian "reason within the bounds of faith."

Conclusion

In conclusion, Caputo's project is the kind of bold envisioning, the kind of hazardous adventure that needs to be undertaken by all who cherish that philosophy be, in Levinas's words, "the wisdom of love" instead of the love of wisdom. Whether we say religion without religion or, as Derrida might well have said, religion not without (*pas sans* (ON, 81)) religion—or, as I prefer, religion before, in, through, and beyond religion—is not all that important. What matters in the end—as Caputo so vividly reminds us in his closing paragraphs—is the answer we give to the question: "Lord, when did we see you hungry and give you to eat, or naked, and give you clothes?" (338).

That is how I ended my initial draft of this chapter. But I cannot suppress the niggling question that sprang to mind when Caputo follows this biblical citation with his Derridean quotation from Augustine: "Quid ergo amo, cum deum meum amo?" (what do I love when I love my God?), which runs like a refrain throughout PT. Why this emphasis on the "what"?

If "[t]he passion for God renounces the cognitivism" that constantly asks "'what is this?' and 'what is that?'" (334), it seems strange to discover this "what" in his third revision ("*I do not know what I love when I love my God*" (332)) of his sentential confession. In the same way that Caputo says that *différance* "does not answer to a 'what' or an 'is'" (DN, 99), I suggest that God doesn't either. God is not a "what" that we can know. Yet, for me at least, this translates not into a lack of knowledge of God, but into the knowing-otherwise of faith. This leads me to propose that a fourth version of the sentence Caputo has been trying to say throughout PT suggests itself: *I know my God in the unknowing of faith.*

I know my God in the unknowing of faith as a God who "seeks us out before we seek it, before we know its name, and disturbs and and transforms our lives" (337). We are not alone, *grâce à Dieu. Oui, oui.*

Notes

1 Edited and with a commentary by John D. Caputo. New York: Fordham University Press, 1997. Hereafter DN in text.
2 Jacques Derrida, "Faith and knowledge: the two sources of 'religion' at the limits of reason alone," in *Religion*, Jacques Derrida and Gianni Vattimo, eds. (Stanford, CA: Stanford University Press, 1998), pp. 80, 126. Hereafter FK in text.
3 Jacques Derrida, *On the Name*, David Wood, trans. (Stanford, CA: Stanford University Press, 1995), pp. 75–76. Hereafter ON in text.
4 Jacques Derrida, *Given Time: I. Counterfeit Money*, Peggy Kamuf, trans. (Chicago: University of Chicago Press, 1992), p. 30.
5 Jacques Derrida, *Specters of Marx: The State of the Debt, the Work of Mourning, and the New International*, Peggy Kamuf, trans. (New York: Routledge, 1994), p. 169.
6 Jacques Derrida, *Points . . . Interviews, 1974–94*, Peggy Kamuf *et al.*, trans. (Stanford, CA: Stanford University Press, 1995), p. 199. Hereafter P in text.
7 Jacques Derrida, *Limited Inc.* (Evanston, IL: Northwestern University Press, 1988), pp. 117, 118.

9 Hoping in hope, hoping against hope

A response

John D. Caputo

Coming to Toronto

As I was winging my way north toward Toronto's Institute for Christian Studies I wondered how I would express my gratitude to my good friend Jim Olthuis and his colleagues, who had set aside two days to discuss this book, who had indeed spent many hours reading and analyzing it, and who then took even more time to write about it. No matter what, I thought, I cannot thank them enough for the high compliment that they are paying this text. How lovely, too, that this institution and a Catholic Augustinian institution like Villanova University can write each other love letters and invite each other to their homes. Scholarly work wedded to a love of biblical hospitality is a rare thing indeed. But Jacques Derrida says that in all hospitality the host remains the master of the house. Did my hosts have something on their mind that they wanted to make sure I heard? Had they decided the time had come to sit me down and have me listen, like it or not, on the grounds that they were not sure I would read my email? Was I being called to Toronto the way Catholic dissidents are sometimes called to Rome, to get an earful? Toronto called and I responded, *me voici*. But what was I getting into? I was starting to worry.

In general, I would say this: at the ICS, the Institute for Christian Studies— that is, the institute for the study of the Christ, of the Annointed One, of the Messiah, let us say, at the Institute for Studies of the Messiah, Who Has Already Come (ISMWHAC)—the claim that is made in *Prayers and Tears* (PT) about the structural futurity of the coming of the Messiah, that the Messiah is, as a structural matter (nothing personal), never going to show up, had a predictable effect. In a series of very incisive and very instructive papers, they gave me a holy earful, pushing me to the limits, sending me home to Villanova well fed, well instructed, and exhausted.

It is not as though I could not see this coming. Some of my best friends are

Ismwhackers of one sort or another (some wackier than others), and I could guess how this would be received. That is why I pointed out in PT that this structural feature of the "messianic" is realized even in Christianity, where we all believe that the Messiah has already made his appearance two thousand years ago. Even here, I say, the structure of the "come" (*viens*) and the "to come" (*à venir*) is realized, because even here, where he has come once before, we all want him to come again. Our messianic appetites are insatiable. No matter that he has come (might he have come in several times and places?), the point is that expecting him to come is the very structure of the future, of time and history. After all, if and when he comes again, actually shows up again in the flesh, by coming down on a cloud, say, then that is the very definition of the end of history, of time. Then it will be time to throw the tools of history on the truck and start preparing the case we mean to present at the final judgment. That is what the early Christians thought was likely to happen any day now, which made for a fascinating sense of time. They did not foresee the need to build churches or train theologians at Institutes for the Study of the Second Coming; they didn't think they had the time.[1] Their sense of the future was of something decisive, short, and intensely charged, whereas we have come to take a longer look at the Second Coming and live with a sense of messianic expectation that needs regular recharging.

As a matter of fact, the question "when will he come?" is alive and well, not only in primitive Christianity, and not only today, but even during the first coming, when he was right there before the eyes of "the contemporary generation," as Climacus called them, in the flesh. For even then the Messiah was not present. What was present was the man from Nazareth, Yeshuah ben Joseph, the carpenter's son, from Nazareth, but the Messiah, the one who is to come, was a different matter, not visibly detectable by a certain messianic gait or bearing, a certain messianic gleam in his eyes, which is paganism.[2] "Who do men say I am?" he asked them. The jury was out, the question raged, nobody got it, everybody was asking "When will he come?" They all behaved like the disciples on the way to Emmaus, not knowing to whom they were speaking until it was over. It was only with the death of "Jesus" that "Christian" communities, texts, buildings, and theologies took shape, and institutes of Christian studies were founded with generous endowments and highly paid faculty and prestigious invited speakers.

"Christians," the people who believe he has already come, are more precisely the people who are situated in the space between two comings neither of which is present, between the memory of the first and the expectation of the second. Both of these comings are objects of faith, and neither of them is or can be present, the one belonging to the time of memory, the other to our sense of futurity. Faith, the very idea of faith, occupies the distance between presence and coming, the gap that is opened up between them, not by chance, but structurally. So whether we are praying and weeping before the weeping wall in Jerusalem for the Messiah who is to come, or celebrating the birth of the Messiah at a midnight Christmas mass in St. Peter's Basilica in Rome while praying for him to come again, the structure of messianic time, its structural futurity, remains in place. If there is time, there is hope and messianic expectation, hope in hope, which, as we Christian deconstructors think, goes hand in hand with hope against hope.

Another problem I saw coming as I winged my way northwards for my rendezvous with my friends at the ICS in Toronto was the reception that the distinction between the pure messianic and the concrete messianisms was going to get. Derrida urged keeping a certain safe distance from the concrete messianisms which in PT took the form of an "attack upon Christendom" (I have always loved Kierkegaard so much). So Christianity gets put in its place in PT not only by insisting that the Messiah is always to come, but because I insist, with Derrida, on delimiting the authority of any of the "concrete Messianisms." I had my doubts about how that would play at the ICS as the plane set its wheels upon the ground in Toronto.

In hot water about cold water

No sooner had the proceedings commenced and I was warmly welcomed, than I was in hot water. I got into trouble right away with Jeff Dudiak, who wants to share a cup of cold water and a piece of bread with the needy, and I am, God forbid, evidently standing in his way. He is worried that there is something about Caputo, Derrida, PT, Caputo's Derrida, or Derrida's Caputo, this entire "corporation," as Jacques would say, to prevent him and others from engaging in such good works. How can I assure him that I am on his side? Perhaps, if he gives me his address, I will send him a check to aid him in all his good works. I would like to think that I am as eager as he is to take the bread from out of my mouth, that I could not enjoy a good meal while the hungry looked on. But he has his doubts, and well he should, for who knows how we will act when the Good comes calling at our door dressed in rags? It is only by doing the truth, *facere veritatem*, that I shall convince him, convince myself, that I love the Good, if there is one. But this benevolent trouble-shooter has found trouble in a distinction I make; well, it is made by Blanchot, used by Derrida, and commented upon by me—the corporation grows—which implies that we will have to break up our corporation and join the ICS, become an Ismwacker, if, like Jeff, we want to distribute bread and cold water on a regular basis.

The distinction that is going to cost the thirsty and the hungry so dearly is that between "messianic time" and "ordinary time." As I understand this distinction, it does not refer to two different worlds or two different spheres of time, or to two different parts of time, but to two different conceptions of time, time conceived messianically as opposed to the ordinary conception of time. In the ordinary view, which has tended to dominate philosophers from Aristotle to Husserl, time is taken as a homogeneous succession of now points in which the present slips into the past, even as the anticipated now becomes present. In the ordinary conception, which as you can see is very boring, time is made of a neutralized succession of presents—a stream of past presents, now presents and future presents. Kierkegaard and Heidegger were the first to challenge the monotony of the prevailing view, and to insist that real time—lived time; that is, the time that anybody cares about—must be more interesting, more charged, than that. So Kierkegaard argued that "existential" time is charged by the passion of seizing upon subjective truth in objective uncertainty in a moment of madness, and Heidegger, hard on his heels, by the authentic moment of anticipatory resoluteness. In the place of a wearisome now-point, they put a very sexy *Augenblick*.

Derrida is very close to both these projects, but he has preconceived time, in the wake of Levinas (more board members), in terms of the messianic demand for justice for the other, and so for him the moment ceases to be a monotonous now-point because it is the moment of the gift, of the expenditure without return, of the in-coming (*invenire*) of the *tout autre*. When time is taken messianically, it loses its neutrality and is charged with justice, which means a messianic hope for justice, a demand and longing for justice, which, as I tried to assure all my friends who want to feed the hungry, is precisely what charges the moment with the imperative to make justice happen now, not next weekend, when we expect to have more time. So my good friend Jeff will perhaps sleep more easily, or rise even earlier in doing good works, knowing that the hunger of those who are starving, which appeals for the bread out of my mouth, is just what constitutes messianic time, that the moment one is overtaken by that demand one is in the messianic moment. Messianic expectation charges the moment and constitutes it as the *Augenblick* in which everything is demanded of me, here, now, in an expenditure without return. Charging time with justice, charging us to make time a time of justice, is just what constitutes messianic time.

Justice here and now—even though and precisely because I cannot do everything, even though and precisely because I know that the poor and the hungry will always be with us. That means that feeding the hungry and attending the poor is a task structured by the to-come of a bottomless obligation, by the obligation to a justice that will have always been to-come. The to-come does not consign us to despair but intensifies the demands of the moment, injecting the life of justice into the flow of time, exposing the present to the white light of an absolute demand for justice. The slightest imperfection in the present, the slightest injustice, is absolutely intolerable, and cannot be written off as a tolerable progress, the way Francis Fukuyama would say to Jeff that all those poor, ill-housed children in north Philadelphia, going to some of the worst schools in the nation, are moments in the progress of free-market capitalism towards the City on the Hill, so relax, they'll get by. That Fukuyamistic sanguinity about the poor is what drives our corporation's insistence on the structural to come: justice is to come; it is not here, not now, not in the Bronx or north Philly, not in Manhattan's sky-scrapers or Silicon Valley. The intensity of the demand for justice is set by the tension between the moment and the to-come, by the absolute pressure exerted upon the present by the relentless demand for justice, the demand to make justice come, which we can never meet. For we will never have done enough, and it is only a complacency with the present, the pleasure that a good conscience takes in the present, that allows us to think otherwise.[3]

But Jeff Dudiak, feeling prevented from distributing cold water to the needy, and suspecting where the trouble lay, decided to pour the same cold water on this distinction, which he construes as a distinction not between two different conceptions of time, but between two different times, or spheres of time, or parts of time. Sometimes his language suggests that he is thinking of two different times occurring in two different places: if one gets hungry, "one had better hope that one is not hungry and thirsty in ordinary time, in lived time" (p. 12), the implication being that no one gets a cup of cold water in messianic time, but only over there, in real time (p. 13), where justice really "takes place" (p. 13). Do they "dovetail," he wonders (p. 13)? Are they parallel? Weak man that I am, I have trouble grasping the coherence of this suggestion: where would these two times be? Would one be "here," the other "there?" One high above in an upper world, the other down here? Would they be simultaneous or successive? Since that is a very baffling possibility to meditate, I am fortunate that Dudiak for the most part pursues a different suggestion, that ordinary time is now ("a concrete today") and messianic time is later ("a messianic future") (p. 13), that ordinary time is to be identified with the real lived time of the present, where only the present are living, and only the living are present, whereas messianic time lies lodged in a future never-never land where nobody lives (yet); or even, most amazingly, that ordinary time is a humble little part, while messianic is a big totality (p. 16). But alas, if only I could bring Jeff Dudiak to see that this is not what we all intended to say, not our corporate *vouloir-dire*, then we could all spend more time in good works and less time trying to show that these two times must be "co-implicated," or insisting that they must "intersect"(p. 15); that is, solving a problem that is not there, experiencing trouble where there is none.

For it is the messianic demand made upon us now, in the present, in the demand for justice now, that constitutes the present as "lived" time, as the moment in which everything is demanded of me. This is a demand that is issued from flesh to flesh, from the flesh of those laid low which comes over and lays claim to my flesh, as I argued in *Against Ethics*.[4] In the neutralized, disinterested flow of ordinary time, on the other hand—that is, in time as it ordinarily taken from Aristotle to Husserl—now-point succeeds now-point in a tranquilized succession, devoid of the *Augenblick*, devoid of the time of the gift, devoid of the time of the other, of the "event" (*à-venir*) of ethics. Messianic time comes out of the future, out of a hope for the future, as the demand to make justice come, which means to make it happen now and thereby transform the present. Let justice come now, let it begin to come, now, let it begin with me, *me voici*. When, occasionally, Dudiak notices this argument protruding there, in the text, conspicuously present and not to-come, he says: "I am not entirely dissatisfied" (p. 18). *Oui, oui*: we should never be satisfied, our love of justice must be unsatisfiable, for justice is always to come!

One last point: since we cannot feed the dead or give them to drink, and since we should let the dead bury the dead, Jeff Dudiak seems to think there is something totalizing about including memory in messianic time. I am scandalized. Now apart from the fact that everything in Christianity is organized around doing things in memory of Jesus, it seems to me that the memory of all those who are persecuted and who died at unjust hands, what Metz calls the "dangerous memory of suffering," has everything in the world to do with handing out a cup of water to the poor whom we will always have with us, which is why Levinas begins *Otherwise Than Being* with a memory. Taking time messianically transforms the past and memory no less than the future and hope, which is something that is very powerfully worked out in Walter Benjamin (another chair at the board table), who usually accompanies Derrida's invocation of the messianic.[5] We today are the messianic generation, Benjamin says; that is to say, we are marked by the "to come" of the dead: we are the ones who were expected, and we have a duty to the dead, to the specters of the past, to the Holocaust and all the holocausts, to their memory, to realize what they died for. Justice is never present, as Derrida shows in *Specters of Marx*, just because it is always owed, not only to those who are present, in the *Augenblick* of justice, but also to those who are not, by which he means both to the ones to come, the future, the children not yet born, but also to the dead, who shall not have died in vain, who shall not have gone thirsty and hungry in vain. In messianic time the demand for a cup of cold water stretches across the length and breadth of time, not because messianic time is totalizing, which would mean that it erases the secret of our singularity in the name of the larger sweep of some world-historical spirit, but because the demands it makes upon us know no limit. Messianic time is set in motion by a love of justice that is unsatisfiable; it prays and weeps over every lost sheep, every lost coin, every lost son and daughter, counting every tear.

Saving the name of the concrete messianisms

It is perhaps a sign of the vigor with which I pursued the problem of the dangers of the determinable faiths that I have driven a man from my own camp over to the other side, at least temporarily, strategically. Ron Kuipers is a good man and true, somebody I was counting on to help me out when I was surrounded on all sides by Ismwhackers, by advocates of the very concrete messianism named in the name of this venerable institution. But Kuipers has found it necessary to swim the river and, emerging on the other bank, to wave his arms frantically shouting "Enough, enough, stop firing, before you wipe everything out!" That is a sign of a certain failure on my part to maintain a tension, and I am grateful to Ron Kuipers for pointing this out and allowing me to refine my position, which rightly troubled others during this meeting.

Deconstruction does not resolve contradictions by means of a happy, Hegelian *Aufhebung* which sends all the parties to a dispute home happy in the belief that they have at least negotiated themselves a piece of the pie. Rather, deconstruction defines and stresses the tension in a phenomenon; it might even be thought of as a kind of phenomenology of torques, of phenomena that are not only "disturbed" but in fact constituted by their stresses and strains. Then, situating itself inside that tension, settling into the distance between the opposing poles, all the while maintaining the tension, deconstruction tries to make the most of the impossible situation in which it has inserted itself. Accordingly, the first thing to do in dealing with the divide between the dry, desert-like messianic and the living, concrete messianisms is to stress the tension between them. On the one hand, there never was anything except the concrete messianisms, the determinable faiths, the particular, historically situated, datable and locatable beliefs and practices of real people, while, on the other hand, the pure messianic, or messianicity of the concrete messianisms, has a kind of unreal formality, a structurality, that relieves it of the need to certify its existence. But, on the other hand, the desert-like messianic protects the purity of messianic expectation and the *tout autre*, while the concrete messianisms, by taking determinate form, contract hope and expectation down to historically limited terms that cut off everybody else who has not been initiated into the local revelation. On the one hand, a concrete but too determined and local faith; on the other hand, an open but too empty formalism. And it will never be possible to choose between them.

I would address this problem as follows. The messianic is always the messianicity of some concrete messianism. It is the messianic impulse in the concrete messianisms, and the point of making this distinction is to remind us that the messianic can always take another form. The point is to remind the concrete messianisms of their own contingency, to attach a coefficient of contingency to any credo. The messianic is the impulse of expectancy in concrete expectations, the structure of hope in determinable hopes, the energy of longing in given and specific longings. The concrete messianism is always given; the messianic is the structure or the impulse of *au-delà* by which any given messianism is inhabited, which cannot itself be contained in or constricted to any determinate form. The messianic is the very uncontainability of the beyond, reminding us that even as we inhabit this body of beliefs and practices, we are not protected by it, are not kept safe, for our beliefs and practices are inwardly disturbed by a beyond that makes it impossible for us to close the circle and say that this is the final form, the last word, that we have "a corner or lock on the promise, that we own the truth or the promise" as Kuipers puts it (p. 25). Whatever we hope for, we are always hoping in hope itself, even as we find ourselves hoping against hope. The messianic is the *inquietum est nor nostrum* muttered not by a North African bishop but by an Algerian *pied noir* who rightly passes for an atheist, but who hopes in hope. That is what deconstruction is, if it is. If deconstruction were something, somewhere, if it did or did not do things, if it were a hypostasis with a proper name, none of which is in the least bit true, we would say that what "deconstruction" does is keep the future open, and, by exposing the concrete messianisms to danger, protects them against themselves. I do not see how anything is safe, how any body of beliefs or practices, how any institution, of any sort or whatever sort, is safe, unless it exposes itself to the danger of deconstruction. For the lethal threat posed by religious fundamentalists of every sort, from devout Christians who are ready to kill pro-choice physicians, and Protestants and Catholics in Northern Ireland who have been killing each other for far too long, to Jews who are ready to kill Palestinians in the name of the Holy Land—in short, the madness that drives "people of God" to kill in the name of God, the giver of life—is a far greater danger than deconstruction or dissent.

I do not think the messianic can exist as such, that it can assume a real form as such, that it can define the lives of real people, of socially, historically, politically situated communities, not as such. That is why I argued, and Ron Kuipers observed this, that even deconstruction is itself one more messian-

ism, of a late modern democratic sort. The messianic always comes embedded in a concrete messianism, as the structure of contingency within it that
pries it open even as it allows it to take determinate shape, as the "it could
always be otherwise" in any specific messianism. The messianic in the messianisms is the pronouncement that our credo, the several credos of the many
faiths, are never the definitive word, the last word, that we are all more or less
children of the cosmic moment in which we have been born and are unable to
lift ourselves up and out of that cosmic constraint. On the other hand, we
stand a good chance of being cut off from any messianic expectation at all, a
good chance of being swallowed up in the consumerism and shopping malls
of North America, or crushed by grinding poverty in the Third World, if you
have not been born into, or moved into the neighborhood of, one or the other
of the concrete messianisms. So I would say that the concrete messianism is
or should always be inwardly disturbed by the "beyond," by the messianic
formality which prevents its closure. Accordingly, the idea is not to denounce
the concrete messianisms utterly, or to leave everyone with the idea that they
are "essentially poisonous," in Shane Cudney's felicitous formulation, or "by
their very nature violent" (p. 23), as Ron Kuipers puts it, but to maintain the
tension, to maintain them in their pharmacological undecidability, which is
the structure of the Gift/gift, the poison/remedy. The failure to do that is the
main rhetorical failure of PT, which is a serious failure for a book that takes
rhetoric and the flow of prayers and tears very seriously. PT appears to have
broken the tension, the undecidable fluctuation of the messianic/messianism,
which is what is truly productive in any concrete messianism. For even as the
community must take the risk of hospitality, must put itself at risk by opening its doors to the other, so deconstruction, if there were such a thing, must
take the risk of community. That is why it has always been possible—and this
is its finest hour—for a given messianism to nourish the likes of Dietrich
Bonhoeffer, Martin Luther King, and Dorothy Day, and beyond them count-
less other peacemakers, in parish basements and crime-infested neighbor-
hoods everywhere, who do not make headlines but who do make peace and
justice flow like water across the land, which is the best flow of all.

Deconstructive head, Thomistic hats

Shane Cudney, whose concerns are similar to those of Ron Kuipers, tackles
one of the most difficult problems addressed in PT: how to deal with the truly
dangerous idea that religious people allow to get inside their heads, viz. that
God has singled out a particular people, in a particular time and place, and
given them (well, in all modesty, usually "us") a privileged access to a divinely
revealed truth to which other people, who do not or did not live in that time

or place, or share that language, who may have never so much as heard of that religion, are denied. God has pitched his tent among "us," while the others, the Canaanites, are just going to have to learn to deal with that. Or else! In support of their privilege, the believers offer their belief—and their swords.[6] Derrida, following Levinas, tries to deal with this particularism—to my surprise, I must say—in a somewhat modernist way, by invoking the language of universal reason, of a formal, universal messianic. In this, I would say, he is following Levinas's idea that the Bible is a "good book," which needs to be translated into Greek. Thus the "chosen people," when properly translated for Levinas, means that we are all chosen, all responsible to the neighbor and the stranger, addressed by the trace of God that is inscribed on the face of the wayfarer who knocks at our door. That, as Levinas, Derrida, and Cudney all recognize, smacks of Kant, and the universal ethical content that can be unearthed by analysis of the historical particularities of Judaism and Christianity. But would that amount to the new Enlightenment for which Derrida strives, which is enlightened about the axioms and certainties of the Enlightenment, or would we end up with pretty much the old Enlightenment all over again?

I have dealt with this by way of my proposing my one major criticism of Derrida in PT, by saying that his distinction between the messianic and the messianisms turns on a set of classical distinctions—like that between fact and essence—which deconstruction bends all its efforts at deconstructing. On Derrida's own terms, one should say that each of the concrete messianisms is a singularity unto itself. But even that is a fiction. For again, on Derrida's terms, both the Tanach and the New Testament are not books but libraries of books, swarming with competing theologies, spiritualities, dissident voices, different historical audiences, etc., the proof of which is the formidable body of literature that has grown up over the centuries trying to interpret what is going on in these texts. Consequently I argue that the distinction wilts and we must concede that there are innumerable messianisms, more than we count, that the "messianic" is simply a finger pointing at the moon, what Heidegger called a formal indication, not a universal that contains or circumscribes them. Accordingly (and this reflects my suspicion of a purely formal messianic), deconstruction itself is one more late modern messianism that repeats Jewish messianism with a democratic difference, constituting a democratic messianism with a Jewish or prophetic difference. But Shane Cudney finds here not only a good Protestant like Kant but neo-scholasticism, and the Thomistic distinction between faith and reason. My friends at ICS, knowing my great love of the Angelic Doctor, who first lifted my mind out of the streets of Philadelphia into the sphere of thinking, to whom I am endlessly grateful, take a singular pleasure in setting a Thomist hat on my deconstructive head. But this is a distinction that he wants to deconstruct on the grounds that faith is a kind of knowing and "permeates every mode of human experience" (p. 45), a point that is made by both Derrida and PT, and that is also, he says, a project of love. I have already owned up to having given the historical messianisms a very hard time. I did not want to leave my readers with the impression that I write them off as "essentially poisonous" (p. 46) or that I have resolved their undecidability into decisively poisonous places to do business—a matter that I have already discussed in my response to Ron Kuipers. For I do agree: we must, in the end, all pitch our tents among one historical messianism or the other; we have no other choice—we have not dropped from the sky. That is my criticism, if it is one, of Derrida. We are all nourished, as also slightly poisoned, by our various traditions. I accept, too, the Cudneyite proviso, that we inhabit the concrete messianism in which we find ourselves in such a way as to "cultivate a religio-ethical vigilance that has an ear bent toward the other" (p. 46). *Oui, oui.* That is exactly what I would say, but I would add a word of questioning gratitude to Shane Cudney for his chapter.

When Shane Cudney invokes the ethics of alterity at the end, when he asks us, very eloquently, to cultivate an ear for the other, he has implicated himself in this problem and started it up all over again. For now he must write his own book and, without distinguishing faith and reason, for he will evidently not allow this distinction, explain to us how we can all share a faith in messianic expectation, justice, hospitality, or the gift, but we cannot all be expected to share a faith in Jesus or Muhammad. For there are always these others for whom we must keep an open ear, and we must do so without producing the violence toward dissent for which the churches are legendary. Perhaps, since faith is ubiquitous, Shane Cudney will be led to distinguish between common faiths and particular faiths. But then he will have to explain to us how his new distinction differs from the distinction between reason and faith, or the messianic and the messianisms, or religion without religion and just garden-variety religion. I look forward to his book.

Tragic and religious hermeneutics

I suspect a certain collaboration between Shane Cudney and his friend Jamie Smith. Jamie is interested in Derrida's Jewish Augustinianism. He singles out the yes to the call of language itself in Derrida, who thinks, in a way that parallels Heidegger's notion of human language as a response, that our first word comes second, as a response to something that calls to us in advance, a deep yes, or Amen, that precedes every determinate yes and no. This structure of response, responding, and responsibility is also found in Levinas, and this because it is ultimately a Hebraic idea, for in Genesis the whole world arises as a response to the word of God, who by speaking calls it out of the void, creation being, in Levinas's beautiful expression, a response to a call that we never heard. Jamie Smith links this with the beautiful text in II Corinthians 1:19–20, that in Jesus "every one of God's promises is a yes," an Amen, *oui, oui,* to the promises that God extends to us. In the biblical tradition, he claims, the undecidability that fluctuates between any determinate yes and no is a contingency due to the fall (p. 54). But for Derrida, this promise and commitment, this yes, is of a piece with undecidability, which is a structural matter, not a contingency. As Jamie Smith himself says later in his study (p. 58), undecidability goes all the way down, which means there never was a language that was inoculated against undecidability. It would be very difficult to understand how a real language, in all its spacings and differentiality, would not be subject to such undecidability; or better, how anything that is not subject to such differentiality could be called a language except in some honorific sense. Indeed, what is the need for promise and commitment unless one has to make one's way through the flux of undecidability? That is also why we need faith, which for Derrida is ingredient in what we call reason, not opposed to it, which is why postmodernism, if there is such a thing, is a postsecularism, having jettisoned the opposition of faith and reason which defines and inaugurates modernity and Enlightenment. But just when I was being lulled by this lovely exposition of deconstruction as an Augustinian science (or faith?), Jamie Smith put two questions to me.

First, he asks, if this is an Augustinian reading of faith and reason rather than a Thomistic one, is not the author of PT himself still a crypto-Thomist who maintains a faith/reason distinction? You see what I mean. Up here in Toronto, in the vicinity of the Pontifical Institute of Medieval Studies, Catholic philosophers, even if they are deconstructors, are always already crypto-Thomists. If my Thomistic friends in the American Catholic Philosophical Association think I have lost my faith, my Protestant friends at the ICS and elsewhere think that if they don't keep a close eye on me I will slip them a Thomistic Mickey and when they wake up in the morning they will all be speaking Latin and referring to the "Holy Father." For in Augustine—and Jamie Smith puts this very nicely—faith is not "beyond" reason, as its crown, as Thomas would have it (*gratia perficit naturam*), but "before" reason, as its font (*fons*), its primordial, energizing pledge. We begin by (*par*) the impossible, by faith. I agree. But I ask Jamie Smith the same question I ask Shane Cudney, whose collusion I suspect. If we say that everything is embraced by faith, then there are only different sorts of faith, ranging from our Husserlian faith in perceptual expectations, through Kuhnian faith in scientific paradigms, to fundamentalist faith in the Lord Jesus who will come down on a cloud at the end of time to raise holy hell. But then we are going to have to find a way to distinguish the common faiths that we can expect everybody in a democratic society to share from the particular faiths that Christians, Jews, and Muslims have, which we certainly cannot expect everyone to share. If you cannot make that distinction, you will endanger the civil rights of people who do not share "our" faith, as do the politicians of the Christian Right who want everybody to share their faith that homosexuality is a dastardly perversion condemned by God, nature, St. Paul, and the Southern Baptists, while not everybody agrees (not even at ICS!). That problem is not unknown to Augustinian political theory. It is, after all, one thing to say that all knowing comes back to a certain faith, as Derrida does, and another thing to say that by my faith I know certain things and the rest of you better fall in line with what I know (read: take on faith), or else. This "or else," if I recall, is not absent from *The City of God*, and it has cost a lot of "infidels" their hides.

To deal with that line of objections, good pluralists like Shane Cudney and Jamie Smith, and, in Chapter 8, Jim Olthuis (pp. 110–19) will find themselves scurrying back to their drawing boards, their lights burning long into the early morning hours, making distinctions that do the work of the now abandoned faith/reason distinction, and that may even start sounding like it. Otherwise, they will start receiving speaking invitations from Southern Baptist conferences to denounce the homosexual takeover of America, and they may even get an invitation from Jerry Falwell to visit to Liberty University. Will they then, in the dead of the night, when everyone is asleep, sneak a peek at the *Summa Theologiae*? Or maybe even Kant? *Je ne sais pas. Il faut croire.* My point is this: the interweaving of faith and reason demonstrated by Derrida, showing the way each bleeds into the other in the manner of *Memoirs of the Blind*, does not require us to drop the faith/reason distinction but to redescribe it, which means to redescribe reason without opposing reason in a binary way to faith. After all, is not Derrida the author of an article entitled "Faith and knowledge: the two sources of religion within the limits of reason alone"?

Jamie Smith's second question is this: in *Radical Hermeneutics*—and, I would add, *Against Ethics*—is there not a tendency to treat religious faith as a "construal," a hermeneutic rendering, while the "tragic" view (Nietzsche), or the view taken by "Felix Sineculpa" (*Against Ethics*) on the flux or the abyss, on the vast cosmic stupidity, is treated as uninterpreted fact of the matter? The tragic is real, while the religious is an interpretation. But is not the "tragic" also a faith and an interpretation, Jamie Smith asks? Isn't interpretation always inescapable? Is it not necessary, then, to revise this distinction? For this question I am very grateful, and I must respond yes, yes. To the extent to which my formulations have exposed themselves to this objection, to the extent to which I have drifted in that direction, this distinction needs reworking. For on the terms of any genuinely radical hermeneutic, everything is an interpretation, and it is always a question of knowing how to sort among the better and the worse interpretations. Both the tragic and the religious are opposing faiths, opposing evangelical words, of which Augustine and Nietzsche are the bearers or the apostles.

What I called the religious and the tragic in *Radical Hermeneutics*, the sides that are taken in the debate with Felix Sineculpa among the pseudonyms in *Against Ethics*, are positions struck within *différance*, directions taken within the *khôra*, which of itself has a certain ahistoricality, not because it is a thing in itself, an uninterpreted fact of the matter, but because it marks a certain condition that inhabits all or beliefs and practices and in just such a way as simultaneously to make them possible and, in the same stroke, to destabilize them. Allow me to cite a passage on the *khôra* from Derrida's debate with Marion at Villanova. The *khôra*, he is saying, is neither biblical nor anti-biblical:[7]

> [W]hen I refer to *khôra*, I refer to some event, the possibility of taking place, which is not historical, to something non-historical that resists historicity. . . . That is why I refer to what I call the "desert in the desert." There is a biblical desert, there is an historical desert. But what I call a "desert in the desert" is this place which resists historicization, which is, I will not say "before," because that is chronological, but which remains irreducible to historicization, humanization, anthropo-theologization of revelation. . . . But this place of resistance, this absolute heterogeneity to philosophy and the Judeo-Christian history of revelation, even to the concept of history, which is a Christian concept, is not simply at war with what it resists. It is also, if I may use this terrible word, a condition of possibility which makes history possible by resisting it. It is also a place of non-gift which makes the gift possible by resisting it. It is the place of non-desire. The *khôra* does not desire anything, does not give anything. It is what makes taking place or an event possible. But the *khôra* does not happen, does not give, does not desire. It is a spacing and it remains absolutely indifferent. . . . I think that this reference to what I call *khôra*, the absolutely universal place, so to speak, is what is irreducible to what we call revelation, revealability, history, religion, philosophy, Bible, Europe, and so forth. . . . This place is the place of resistance—perhaps resistance is not the best word—but this non-something within something, this non-revelation within revelation, this non-history within history, this non-desire within desire, this impossibility. I would like to

translate the experience of this impossibility into what we could call ethics or politics.

The *khôra* is neither tragic nor anti-tragic, neither religious nor anti-religious, but the inescapable necessity we live under to make sense in signs, to mark out sense, and even non-sense, in traces, so that whether we make tragic signs or religious signs, or like Richard Rorty shrug off both as too much hype, we do so under the conditions of *différance*, against a barren *khôral* landscape. The mistake of *Radical Hermeneutics*, which Jamie Smith's second question exposes, is to have collapsed the distinction, or at least not to have insisted on a distinction, between the tragic and *différance*, since the tragic is no less a way of construing the flux. That is a point that follows from what is called in PT the "neutrality" of *différance* (12), to which I will return in discussing Jim Olthuis's chapter, viz., the notion that *différance* constitutes neither some kind of "ontological argument" for God, as in Anselm (if that is what Anselm was doing, which I doubt) or against God, as in Sartre. *Différance*, which is "altogether too meager and poor a thing to settle the question of God" (13), is the quasi-transcendental condition under which our various beliefs and practices are made and unmade. If, in Derrida's early writings, his readers were inclined to think that *différance*, and the critique of the tran-scendental signified, was the very undoing of God, the last ultra-Nietzschean nail in the coffin of the old God, we must also resist the opposite temptation, which is perhaps something that we might be lured into by PT, that on the contrary *différance* is of a piece with messianic religion, that it is the watch-word of a certain Jewish Augustinianism. It remains forever indifferent to the religious and the tragic, to Nietzsche and Augustine, who are all on their own and cannot claim its authority, for it has none.

Jesus loves parties

Keith Putt thinks I am too happy, and that I do not have enough sorrow, while David Goicoechea thinks I am too sad and abstemious. Since I prefer happiness to sadness, I will take up Keith Putt's claim first and then, if my spirits are not too low, David Goicoechea's.

When my daughter attended Confraternity of Christian Doctrine classes as a young child years ago, she brought home a textbook full of colored draw-ings of Jesus, one of which said "Jesus had friends and loved parties." I remarked upon the theological profundity of the point, telling her that it went to the heart of the difference between Jesus and the Baptist, for while the Baptist mourns, Jesus pipes. Jesus changed the tune of *metanoia*, asking us to retune, to change our *Stimmung*, our nous, and be of a new heart, to play a new tune, one that is alas drowned out by translating this magnificent word as "repent," which is a Baptist (as in "John the," and "Southern"!) translation. Cast in Derridean terms, Jesus loved the gift, not the economy of exchange and retribution. When someone says *metanoo* in the New Testament, they are saying "I have turned around, I want to dance." Now as my dear Baptist friend Keith Putt points out in a thoughtful and provocative essay, *metanoia* also has the sense of an "after-thought," a reconsideration, particularly one in which one looks back with regret. Hence, Baptists of every stripe, from biblical Baptists to Texas Baptists, are not whistling in the dark when they render this word as "repent," which is in fact the NRSV translation, and link it with the Hebrew *teshuvah*. Indeed, Putt is quite right: no one would have a change of heart without sorrow for the wrong he or she has done (p. 67), which Levinas would express by saying that we are always worried by the murderousness of our own freedom, by the threat posed by the "same" to the "other."

We are never simply going to walk away from economy. There is no simple exteriority to the circle of exchange, but only a mad moment of interruption which widens the circle and tries to keep it loose and open-ended. Indeed, as Derrida says, it is the gift that creates economies to begin with and keeps them going. Once again, I come back to the idea of maintaining a tension, this time between gift and economy, and situating oneself in the difference between the two. We can no more imagine the nightmare of a world in which nobody ever did anything except for a price, a world of pure economy, than we can imagine a pure gift, where somewhere someone made an expenditure without return without setting off the smoke alarm of the circle of economy, by giving a gift that did not get drawn back into the circle after the moment of madness. The gift is very nicely formulated by Putt as an "improvisation" (p. 68), an unexpected move—in a dance or a musical performance—and he very rightly insists that I allow for both Hallelujah choruses and *Dies Irae*. Putt's model of an improvisation has the dual advantage of both presupposing a preexisting practice (economy) and allowing for a new move, a mad and unexpected interruption of the economy, which then is threatened by imitation and could always be written into the score. But this model does not, however—and here I disagree with Keith Putt—provide for a peaceful Hegelian reconciliation, a happy *Aufhebung*, as I said above. It depends upon taking a risk, upon a restless tension or tossing to and fro between the settled tendency of the score and the transgression, which is why a lot of improvisations fall flat. Either way, sorrow and the dance, grief and grace, belong together, for par-doning must not be confused with con-doning, he insists, because grace always interweaves with grief in anyone who has turned around. I agree, and I am grateful for a point well made.

But I will not be drawn into the confessional cross-fire Keith tries to set off with his shot at my beloved St. Thomas, to whom I have sworn an oath of undying allegiance (even though I sometimes disagree with him). It would be difficult to decide whether Protestants or Catholics have been more successful in torturing themselves half to death (and sometimes not half) with their sense of guilt and self-recrimination. I will not be seduced into arguing that Protestants, taking a point of departure in Augustine, have been, from Luther and Calvin to the present, immensely successful in convincing a lot of people about the essential corruption of human nature, and they have gotten it into their head that total abstinence has something to do with Jesus, whom they regularly confuse with the Baptist. Nor will I be drawn into pointing out that Thomas Aquinas was a level-headed Aristotelian realist who never gave such nonsense the time of the day. Nor will I draw attention to the fact that Catholicism produced Jansenism and Irish Catholicism, and alas American Catholicism was founded by and overrun by guilt-ridden Irish priests who set out to coat and colonize the New World with their morbidity and melancholy—remember the retreat young Stephen Dedalus attended in *A Portrait of the Artist as a Young Man* —instead of by Italians who prefer Puccini and pasta, *vino* and *amore*, on the sound theological point that Jesus had friends and loved parties. I will not be drawn into this contest. I will settle for a tie.

I agree that we require sorrow for wrongdoing, against the neighbor, against the stranger, against God, whose trace is inscribed on their face, and, as Keith Putt shows, I strongly defend the notion of our responsibility to the other as a paradigmatically biblical virtue. But I want to make two points in this regard. First, as I am interested in the gift beyond economics, I argue that the affirmation of the other means a responsibility that cannot be contracted to duty, and a duty that cannot be contracted to debt. If you come to my aid because you have to, or will fall into debt otherwise, well, don't bother; I would rather lie here and bleed while waiting for a good Samaritan to come along who will not feel so guilt-ridden in helping me out.

Second, as I am interested in the God of all good gifts beyond economics, the difficulty I am raising has to do with the mainstream—both Catholic and Protestant—conception of God. In the mainstream view, in which I think Keith Putt is happy to swim (p. 75), God is thought in terms of an economy of debt according to which the Crucifixion is the only way that God can be appeased for the enormity of the guilt humankind has incurred. God sent Jesus into the world to suffer crucifixion just so as to pay off the debt of sin (or even to pay a ransom to the devil); we can't do it by our works, because we are too far in debt. God wants sacrificial blood, infinite blood, and the devil wants a ransom, and with a debt this large only the blood of Jesus will do, otherwise the debt stands. That, I say, leaves the reader of the parable of the prodigal son, and the followers of the master of forgiveness, as Hannah Arendt calls Jesus, at a loss. Apart from the fact that any such earthly father— or mother—who demanded such retribution of their children would, to say the least, raise an eyebrow or two, this economy flies in the face of the parable of the prodigal son. When the prodigal son comes home, his tail between his legs (sorrow), the father throws a party. Jesus loves parties! He does not execute the son, or execute someone or something else, to appease his injured self-esteem. Then, does the father's gift of forgiveness to his son "condone" the son's prodigality? Is it an insult to his fatherly self-esteem? The elder brother thinks so, economists everywhere must think so, but the author of this story does not, nor does the father, whose only concern is that his son has returned. Is he being foolish? Might the son do the same thing all over again? Maybe. That's the risk. Are there measurable criteria for differentiating pardoning/condoning? Would the gift of forgiveness ever not look like con-doning? Would it not always be the risk? We need Keith Putt's gloss on this story.

Keith Putt knows very well that we need to think about forgiveness without getting caught up in the need to "retire . . . debt and purchase forgiveness" (p. 73). If you have to earn forgiveness, it is not a gift, not forgiving, but a fair exchange. So we must keep several tensions alive: between the great and sweeping "forget it" of forgiveness and the great anamnesis, the "never for-get" of the dangerous memory of suffering, about which I reminded Jeff Dudiak (p. 125); and also the tension between giving forgiveness and earning it, between showing mercy and showing sorrow which, I agree, is not mere lip service. The gift of forgiving transpires in the midst of these tensions, as the mad moment in which we give away what we are owed, go beyond the equi-librium of fair exchange, and do what we do not have to do, are not duty bound to do, and run the risk of looking as though we condone evil. After all, you cannot make a gift of forgiveness or of anything else to someone who has earned what you are giving. Accordingly, does not forgiveness always involve forgiving those who have not earned it? Does it not include, contra Keith Putt (p. 67), forgiving those who are precisely unrepentant; that is, who do not deserve it and have not earned it? Is that any more paradoxical in the Gospels than the gift of loving those who hate you, of turning the other cheek, or of hating those who love you (your father and your mother)? Sorrow and repentance are rightly expected of the offenders, but that is their business and their loss if they do not turn around, but inasmuch as they cannot give themselves forgiveness, forgiving them is our business. The business of forgiv-ing is the business of the offended, which is the gift, which is not a business, but a grace. Who are more unrepentant than the soldiers at the foot of the

Cross, taunting Jesus and dividing up his garments? "Father forgive them," these unrepentant Roman soldiers, "for they do not know what they are doing" (Luke 23:34). Isn't this paradigmatic case of forgiving a matter of forgiving those who have not earned it? So I would say that Keith Putt should reconsider not only what he says about Caputo at this point, but more importantly about Jesus.

A song to *sans*

If I have convinced Keith Putt that I make room for sorrow, I must convince David Goicoechea that I love to dance! I must prove that the tears in PT are both tears of sorrow and tears of joy; that if Derrida can write with both hands, I must know how to cry with both eyes. From the outset, I want to go on record as stating that in my opinion, if the world were full of people like David Goicoechea, it would be a happier place for everyone—except perhaps for those who are experts in conflict resolution, who would be unemployed and would need job retraining, all conflicts having disappeared. David hears a great deal of harmony among Nietzsche, Derrida, Heidegger, and Levinas, as though they are all singing together in a great polyphonic voice, like members of the Robert Shaw Chorale belting out the final chorus of Handel's *Messiah* (which Keith thinks is one of two voices we need). To this we must add, in view of David's love of angels, a heavenly choir singing overhead. David thinks that I have pictured Derrida too negatively, as doing "without" too many things, with too many "withouts"—without God and the pope and angels, that Derrida, at least Caputo's Derrida, and I, Derrida's Caputo, are trying to do without too much. He complains that I am singing the Derridean blues, wailing a sad song to *sans*, even though I have just put on record that I stand with Jesus's love of parties and I prefer my Christianity with Puccini, pasta and *vino*. (I am against totalization and tee-totalers!)

To cut to the chase, I cannot agree with David that there is a parallel logic of the "with" (*avec*) that goes along with the logic of the *sans* in Derrida, and I do not see that David produces a lot of evidence for such a hypothesis. The logic of the *sans* is ubiquitous in Derrida's text. It leads us off into desert sands, destinerrant, leaving us to pray like mad without knowing where our prayers are going, without a *hyperousios* to direct them towards, astray in the *khôra* rather than rising in steady ascent toward the *agathon*. But by siding with the *sans* I am not (nor is Derrida) deciding the undecidable, as David suggests, and as Jim Olthuis intimates, but I am injecting undecidability into what would otherwise be an uninterrupted positivity or identity (religion, faith, community, nation, etc.), without which, without this without, they would all be very dangerous for Derrida because, as self-identical, they reject difference. That is why we have excommunications, heresy trials, holy wars, immigration laws, deportations—and the list goes on. So allow me to inject some dissonance into this beautiful choir of Goicoechean angels and to defend my song to *sans*.

I think that David is right to say that Derrida has emphasized the leap in which Abraham gives up Isaac to death, but without the result (the leaping back), in which Isaac is returned by God in faith. That is because Derrida is engaged not in establishing an exegetically correct interpretation of Genesis, but in allegorizing the story to emphasize his account of the gift. By the same token, Kierkegaard underlines the result by telling the story in a very Pauline manner in order to emphasize his very Lutheran account of faith. As a strictly exegetical matter, they are both grinding their own axe, and Levinas is closer to the mark: the point of the story is that God stays the patriarch's hand and announces that the ethical demands the end of human sacrifice. That is the one version that really sticks with the point, if I may say such a thing about this delicate matter, of getting Isaac back. Still, Kierkegaard and Derrida have both put a nice spin on the story and made their respectively different points.

Again, I think that David is right to say that Derrida puts a kinder, gentler spin on Nietzsche than I do, but that is because Derrida is producing a Nietzsche without Nietzsche, or following Nietzsche without following him. For Derrida also puts a kinder, gentler spin on Nietzsche than does Nietzsche, and he admits it. As Derrida tells us in *Politics of Friendship*,[8] he is speaking only of a "certain Nietzsche," one whom he has carefully selected, and only one—"one Nietzsche, in any case (for there is always more than one)" (PF, 297)—who is given a very generous and very friendly reading, "an active and hazardous" (PF, 70) interpretation. Thus Derrida is compelled to "quickly inform the reader that we will not follow Nietzsche here. Not in any simple manner," that this will be at most a "following without following" (PF, 33). Derrida does well to find Nietzsche's other voices—that is what deconstruction always does—but my point is that Nietzsche loses all interest to me if he becomes a proto-feminist, proto-left-wing, left-bank Franco-intellectual, of whom I already have an adequate supply. What I love about Nietzsche is that he is bold enough to say that he philosophizes with his nose, that democratic and egalitarian values have the smell of putrefaction to him. I love Nietzsche because he is bold enough to say that he affirms the innocence of becoming, that you cannot separate the doer from the deed, that the forces are what they are, that they discharge as they do, and that is all. That means that the Nazi executioners are no more responsible to their victims than are the waves smashing against the shore, or the hawk swooping down on its prey. This is all of part of the great cosmic necessity, and we must love it all, without attenuation, selection, or subtraction. *Amor fati!* That is the most frightening hypothesis propounded by any philosopher the West has produced, and it is a great loss to duck that challenge, to purge his text of its terror, and to make Nietzsche look like St. Francis. We already have St. Francis.

The difference between my *sans*-oriented reading of Derrida and David's both/and syncretizing approach shows up clearly when you get to Levinas and his Good beyond Being. In Levinas, I am not simply approached by the neighbor, but rather I desire the Good, and the Good, Levinas says, deflects the direct approach I make to it and orders me to the neighbor, sending me on to the stranger. In my view, which cannot be debated here, that gives the ethical relationship a backup in the Good, which enjoys a metaphysical, even Neoplatonic status for him. In Levinas, the phenomenologically accessible ethical relation with the other is given a metaphysical grounding in the Good. But in Derrida—and I believe David's both/and approach suppresses this very important distinction—the claim of the other has a more starkly *khôral*, more radically *ankhôral*, quasi-phenomenological status. The wholly other comes over us, overtakes us, not from out of the *agathon*, with all of the backing and prestige of God or the Good, but in the midst of a *khôra*, more like a stray sheep, without a deep source in an ordering Good that orders us to the neighbor, and I fear that David's love of harmony and heavenly choirs obscures that crucial difference.

But I am not singing the Derridean blues (if there are any) with my song to *sans*. David is hearing only one side of what I want to say, what the lovers of *Star Wars* might call the dark side. But I am always writing with both hands, as Jacques would say, always writing two different texts, the one painting the dark side, the great cosmic stupidity, which steals over me with a merciless persistence and keeps me awake at night, while the other one is about a Jewish deconstructor named Yeshua, who heals the man with the withered hand and thereby deconstructs the law in the name of justice. Hallelujah! My idea is, like Yeshuah's, to pipe, not to mourn. I want to sing and dance, and I love parties and pasta, not locusts and deserts. The prayers and tears I advocate are tears of joy and hope. But for me that always means to have the courage to choreograph an inescapable *khôral* scene, which is for me the context of the gift, for hospitality is the virtue of a desert wanderer whose setting out is made only because he can depend upon being made welcome. That requires hope, hoping in hope, hoping against hope, *ankhôral* hope, hoping like hell.

Repetition and de-Hellenization

Avron Kulak is very much attached to the project of de-Hellenization that runs throughout PT, a project that is very much alive, *mutatis mutandis*, in Kierkegaard, Levinas, and, *mirabile dictu*, in Derrida himself, and I would say in a general way in the whole idea of "overcoming metaphysics" in Continental philosophy today. He focuses this project, as I also did in *Radical Hermeneutics*, on the distinction made by Constantine Constantius, between Greeks who "repeat backwards," which refers to the Platonic theory of recollection, in which the eternal is always behind us and nothing radically new or "event-ful" ever happens, our life being a fall from a lost origin, and Christians who "repeat forwards," for the eternal is up ahead, in the *vita ventura*, the life that is *à-venir*. Repeating forward, as Kulak and I would both argue, is pretty much what Derrida means by iterability, which is a repetition that produces what it repeats, as opposed to repeating something that is already there. Kulak links this line in repetition with the concept of anxiety, in which Vigilius Haufniensis distinguishes between the quantitative and qualitative interpretation of original sin. As a quantitative first, which Vigilius rejects, we all incur sin just by being born and descending from the first parents ("inherited" sin). That account undercuts our freedom while driving Adam out of the race. Since his own sin then is "before" the human race, he is detached from the race, while our sin is rendered in a way that is indistinguishable from the pagan conception of fate. As a qualitative first, original sin occurs when each of us individually, from Adam to the present, in the inner recesses of our freedom, crosses the abyss dividing innocence from the knowledge of good and evil. That makes for a kind of "originary" sin, where freedom is the origin of sin, so that sin comes into the world not by fate, but by sin; that is, by freedom. That means that original sin occurs again and again, within each individual, who makes themself to be what they are by freedom, by repeating forward, but without a quantitative coefficient. No one is first in a quantitative sense, which means that someone else's act does not make me guilty or innocent. This necessity that freedom is under to repeat forward is risky business, Kierkegaard and Derrida agree, being structurally exposed to failure, to rote repetition, or even to infidelity, which is the failure to repeat the yes from day to day. But, for better or worse, that is the very structure of faith, or of the vow. For Kulak and me, biblical categoriality circulates around this creationist model of productive freedom and productive repetition and the invention, the in-coming, of something new, which shows up in Kierkegaard's repetition and Derrida's logic of iterabilty.

Now that logic, Kulak rightly observes, is already at work in the title *Religion without Religion*, where religion is repeated—in and as deconstruction—but without the determinate religions. "What does Caputo mean by 'determinate'?" (p. 102), Kulak asks. That is not difficult: the dogmas, rites, and institutional structures of the historical religions like Christianity, Judaism, and Islam, the determinate beliefs and practices of historically identifiable religions—like Yahweh and the Blessed Virgin, the Trinity and the parting of the Red Sea. In short, I mean all the things whose absence, in virtue of the logic of the *sans*, David Goicoechea was complaining about when he lamented that there are no angels, popes, or Vatican City, no weeping wall at which to weep in this *ankhôral* religion. But how can that be absent, how at least can Judaism be absent, from deconstruction, Kulak asks, since my whole argument has been to show that it is not absent, that Derrida has all along maintained secret negotiations with Judaism, something that he himself confesses in *Circumfession*? Avron Kulak proposes that, in the face of this question, it would be necessary to distinguish an idolatrous from (let us follow Marion, here) an iconic conception of the determinable religions (p. 105). That, I think, is a very nicely made point, and it provides something that a lot of us were all looking for these two days. It offers a way of thinking about the determinable messianisms which keeps them open-ended, which prevents them from closing in upon themselves in a way that is nicely described, I think, as idolatrous, the risk of idolatry being built right into the very structure of repeating religion. The dead, narrow, literal, exclusionary repetition of the faith is, Kulak says, "finite," constricted to the finitude of its human-made limits, and does not let faith move or repeat forward. That non-idolatrous way of thinking about Christianity is exactly what Ron Kuipers wants; what all of us want, I think. It also goes hand in hand with my argument that a rigorous distinction between the messianic and the concrete messianisms cannot be sustained, and that deconstruction is itself, if it has an itself, another concrete messianism, of a quasi-prophetic, very late modern, hi-tech democratic sort. Deconstruction, too, has an identifiable historical pedigree; it did not drop out of the sky.

Kulak pushes on: but given what is said about the infinite slippage of the signifier that shows up in the deconstructive notion of exemplarity, according to which we must confess that we do not know what is an example of what, does not Caputo admit that we cannot tell whether deconstruction is an example of religion or religion is an example of deconstruction, because in any repetition worth the name, both are first (or neither is first)? Is deconstruction a case of the passion for God, or is the passion for God a case of deconstruction? (114). Is God an example of undeconstructible justice, if there is such a thing, or is undeconstructible justice an example of God? If God is love, is God an example of love, or is love an example of God?

I am very grateful to Avron Kulak for drawing attention to that text, because it belongs to the second "edifying divertissement," where I have the audacity to speak in my own name, if there were such a thing. The one thing in PT that so far no one, either at Toronto or anywhere else, has thematized for discussion is the distinction between the "edifying divertissements" and the "main text," a division over which I labored in composing this text. I did not know where to put these heretical "supplements," which contained my most scandalous suggestions, ones not entertained by Derrida or what I like to call, with a bit of irony, his "secular admirers," or by advocates of the concrete messianisms, by the several sorts of Ismwhackers. (Do the "edifying divertissements" belong to Caputo's Derrida or Derrida's Caputo?) Avron Kulak has singled out an important and audacious claim: the suggestion I make here that perhaps deconstruction does not have the upper hand in the distinction between the messianic and the concrete messianisms, that perhaps deconstruction is not the messianically distilled truth, the essence, of religion, of which the concrete messianisms are the manifestation, but that deconstruction is an example of religion, a case of the passion for God. I will get an earful about this, but not at the ICS

Finally a word about the Greeks and modernity. Avron Kulak's love of de-Hellenizing is so great that he is not quite sure of what to do with the Hellenes. He wonders if Greek texts are iterable (p. 106), if there can be any deconstruction at work in Greek texts, at least any that would not have been imported from Jerusalem (p. 107), and that leads him to wonder even at the value of the "Jewgreek" miscegenation. Here I would say we should recall that for Derrida every text, in virtue of being spun from *différance*, is structurally iterable and deconstructible, is auto-deconstructible, with or without Jerusalem, a point that is based largely upon a creative reading of Saussure and Husserl. In virtue of the auto-deconstructing trait of the text, Plato's *pharmakon* is caught in the undecidability of poison/remedy with or without Jerusalem or the Septuagint. But the passion for the justice and for the impossible that beats within the breast of deconstruction is a biblical and messianic spirit that orients Derrida's rendering of *différance*. Without this Jewish and messianic motif, *différance* would tend to have a flat, lateral significance, simply allowing a kind of lateral, rhizomatic proliferation of alternative possibilities. Without its biblical heart, deconstruction would lack a messianic passion, a passion for justice, which of itself *différance* does not supply, and which thus represents another layer or structure in deconstruction. That is an important point that becomes increasingly evident from the 1980s on, the failure to see which, Derrida says, causes him to be read less and less well. Thus, I would say that Derrida has indeed situated himself in the difference between the Jew and the Greek, and that deconstruction is nicely described as Jewgreek, without reducing him to one or the other. Having demonstrated the prayers and tears in Jacques Derrida, I do not want to reduce him to prayers and tears. As to the moderns, I remain a little puzzled about why Kulak attributes a project of de-Hellenizing to "modernity," whereas most of us think it is the postmodern, which is postsecular, which has helped liberate us from the modern, itself the "repetition" of Hellenization, the modern Enlightenment being the repetition of the Greek Enlightenment.

The casino of the good

My dear friend Jim Olthuis pronounced the final word, and well he should, for he alone took note of the "frame" of the book (p. 111), which also describes its movement, its repetition forward: from "A passion for the impossible" (the "introduction") to "A passion for God" (the "conclusion"). In the conclusion of PT, as Jim Olthuis points out, I argue for the undecidability of these "two" passions; one of them is the example of the other, but I don't know which, a point that Avron Kulak, I am happy to say, also stressed. This undecidability rests on the Kierkegaardian and Augustinian grounds that in the biblical tradition truth is not something to write books about but something to do, *facere veritatem*. If you make justice flow like water over the land, for the widow and orphan and the stranger, then you can check your theologies at the door. And your "religion." That, in a nutshell, is what is mainly astir in the book; it is the theme that is being continually varied, rehearsed, rephrased, and repeated, sometimes with a full orchestra, sometimes in small private chamber music sessions, sometimes joyfully, sometimes sorrowfully.

Now, after the claim that the Messiah was never going to show up, the thing that got me in the most trouble with the Ismwhackers, or me and Derrida, or me because of Derrida (I think we should blame everything on Derrida), was the *khôra*, whose undecidable relationship with God Jim Olthuis explored in a very challenging argument. The *khôra*, which Derrida describes in terms of a cousin/*cousine* relation with *différance*, as a surname for *différance*, is the very spacing in which all our beliefs and practices are inscribed. I would say that *khôra* is actually a Jewgreek transcription. Its Greek version is overt: the account given in the *Timaeus* of the irreducible "place" in which the Demiurge inscribes the likenesses of the Forms for the sake of the Good. One might think of sensible things as occupying a middle ground between two extremes, the Good (*agathon*) in the upper world, the *khôra* down below (way down). But these two extremes are so removed from each other and from ordinary experience that they actually start to look or sound alike, to enjoy a certain isomorphism (they are both ingenerated, eternal, and invisible, for example), constituting a kind of *coincidentia oppositorum*. While the Western tradition has been utterly charmed by the Good, has made her the hit of every metaphysical and theological ball it has thrown, poor *khôra* has been left at home to do her household chores. Needless to say, then, Derrida, who always sides with cinders and Cinderellas, with everyone who is left out, of whatever sort, wants to say a word for *khôra*, which he transcribes as *différance*.

But the other reference, the biblical version of *khôra*, is not hard to find, the *tohu wa-bhohu* of Genesis 1:12: the vast formless void, the darkness that covered the deep, from which, or upon which, God began the work of the seven days. Creation was a work of differentiation, making light to differ from darkness, seas from land, day from night, sky from earth, living creature from non-living, humans from non-human, male from female, all by the power of his word. The world, then, is like a word God has spoken, a response to his call, and creation is, as Levinas says, the answer to a word that we never heard spoken. It is through Levinas, ever present on the Derridean horizon, who has transcribed the *tohu wa-bhohu* as the *il y a*, that *khôra* receives a biblical charge. Now what interests Derrida, and what interests me, is what Levinas calls the "point of possible confusion" between God and *il y a*, God and *khôra*. Once we leave behind the medium-sized chunks of reality with which phenomenology is equipped to deal, which is where we pass the better part of our day, once we pass to the limits (*passage aux frontières*), to God and *khôra*, we start to get a little lost. How can we tell the difference between them? "Let's call this the test of *khôra*," Derrida says, and that is the test that Jim Olthuis wants us to take (p. 113).

God and *khôra*: I would say that the factical situation is that we are situated in the interval between them, sometimes twisting in the winds that blow across that dark and ominous space, sometimes lifted by its light and gentle breezes. Either way, we are not going to reduce the distance, close it down. We will never make one an effect of the other. Not at least as a phenomenological matter. Of course, it belongs to the most ancient faith of the religions of the Book that it is God who has created the world, so that these opening verses of Genesis were theologically glossed in terms of the *creatio ex nihilo*, which represents the utter victory of God over the *tohu wa-bhohu*, who called the world out of the abyss and saw that it was good. But that is a matter of the faith of the followers of the various religions of the Book, and there are lots of people who do not share that faith. My hypothesis, my bet, is that we are all—believers and "infidels" alike—the subjects of those midnight visitations in which we are sure that we are alone in the cosmos, adrift on a spec of cosmic dust, going nowhere but in circles in a great comic stupidity. That is another interpretation, another faith (*nota bene*, Jamie Smith). Each faith is what it is as the rejection of the other, each is the stand taken against the other; my belief in a God who called things out of the abyss and called them good is made over and against another possibility, and in the face of the faceless of the *tohu wa-bhohu*, whose victory would represent the nightmare of being swallowed alive by an abyss. Each requires the other, like two men tugging on a rope and thereby holding the other up. Religious faith requires the permanent possibility of the possibility it refuses, even as the Nietzschean night of *amor fati* is made against the faith it rejects.

Two possibilities (at least; there are certainly more), at least two faiths, the affirmation of justice and the innocence of becoming, of a weepy Jewish Augustinianism, a woman weeping at the foot of the cross, and Zarathustra, evangel of a phallocentric *Übermensch* who never sleeps, the one against the other, the one irreducible to the other. Each one is put at risk by the other, always already exposed to the other, irreducible to the other, and the risk or exposure is constitutive of the faith, which would otherwise fall back into certainty, dogmatism, triumphalism. The condition of their irreducibility, the irreducible condition in which both are inscribed is *différance*, and *khôra* is its surname. The *khôra* is neither the tragic nor the religious, neither Zarathustra nor Augustine, which is the point that Jamie Smith has wrung out of me, but the irreducible matrix, condition, or spacing in which each is inscribed, making each possible and at the same time rendering each an unstable formation, a form traced in the sand of traces.

But I think my dear friend Jim Olthuis wants to stack the deck in favor of the good, to make of *khôra/différance* something justice-friendly, a loving matrix, "already primed toward the good" (p. 117), like a madly benevolent casino operator who has loaded all the dice and stacked all the decks in favor of the customers! *Haec dies!* If he wants us to take the test of *khôra*, he also wants to rig the results. His *khôra* test is a casino of the good, a sea of prayers and tears whose tide sweeps us toward the good, instead of being the inescapable spacing of and between good and evil, of the one and the other, the condition of their undecidability. He would even have "the call to justice" be the "condition for *différance*" (p. 114), instead of seeing the call to/of justice arise in the midst of *différance*. He wants me and Derrida to renounce *khôra* and all her (non)works. But alas, *hier stehe ich, ich kann nicht anders*. Besides, even though the devil is in Derrida's eye, *khôra* is not the devil, but a neutral yet necessary condition, which Jim Olthuis is too inclined to reduce to a kind of necessary empirical evil. It is true that I say this neutral is preliminary, for deconstruction is ultimately affirmative, but the neutral *khôral* matrix is the inescapable condition of that affirmation; it is why one would have to be affirmative.

Let me be more specific. By consigning us to the inevitability of spacing, which constitutes an archi-violence, a structural condition, I am not, nor is

Jacques Derrida, thereby consigning us all to ethical violence, acts of ethical violence, as Jim Olthuis suggests (p. 115). For these are different things and must be distinguished.[9] For good laws, laws that embody justice, that protect the weak against the strong, which is the very thing that made Nietzsche's patrician nose twitch, are spaced, constructed, inscribed in *différance*. "Archi-violence" is what makes just laws possible and revisable—even as it make possible tyranny and oligarchy and unjust laws, making them all possible and impossible, constructed and deconstructible. Indeed, being on the alert to the constructibility and contingency of our beliefs and practices, which is the reminder that "archi-violence" serves on us, is just what can best protect the peace. So I would beg my friend Jim Olthuis to observe the distinction between archi-violence, which is really just the necessity we are under to make sense with signs and traces, and ethical violence, which spills blood, and to remember that Derrida first used this expression in a critique of the Rousseauism of Lévi-Strauss, whose myth of innocence he was trying to disturb. Although the word "archi-violence" rubs a peacemaker like Jim Olthuis the wrong way, we should remember that Derrida was just trying to say the following: do not get teary-eyed about the pristine innocence of native populations; they have their laws, their politics, their limited way of carving the world up, just as much as do people holding onto the straps in subways roaring beneath the streets and buildings of Manhattan. So it is certainly true that "the risk of violence is not the same as necessary violence" (p. 115); that means that *différance/khôra* does not inevitably imply injustice, which is empirical violence. Still, the one devil I do renounce is the devilishness of my attack upon the concrete messianisms in PT, which I discussed in response to Ron Kuipers, which seemed to crush the undecidability of the concrete messianisms and to identify them with the violence for which they are so well known. That identitarianism not only violates the terms of a philosophy of difference, but insults the memory of the extraordinary achievements of unselfish men and women of religious faith, which really would amount to throwing the baby out with the wash. That was a great rhetorical failure in PT, but it was not my *vouloir-dire*. (That is why I stress the notion of forgiveness in deconstruction!)

Next, I have to say that Derrida, and I in his wake, do not reduce the subject to capitalistic aggrandizement, which would destroy the undecidability of the self and turn it into an identitarian machine. That puts too cynical and deterministic a reading upon the idea of the subject. Derrida's view of the subject stands in the tradition of Aristotle, who for my money still offers the best way to approach the acting subject: every agent acts for its own good, and the moment an agent sees no good, no point, to acting, the agent won't act, even if and especially when my good, what I want, is the good of the other. For if nothing matters, which is what happens when I stop loving myself, then the good of the other doesn't matter either. Derrida's point is that the subject's love of its own good cannot be disambiguated, inoculated, sanitized against that built-in structural tendency of the ego to turn everything over to its profit. That means that the gift, the affirmation of the other, the yes to the in-coming of the *tout autre*, always comes in an *Augenblick* of madness, in which I throw profits to the wind and make an expenditure without return, knowing full well that the circle of economy will eventually catch up with me. The expenditure without return is structurally dependent upon the self's love of a good investment, the structural tendency to self-aggrandizement; the gift structurally requires the economy as the very thing that offers resistance to the gift, to which the gift is never simply exterior.

"We are not alone, *grâce à Dieu. Oui, oui*" (p. 119). Those are the final words of this powerful last word. That is my faith, too, our common faith, I who own up to being something of an Ismwhacker myself. But that faith does not extinguish *khôra/différance*, or domesticate it into a force for the good, or settle the flux, or rig the game in the direction of a favorable outcome. Rather, it is the word I speak in midst of the anarchic and *khôral* energy of *différance*, through a *glas* darkly. For *khôra/différance* makes the word of faith possible and impossible, makes it possible even as it destabilizes it, leaving it, and us, to take what Levinas calls *un beau risque*, a good risk, a good bet, a bet on the good, but without any assurance that the deck is stacked in our favor. For even if I say that the Good who called all things from the abyss and saw that they were good, that this Good has stacked the deck, I would insist that that too is part of the bet. Hope is always hope in hope, hope against hope, hoping like hell.

Back home, safe in Villanova
Summer 1999

Notes

1 That is the argument that influenced the young Heidegger, made by Franz Overbeck, *Über die Christlichkeit unserer Theologie* (Leipzig, 1903; photographically reproduced, Darmstadt: Wissenschaftliche Buchgesellschaft, 1989).
2 See Soren Kierkegaard, *Kierkegaard's Works*, vol. 7, *Philosophical Fragments*, H. Hong and E. Hong, trans. (Princeton, NJ: Princeton University Press, 1985), pp. 55ff.
3 Perhaps the best place to see how this works in Derrida is the description on the three aporias of justice in "The force of law: the 'mystical foundation of authority'" in *Deconstruction and the Possibility of Justice*, Drucilla Cornell *et al.*, eds. (New York: Routledge, 1992), pp. 22–29, and in the critique of Fukuyama in *Specters of Marx: The State of the Debt, the Work of Mourning, and the New International*, Peggy Kamuf, trans. (New York: Routledge, 1994), pp. 56ff.

4 John D. Caputo, *Against Ethics: Contributions to a Poetics of Obligation with Constant Reference to Deconstruction* (Bloomington: Indiana University Press, 1993).
5 Walter Benjamin, "Theses on the philosophy of history," in *Illuminations: Essays and Reflections*, Hannah Arendt, ed., Harry Zohn, trans. (New York: Schocken, 1969), pp. 253–64. See Derrida's comments on Benjamin in "Force of law" pp. 64f., *Specters of Marx*, p. 55, and see Peter Szondi, "Hope on the past: on Walter Benjamin," *Critical Inquiry* 4 (1978).
6 See Regina M. Schwartz, *The Curse of Cain: The Violent Legacy of Monotheism* (Chicago: University of Chicago Press, 1997).
7 See "Roundtable on the gift" in *God, the Gift and Postmodernism*, John D. Caputo and Michael J. Scanlon, eds. (Bloomington: Indiana University Press, 1999), p. x.
8 Jacques Derrida, *Politics of Friendship*, George Collins, trans. (London and New York: Verso, 1997). Hereafter PF.
9 Jacques Derrida, *Of Grammatology*, corrected edition, Gayatri Chakravorty Spivak, trans. (Baltimore: Johns Hopkins University Press, 1997), pp. 112, 139f.

10 What do I love when I love my God?

An interview with John D. Caputo

B. Keith Putt

B. Keith Putt: You state in *Prayers and Tears* that deconstruction has always been driven by a passion for God, a love for God. Does this statement corroborate Derrida's claim that everything is autobiographical? Have you not also always been driven by that same passion?

John D. Caputo: I think that Derrida is right to say that we can never make a clean cut between the inside and the outside, the personal and the objective. Any such sharp division is questionable for him. It would be inconceivable for someone, particularly in philosophy, to simply abstract from their own personal concerns. There would be no passion, no creation, without personal involvement, and so there will always be an autobiographical element in the process of creation. From the point of view of the reader, I think it remains true that the "death of the author" is a valid notion, because that has to do not with creation, but with reception. A reader can read a text without worrying about the personal passion and trauma and joys that give birth to the text. The text has a life of its own. The whole idea of the death of the author, which is valid enough, proceeds from the point of view of a reader or reception. But for the writer, the author, this is meaningless; it is nonsense. As an author I write with my blood, with my heart, passionately, from a deep concern, which Augustine and Derrida, each in his own way, call "the love of God." Otherwise I am not interested.

Putt: So your recent work in the past few years, which has focused so much on religion, is not really new. From the inception of your philosophical career, this concern for God, for the religious, and for the mystical has been a passion that has driven you?

Caputo: Yes, although for a while I kept it concealed. I have always been writing about the intersection of religion and philosophy, but in the beginning I undertook a more scientific, a more exegetical interpretation of the relationship between Heidegger and the religious tradition. Those first texts—*Heidegger and Aquinas* and *The Mystical Element*—were written with a kind of traditional academic propriety, a calm, professional style. My own personal voice was muted there. Then, in *Radical Hermeneutics*, I found my own voice. But even then I did not pass myself off as someone who was explicitly working with questions in religion. Religion was a part of the problematic of *Radical Hermeneutics*, but it was not the principal concern. It is only in the last ten years that the question of religion finally came to the surface for me. At first it was a strictly personal issue for me. I was a philosopher and philosophers are antagonistic to it, allergic to it; they do not want to hear it or talk about it. But now, if you ask me what I am doing, I would say that I work in Continental philosophy and religion. Ten or fifteen years ago I would have said I was working with hermeneutics and deconstruction. But the issue has always driven my work in one way or another.

Putt: In an article entitled "Confessions of a postmodern Catholic: From St. Thomas to Derrida," forthcoming in *Faith and the Intellectual Life*, a book of confessional statements by Catholic theologians and philosophers, you argue that you now see yourself as a midwife giving birth to religious ideas in philosophical parlance.

Caputo: Levinas says that he is transcribing into "Greek"—that is, into philosophical language—what he has learned from reading the Bible. I think that there is a lot to that. Religious experience is an elemental, fertile, and rich part of human experience, and most philosophers pay no attention to it. They blind themselves to it, perhaps because of the many troubles that religion has visited upon us over the centuries, and because of a kind of rationalism that is endemic to philosophers. But Heidegger's project back in the early 1920s was to go back and reexamine the experience of time in primitive Christianity, which he regarded as a rich source for phenomenology, for what he was calling in those days the "hermeneutics of factical life."

Putt: He claims he got this idea of facticity from the New Testament.

Caputo: Yes. Two sources, actually: the New Testament and Aristotle's ethics. He often tells us that his path of thought was set in motion by Aristotle's *Metaphysics*. That is a kind of retrospective illusion. When you examine it closely, what really drove his earliest work was Aristotle's ethics, not the metaphysics. Heidegger thought that Aristotle's ethics and the New Testament are wired up to the deepest and most elemental "pre-theoretical" experiences of human life. Theory had not yet gotten its hands on these experiences, had not yet distorted them with its own conceptual apparatus. The New Testament, in particular the earliest letters of Paul, was among our best resources for tapping into those experiences. The young Heidegger shows that philosophers cut themselves off from a rich phenomenological vein by ignoring religion. I do not mean to say that we simply want to exploit religion for phenomenological ideas. Religion is, like art, an elemental human experience. It needs to be understood in its own terms and brought to life philosophically in a language that respects its integrity. That is exactly what is happening, I think, in contemporary Continental philosophy right now. Philosophers today are fascinated by Levinas, and anybody who knows the biblical tradition recognizes what Levinas is saying. But he has given it a powerful philosophical conceptuality, which has stimulated a whole new wave of philosophical work.

Putt: That wave seems to be uniquely American. American Continentalists, such as you, Mark Taylor, and others, are dealing with this religious turn in Continental thought. Why do you think that is?

Caputo: It is an interesting phenomenon, isn't it? Things are said in France and they are heard in the United States. We pick them up and run with them. We invite leading philosophers from the Continent over here, and they spend a lot of time in American universities. There is a tremendous reception here. American Continental philosophy has its own integrity and its own life and its own institutional structures. It is in some ways more vital than Continental philosophy on the Continent, because there are just so many people and institutions involved, so many texts being produced, and so many conferences and so much work being done over here. In some ways it overshadows the font, the Continental origin of the work. I would say that the rekindling of interest in religion in particular that is taking place among American Continentalists clearly goes back to France, although Germany historically is the deeper resource because of Kant and Hegel, Marx and Nietzsche, Husserl and Heidegger. But not only to France. The English translation of Vattimo's book *Belief* appeared not too long ago. There he describes his return to Christianity—he is very critical of the Catholic Church in Italy—but he finds himself returning to the Christian faith and stressing the notion of the Incarnation. He has a liberal interpretation of the Christian faith, and he describes his return as part of a more general rebirth of interest in religion in Europe. Even among analytic philosophers in the United States you see the same thing. Hilary Putnam has rediscovered his Judaism. Part of the movement beyond the Enlightenment, beyond the narrow definition of reason and rationality in the Enlightenment, has been a movement beyond the secularism of the Enlightenment and an appreciation for the polymorphic quality of human experience from which religion can no longer be excluded. There are no good philosophical arguments against religion of the sort that the eighteenth and nineteenth century constructed. Those arguments have been attacked on purely philosophical grounds. The critique of rationalist ideas of reason proceeded on purely philosophical grounds. But the upshot of this critique was to show that when that Enlightenment notion of rationality collapses, then the critique of religion that was rooted in that idea of rationality also collapses.

Putt: How would you contrast the Anglo-American analytical tradition in philosophy of religion with this "new Continental tradition in philosophy of religion"?

Caputo: The Anglo-American philosophy of religion is still linked to what Continentalists would call "onto-theo-logic." It still turns on tight discursive argumentation and, as in the case of someone like Richard Swinburne, is still interested in offering rigorous demonstrations of the existence of God. Swinburne thinks these arguments can be formulated in the language of symbolic logic. He can fill a blackboard with arguments that have been cast into the well-formed formulae of symbolic logic, which go to prove the existence of God, or the greater probability of the existence of God than of the nonexistence of God. The Reformed Epistemologist offers us very tightly argued demonstrations of the credibility of faith, of the reasonability of properly basic beliefs. That style is tied to what Continental philosophers consider "onto-theo-logic," a rationalistic mode of argumentation and discourse, whereas Continentalists are, in some form or another, phenomenologists, post-phenomenologists, quasi-phenomenologists, or hyper-phenomenologists. They have all adapted, each in their own way, something of a phenomenological style, even though someone like Derrida criticizes phenomenology.

Putt: But is the Continental philosopher of religion lacking in a kind of rigor of argumentation?

Caputo: No. In each case you are dealing with disciplined thinking, but the disciplines are different. (The old saw is, Continentalists are people who can't learn logic and analysts are people who can't learn foreign languages!) The attention to detail and the rigor of a phenomenologist are quite different from analytical discursive rigor. It has to do with a sensitivity to experience and insight, the sort of discipline that is required when reading literature, like the discipline of a careful, sensitive reader. It is not a matter of logical argumentation, but it is every bit as rigorous in its own way. Now a phenomenologist is like that. A phenomenologist is someone who is trying to capture the structure of experience in a sensitive way and to describe it in a language that does not distort it. This is difficult. You are dealing with more subtle features of the landscape of human experience. It does not mean Continentalists do not have a head for logic; it means that they require a different sort of head, a head for a different sort of discipline.

Putt: If you look at the two traditions, you could contrast them on this point: that there seems to be in Continental thought more of an openness to mystery, to the mystical, to that which transcends the rational. In your own thought the mystical tradition has been quite significant. From the very beginning through your recent work and even work in progress, you are still struggling with what is beyond reason, the *tout autre*, the otherwise than reason. That was expressed in *Radical Hermeneutics* as an "openness to the mystery," using Heidegger's expression, or in *Prayers and Tears* as a "passion for the impossible," using Derrida's expression. Do you have a love–hate relationship with mysticism?

Caputo: It is more love than hate. One of the most interesting philosophical questions, and a question that I have always been trying to work with, is the question of limits and of the movement beyond limits. The question of the limits of what can be discursively, demonstratively established by rational argument and what lies beyond or eludes those limits has always provoked me. My first work had to do with the relationship between metaphysics and mysticism. I was very interested, like all the Catholics of my generation, in Jacques Maritain, in particular in his *Degrees of Knowledge*, a book that treated the ascent from philosophical knowledge up to mystical experience. Maritain had very powerful and beautiful analyses of the nature of mystical experience. So when I first began to study the later Heidegger, I was struck by the presence of the same mystical motifs that I had studied very carefully as a young Catholic. I had not studied the medieval mystic Meister Eckhart in particular before I encountered his sermons in Heidegger, but I knew at once where Eckhart was coming from. I recognized immediately what Heidegger was talking about when he began to refer to Meister Eckhart. The first really serious research project that I undertook was to investigate the later Heidegger's delimitation of rational calculative thinking and the mystical relationship of the soul to God in Meister Eckhart. The more general philosophical point that is at stake here is what I call "not knowing who we are," an expression I used in an essay on Foucault a few years ago, which I also used as the title essay in *More Radical Hermeneutics: On Not Knowing Who We Are*. Who are we? We are the ones who do not know who we are. So we have this Augustinian motif of *quaestio mihi factus sum*, I have become a question unto myself. I think that is a very beautiful and powerful characterization of exactly who we are—the ones who do not know who we are, who are a question for themselves. Consequently, there is a mystery surrounding us and an unknowing that are not simply a matter of an ignorance that we have to dispel. In fact this unknowing constitutes in a positive way the structure of our life, because it requires some movement of faith, some decision or orientation in our life not founded on rational argumentation. I am not saying we should not use rational arguments or that we should not try to know as much as we can know and demonstrate as much as we can demonstrate. But I think that there is a kind of structural darkness, a structural unknowing in our life, in the midst of which we need to take a stand, without having any sense of foundation; we cannot get foundations in a thing like this. It is beyond us, but it is an elementary mystery in our lives that everybody has to deal with. Some people deal with it by walking away from it, some people deal with it religiously, some people deal with it cynically or skeptically. But we are all faced with a deep unknowing, and that to me is the most interesting philosophical question of all. What is this thing that we do not know? I do not know—that is what it is; it is what I do not know that constitutes me. But how do I relate myself to that?

Putt: In your thought there has always been a tension in the ways you have characterized that mystery. Sometimes it is the meaningless—the tragic in *Radical Hermeneutics* or the heteromorphic in *Against Ethics*—the position put forward by the pseudonym Felix Sineculpa. In *Prayers and Tears* it is Derrida's desert. But at other times that mystery is religious—the hermeneutics of faith that finds loving eyes looking back from the abyss in *Radical Hermeneutics*, the heteronomic in *Against Ethics*, or faith in *Prayers and Tears*. You often speak in a number of works both of being "haunted" by what may be nothing more than the abysmal nothingness of the playing out of the cosmic forces and of a loving presence, a divine presence, almost a holy spirit.

Caputo: That is true. In *Radical Hermeneutics* I speak of a "cold" hermeneutics . . .

Putt: . . . but with a warm heart.

Caputo: Yes. We can give a completely cold or heartless rendering of our situation. We find that in Nietzsche, who is for me the most terrifying philosopher that we have come up with yet. He has thought the most abysmal thought. I do not like to rehabilitate Nietzsche and turn him into a sort of vanguard of the academic left, the hero of those people who, as Rorty says, read unintelligible papers to each other about emancipation based upon Nietzsche and then feel they have made their contribution to alleviating the suffering of the wretched of the earth. I do not like to do that with Nietzsche. I like to take my Nietzsche straight up, not on the rocks. Nietzsche's portrait of things is well captured in that famous section at the beginning of "Truth and lying in the extramoral sense." He imagines these little animals off on a distant corner of the universe—we know this text very well—in which these proud little animals then invent for themselves noble words like truth and goodness. Then, he says, soon enough all the animals have to die and the little planet, the little star, falls back into the sun and turns to ash. Then the universe draws another breath and moves on, and the little animals and their little planet are gone. No one knows we are here and no one cares, and soon enough in cosmic time we will all disappear and the universe will dance on. Now, that is a haunting specter, it is a haunting, cold, tragic vision of our life.

I do not say that this is the way things really are, that this is the undisguised truth. When I have sometimes spoken that way, that was a mistake. I do not want to privilege that point of view. I simply want to hold it open as a kind of horizon of possibility and see it as a backdrop against which any other position that we take about our lives must be struck. It is there; it haunts us; it is a specter, a horizon of possibility that is inextinguishable. There are no arguments against it, no way to knock it down with a good argument. It is a perfectly sensible hypothesis from a cold-hearted and scientific point of view.

Putt: You know that some of your critics, in reading the last section of *Radical Hermeneutics* and especially the last chapter of *Against Ethics*, accuse you of just that, of privileging the abyss.

Caputo: I think to some extent I may have. That has been pointed out to me and I think that it was a mistake on my part. All I want to say is that there is something irreducible about that view, and that interpretation is always made in the face of it. So if we have an interpretation of life as religious, or ethical, or whatever interpretation we may have, it must always be "haunted" by this more disturbing perspective. I have sometimes portrayed this perspective as not an interpretation at all, but as simply there, an uninterpreted fact of the matter, a kind of raw fact, whereas—the objection goes—it too is another interpretation. Now I think that is a valid criticism of *Radical Hermeneutics* and *Against Ethics*.

Putt: Do you think that the Kierkegaardian character of *Against Ethics* mitigates that criticism a bit? I mean, were you not being somewhat ironic in *Against Ethics*?

Caputo: Yes, I never saw that I was getting myself into that trouble until my critics pointed it out. I did not mean to say that, and as soon as the objection was made, I saw that I needed to reformulate it. I do not want say that this abyss is what is "really there" and then we cast interpretations over it like veils over the abyss, like Schopenhauerian interpretations over the turbulent irrational will. Rather, the abyss too is another interpretation, just like the religious interpretation, but it is an irreducible interpretation, an interpretation that cannot be dismissed, waved off, or laid to rest. It poses itself against a more benign or warmer interpretation of human existence. That is why in *Against Ethics* I put the discourses of Felix Sineculpa—the name, of course, means the joyful innocence, the innocence of becoming, in Nietzsche—both at the beginning and at the end of those discourses, and I sandwiched all the other, more affirmative interpretations of the human condition between it. I meant to say by that not that Felix has the first and last word, that his word is final, but that his word is irreducible and a permanent specter. It is there at the beginning, the middle, and the end. That is not to say that we need to embrace it, but that we need to choose in the face of it. The value of insisting on that point is that it guards us against triumphalism and from an overly dangerous belief in our own legitimacy and self-justification. I say in a couple of footnotes in *Against Ethics* that I am not trying to eliminate religious faith but to establish the framework within which faith occurs. That serves to remind us that faith is faith. Faith can be testified to, but faith cannot be demonstrated or confirmed in discursive, argumentative, rational discourse. We can testify to what we believe, but that does not make it true, and it does not dispel the specter of Felix Sineculpa, which irreducibly haunts our existence—we who do not know who we are.

Putt: In one of those footnotes, you promise to take faith out of the *epoché*, remove the brackets, and treat it, which you do in *Prayers and Tears*.

Caputo: Yes, that is a good way to put it. At least, I started to remove the brackets in *Prayers and Tears*. That book that was not supposed to be about Derrida but about lifting the *epoché* from faith, and it was supposed to be called *God and Anonymity*, which is a book I am still writing. In *Against Ethics*, Felix represents the anonymous—the anonymity of our existence, the idea that no one knows we are here. As I started to write what turned out to be *Prayers and Tears*, I decided that I had to start with Derrida and situate this problematic in terms of Derrida by showing how to put deconstruction to work in the service of religious faith. So, I thought, I will need a couple of chapters at the beginning on Derrida and religion—and that was a hole from which I never reemerged. The result was *Prayers and Tears*, which ended up being for Jacques and about Jacques. I am certainly in there, too, in the "edifying divertissements," in play with Jacques, as if it were "a game of Jacks."

Putt: Derrida says, in responding to that book, that you read him the way he loves to be read. What exactly do you think he means by that? How does Derrida love to be read?

Caputo: I think he likes to be read affirmatively. He wants to make it completely clear that deconstruction is not what its most vociferous and at times, I would say, academically violent critics say it is, namely a vicious relativism and anarchism. He wants everyone to understand that it is an ethically, politically sensitive, "upbeat"—as Rorty would say—affirmative portrait of human existence.

Putt: How about edifying?

Caputo: Yes, edifying, in the sense of trying to "up-build," as the new Kierkegaard translation says so awkwardly, building up, constructive. Deconstructive is constructive. It has an affirmative point, and so Derrida very much appreciates being read in a way that is organized around the deep affirmation, the *viens, oui, oui* of deconstruction. That motif of affirmation in

Derrida is very closely linked to the religious element in deconstruction. The messianic expectation of justice, which has surfaced in his work in the last few years, is quite astonishing to his more secularizing readers. Derrida is a very close companion for me in the project of bringing faith out of the *epoché*, as you put it. But deconstruction is not the final word. I have other things that I am working on, in which I try to articulate more directly and unequivocally a religious understanding of our existence. But this will always be situated within the "cloud of unknowing," this not knowing who we are. Faith is a position we take precisely in virtue of the fact that we do not know who we are, that is why you need faith, which is "through a *glas* darkly," as I like to say. Religion becomes dangerous the moment we forget that. Indeed, anything can become dangerous—religion does not have a corner on this; science can be dangerous, or politics. They all become dangerous the moment they forget that we do not know who we are. We proceed on the basis of our own best insights and we do the best we can. But we operate within uncircumventable limits, which should sober us and should give us a sense of diffidence about our own correctness and openness to the other, who is in the same boat.

Putt: You could say that the first thinker really to shine a light on the theological and religious significance of Derrida's thought was Mark Taylor. How would you differentiate what you do with Derrida from what Taylor has done with Derrida?

Caputo: One of the things that I appreciate about Mark Taylor is that he always makes me feel very conservative. I do not often have the opportunity to feel conservative, so I am grateful to Mark for that. We all work in the wake of Mark Taylor's *Erring* and we are in his debt. My main criticism of Mark is that he has broken the undecidability between atheism and theism; he has erased the slash between the "a-" and the "theological." In his "a/theology" God is dissolved into the world without remainder. Mark's work has never departed from the "death of God" motif that he first took up in working with T. J. J. Altizer. While he has criticized Altizer, it seems to me that he has not really departed from him on this point. I object to the story Mark tells in *Erring*, which is that deconstruction should be conceived as the final nail in the coffin of the old God, bringing the death of God movement to its most radical conclusion. That seems to me to be a misreading of deconstruction, a powerful, ingenious, and provocative misreading, to be sure, and so I deeply appreciate a great deal of what Mark does. I always look at Mark and think that he is doing something that in about ten years I will get around to doing, too. He is always so far ahead of the rest of us. But on this point I think that he has underestimated the religious resources of deconstruction, and in a fairly traditional sense of religion, one that has to do with hope and faith and trust. Furthermore, Mark's rendering of deconstructive theology shows very little trace of Levinas, and Derrida's work has progressively become more and more marked by Levinas. Mark is one of the people who has clearly and powerfully taught us to see the Kierkegaardian element in deconstruction. But the more Jewish idea of messianic hope and hospitality and the Levinasian relationship with the other one are much more powerful in Derrida than in Mark's rendering of deconstruction. Mark has not been writing about Derrida lately, and when he was writing about Derrida he was really looking at the works of the 1960s and the 1970s. Today he would need to say something else about Derrida were he to go back and read the texts of the last two decades. He is not going to do that, because he is an independent philosopher following his own path, which now is focused on the question of the revolution in communications technology and virtual reality, the cyber world.

Putt: You mentioned earlier being surprised when you were reading Heidegger to find some of the themes that you had studied in the medieval Catholic thinkers. Did you have a similar experience with Derrida? You were already dealing with mysticism, and then you heard in Derrida the significance of apophatic theology. You were already reading Kierkegaard and were heavily influenced by him, and then you found in Derrida significant attention being paid to Kierkegaard, especially to *Fear and Trembling*.

Caputo: Yes, the experience was similar. I was quite naturally drawn to these discussions of negative theology in Derrida, which were quite interesting to me. Indeed, Derrida himself, perhaps under the influence of Heidegger, often used Meister Eckhart as an example when he talked about negative theology. But I have to say that the apophatic theme in Derrida is displaced for me by something even more surprising, by the prophetic theme. What really is interesting to me about Derrida is that he has recovered the voice of prophetic Judaism, even though, as a matter of personal belief, he describes himself as an atheist. He says that he "quite rightly passes for an atheist." That is a very tantalizing way to put it. Why does he not just say "I am an atheist"? One way to read an expression like that is to say that to all appearances he is an atheist but appearances can be deceiving. So he is teasing us with this expression, although I suppose that if we had him sitting here with us and we said, "Now give us a straight answer," he would say that he is by conventional standards an atheist. Whatever is true about him personally, that is not the final word for deconstruction. There is nothing atheistic about deconstruction. Deconstruction is simply an attempt to say that we are always driven by an affirmation, by a desire, or a desire beyond desire; we are moved by something that we do not fully understand; it has to do with testimony and action and praxis; it belongs to the sphere of pragmatics and performatives, and it is structured around an act of faith. Now, that description of our relationship to the world is not in any way hostile to religion. Religion would be very happy to be described in those terms. There is nothing at all irreligious or anti-religious or atheistic about deconstruction. I would say that, in fact, deconstruction is structured like a religion, structured around a radical affirmation and faith in something we cannot understand or see or know. That is why I think that the most religiously interesting dimension of his thought is its prophetic character, not its apophatic side. The religious dimension of deconstruction consists in being a repetition of a prophetic Judaism. As a radical call for justice, it has a deeply ethical, political side without becoming self-congratulatory about being on the side of the good and the true, because he is very critical of "good conscience." But its ethical and political aspirations lead us back to prophetic Judaism. The comparison of deconstruction and negative theology is too Christian. It goes back to Christian Neoplatonism, and then you miss the Jewish voice of Derrida.

Putt: But do you think the apophatic has hermeneutical implications? You talk about a "generalized apophatics."

Caputo: Yes, I do not want to erase the apophatical or get rid of it. I like the notion of the apophatical, because it is another way of speaking about the secret or the mystery. Heidegger calls it the mystery; Derrida calls it the secret; the mystics call it the cloud of unknowing. St. Augustine talks about the question that we are to ourselves. These are all different ways of formulating the unknowing that besets us. What the mystic says is true in a deep and generalizable way. When I speak of a generalized apophatics, I mean that what the mystics say about God—when you confess that you do not know what God is, then you are starting to get it right—is true in general and not just about God. I do not want to lose the apophatic. But the limitation of mystical theology is that it is too much modeled around the idea of seeing and knowing, and it wants to say that the highest knowing is unknowing. Derrida—and this is also clear in Levinas, who is suspicious of mysticism—wants to shift from the cognitive or the constative into the performative and the praxical, into the life of decision and responsibility, of engagement with the world, with one another. Derrida would agree with Levinas that justice precedes truth. Of all the words that he uses to describe "the impossible," as he puts it, or "the undeconstructible," I think the most important word is "justice." We need to be cautious in talking like this because we are about to construct a master word, and in deconstruction there is no master word. But of all the words in his vocabulary, the word that most tempts us into making it a master word is the word "justice." It is the first among equals among the synonyms for the impossible. While mysticism and the apophatical are somewhat more concerned with the mystery embedded within truth, Derrida wants to say that whatever the final accounting of things is, which we do not know, we need to be just; we need to respond to the other. This is quite different from the popular caricature of deconstruction as a kind of "onanism," as Graham Ward has recently described it, as simply giving pleasure to oneself by dabbling in ideas that can never be resolved, playing with the play of signifiers, splashing around in a pool of undecidability. Quite the contrary! It is deeply concerned with the urgency of action. Derrida agrees with Johannes Climacus when he wrote that the results of the system will never be in; if we are waiting for the final paragraph of the system to come in before we act, we will never act. But we need to act; the demands of justice are upon us and justice is needed now. Justice is always to come; it is never here and we should never again identify justice with any present structure. But at the same time justice deferred is justice denied; we need to act here and now. So there is this radical shift away from the constative to the performative, away from questions of truth to questions of justice and responsibility, of responding to the other. I do not want to erase the apophatic motif but to organize it around the more primary motif of justice.

Putt: The idea of the messianic, the incoming of the other, the waiting for what cannot be programmed, what Derrida calls the impossible—you could use this nomenclature to talk about his audacious statement you just mentioned from his article "Force of law," where he talks about justice as undeconstructible. This claim of the "undeconstructible" had to be for some Derrideans quite an "other" other! More recently, he has claimed the same for faith in the Villanova Roundtable reproduced in *Deconstruction in a Nutshell* and for the idea of gift. What is the significance of his asserting that all of these "things" cannot be deconstructed?

Caputo: First of all, I think you are absolutely right to single out the "undeconstructible" as an important issue. The first time I can think of him using this expression is in "Force of law." I am not sure that it is found any earlier than that. I think the prevailing view, in fact, in the 1960s and the 1970s, was that there is nothing undeconstructible, that deconstruction is an endless process. Now it is true that deconstruction is an endless process and also true that we would never actually meet any "thing" that is undeconstructible. Nothing undeconstructible would ever be present. Whatever is present is deconstructible, because whatever is present has been constructed, and whatever has been constructed is deconstructible. So the undeconstructible is nothing that exists. But it is an organizing aspiration in deconstruction. It is the heart and the soul of deconstruction, what deconstruction is all about, which reflects the messianic expectation, the hope. That is the point of deconstruction. Now there would have been attempts in the 1960s and 1970s to say that deconstruction has no point. If you give it a point, that becomes a transcendental signifier. That would be a far too Nietzschean reading of

Derrida. His own position is a little more traditional than that. There is a
point, a center, which is the object of desire, but it is never present. To put it in
biblical terms, it would be a kind of idolatry to treat something that is present
as undeconstructible. His critics now say this is the myth of Sisyphus all over
again, a futile passion, nothing we will ever be able to do. If it is impossible,
why bother? First he is criticized for the endless play of dissemination; now he
is criticized for being a dreamer dreaming the impossible dream. But this is a
perverse misreading, because the point of the "impossible" or the "undeconstructible" is to make us intolerant of the injustice of the structures that are
around us, to offset complacency and to raise the pitch of our sensitivity to
those who suffer injustice, those who are excluded, those who are marginalized. He wants to make us discontent with anything that we have now so that
we can do better. For example, when we say grace before meals, we thank
God for the food that is in front of us, but when we say "make us mindful of
all of those who have nothing to eat," then we make a deconstructive gesture.
That is because we are asking that the present structure not be allowed to
close around itself. The present is always marked by injustice; there are always
those who are left out. We are not taking the joy out of the meal, but we mark
that joy with a sense of what remains to be done. Derrida wants to keep us
open to what still solicits us, to make us distrustful of identifying the present
arrangement with justice or with truth because it is not, not as long as we live
in time.

Putt: So justice does not exist, but it is. The gift does not exist, but in some
way it is.

Caputo: Do we want to say "is"?

Putt: That is metaphysical, isn't it?

Caputo: Maybe we should say "Justice does not exist but it calls."

Putt: It calls . . .

Caputo: . . . it solicits and calls us.

Putt: How would you then relate that to Jean-Luc Marion's distinction
between the icon of God in Godself, God written *sous rature*, over against the
conceptual idol of God caught in some conceptual network? In other words,
would you say that God is undeconstructible because God does not "exist"
but "calls"?

Caputo: I think Marion makes a very beautiful distinction and I can embrace
that formulation. I would qualify it, because I would not want to associate
myself with everything that is going on in Jean-Luc Marion. What I like
about his account of the "saturated phenomenon" is that he does say that it is
an experience of anonymity; we do not know what it means and we need faith
in order to identify it. But I worry that it is too much of a good thing, that it
associates itself too easily with a kind of triumphalistic vision of the existence

of God, that God visits himself upon us in some sort of plenitudinous experience that is very close to mystical theology. The thing that Derrida warns us about mystical theology is that eventually the mystics are going to claim to be speaking from the heart of God. I have experienced God, they will say, so listen to what I have to say.

Putt: That is like Marion's Eucharistic hermeneutical theology.

Caputo: Yes. The experience is a little too powerful, a little too authoritative, and then it is linked too easily with authority. But, having these reservations in mind, I love the notion of the God to be crossed out, and I agree that this is a very good deconstructive gesture. In Derrida, the name of God is one of the ways that we name what we desire. It is the name of our desire, of our desire beyond desire, of our expectation. There are many names, and you have itemized a number of them—the gift, hospitality, etc.—but the name of God is one of the most important, and he wants to save the name of God. Heidegger will say that the name of God puts all of our questions to sleep, and that those who believe in God have no more questions because they already have the answer. But in Derrida the name of God functions in exactly the opposite way: it makes everything questionable, because we do not know who God is, and we come back once again to St. Augustine, and to the Augustinian motif in *Circumfession*, when Augustine asks: "What do I love when I love my God?"

Putt: That question "What do I love when I love my God?"—which you argue always comes in tandem with the question of the self, with the Augustinian question "Who am I?"—appears to be a necessity, given the way that you deal with it in *Prayers and Tears*. Do you think that this question is an expression of a religious a priori, some kind of restless drive that is ultimately a drive for God?

Caputo: That is what you mean by a religious a priori?

Putt: Yes. Our souls are always restless until we rest in God.

Caputo: Yes, I think that at that point Augustine enunciates a structure that is basic in our experience. At least for us, for anyone in the West. Augustine is a very Western person, who has a very powerful sense of the will and desire that we may not find in non-Western religion and non-Western culture. But for us, for the Greco-Roman Judeo-Christian West, Augustine is articulating something that is very basic in our experience and that is very difficult to imagine doing without. I think that Derrida associates himself with that restlessness, and so do I. It goes hand in hand with not knowing who we are. In Augustine himself, that restlessness is oriented toward peace, and Augustine has a very strong idea of just exactly what would satisfy his restlessness. Derrida does not, and I too would keep the question open, alive, and moving. Augustine was a bishop, and he had developed a low tolerance for dissent. So I greatly prefer, and so does Derrida greatly prefer, the Augustine of the *Confessions*, the prayerful, tearful, questing, self-questioning Augustine, to the Augustine of *The City of God*, where the bishop in him comes out swinging. But if you keep the question open, then the description of the self, the *inquietum es cor nostrum*, at the beginning of the *Confessions* describes the condition of us all, at least of us Westerners.

Putt: You also claim in *Prayers and Tears* that deconstruction does not have jurisdiction over who or what God is, over who or what is the *tout autre*. In other words, you seem to be saying that deconstruction raises a question that it cannot answer. So does that mean deconstruction is a ladder in the Wittgensteinian sense that you can discard it after you reach that point of asking the question, that you have to go on to something else in order to answer it?

Caputo: I do not think that we could ever reach some point in human experience where we get ourselves on the other side of the deconstructibility of the structures in which we live, beyond the deconstructibility of our beliefs and practices. I do not think we can ever reach that point, not so long as we live in time and history. In that sense, deconstruction is irreducible. But we need to act and decide and choose, which deconstruction also demands. Let us be clear: deconstruction does not exist; there is no thing, deconstruction, doing something. But deconstruction describes the situation in which, in the midst of unknowing, and in the midst of the deconstructibility of our beliefs and practices, we are called upon to act; it describes the setting in which we have to act. We will never get beyond the deconstructible structures of our beliefs and practices but we must act. In that sense you could say it is a ladder that you throw away, not in the sense that you get past it, but in the sense that you need to choose, and deconstruction cannot advise you about that, about what to choose, what to do. It cannot tell you to be a Christian or an atheist or an artist or anything else. It simply gives us some description of what is going on when we act. Religious faith, I would say, is an instantiation of a deconstructive situation in which we are asked to affirm, to make an act of faith, and to make an act of faith which is motivated by love, by the love of justice and what is to come, that mourns for the dead, that hopes for the future. Religion would be a perfectly sensible instantiation of the deconstructive gesture. But there would be other possibilities, too. Deconstruction is not authorized to decide among these possibilities. It has not come into the world to tell humankind what to do. It is a kind of salutary description of the conditions under which we act, but that is all.

Putt: But would you say that although deconstruction cannot prescribe a particular religious content, deconstruction can lead to what Heidegger calls "formal indications" of some content? I ask this question for two reasons. First, you yourself argue in *Nutshell* and in *Prayers and Tears* that Derrida's pure messianic has a definite content, that it is an identifiably Jewish messianic. Second, in your own thought, you practice a Christian deconstruction, and you write a lot about Jesus. So are these two examples not prescriptions, but formal indications of a possible content?

Caputo: That is a complicated question. Derrida does not explain things this way, but I think that we can say on his behalf that what he has done is to have taken certain biblical structures—like biblical hospitality or forgiveness— which he has taken as formal indications, as Heidegger called them, which are not to be confused with universal concepts. The main difference is that formal indications are empty schemata, and they do not really mean anything until you deploy them in the concrete where they get flesh and bones. In that sense the concrete instantiated decisions, which give the formal indications life, are what we are always already caught up in. That is true even of Derrida himself, so that this utterly pure, barren, almost ahistorical messianic would be an unlivable schema even for Derrida himself. This is actually one of my few criticisms of Derrida. I think that the distinction between the pure messianic and the concrete messianisms cannot be rigorously maintained. If it were maintained, the result would be, as you said, a true a priori, a pure transcendental, which is something that is blocked by the very idea of *différance*. Consequently, we are always involved with structures whose historical pedigree we can trace if we read them carefully enough and study them closely enough. That is no less true of deconstruction itself. Deconstruction bears a historical pedigree: it is a late-twentieth-century radical democracy, that among other things has roots going all the way back to prophetic Judaism. So we can mark it, we can find its historical tag. If we search it carefully enough, we discover that it, too, is another concrete messianism, which is the only thing that is livable. I do not think you can live in a pure messianic. The pure messianic is a formal indication of a concrete structure which deconstruction is trying to formalize, but which it is also at the very same time concretizing in an account of a radical democracy.

Putt: And that raises the issue of its Christian structure.

Caputo: Yes, in my case I would give it a more Christian twist, but it is a Christian twist which is very closely tied to Jesus the Jew, to the Judaism of Jesus himself, so that I am never completely comfortable with the Jewish-Christian distinction in the case of Jesus. Jesus never heard of Christianity and, from what we can tell, had no intention of starting a new religion called Christianity. He thought the world was going to end and that his job was to awaken everyone to the coming end and to understand that they are forgiven. I am very closely attached to the "Jesus movement," to what used to be called, before there was such a thing as Christianity, the "Way." If it has to do with Jesus, it must be "Christian," but Jesus never heard of Christianity. As for myself, I am very attached to Jesus. (Laughter)

Putt: In *Radical Hermeneutics* you say, in the spirit of what I think is a methodological agnosticism, "I do not know whether I believe in God." In *Prayers and Tears* the question has become "What do I love when I love my God?" and you seem to love the God of Jesus. When you write about Jesus, do you recognize that there is a divine revelation going on there or not? I raise this issue for a critical reason. When you deal with Jesus and the claims made about Jesus in the New Testament, you reject much of the miraculous and a high Christology, basing that rejection on the work of John Dominic Crossan and the Jesus Seminar, which truly could be considered very modernistic. At this point you seem to abandon your post and become a modernist. When you deal with Jesus, you write about the hard truths of the historical critical method, which is really just another hermeneutics, is it not? I mean in the flux, in the *khôra*, that is simply one way of reading among others.

Caputo: I think that the postmodern does not abandon the modern in order to become premodern. It passes through the modern. Politically, it passes through the Enlightenment, modern science, human rights, the rights of women, the modern social order, separation of church and state and then, after it assimilates them and assumes all these things, it puts them into question and says that in order to be what they themselves want to be, they cannot remain as they are. The desire for emancipation that motivated the Enlightenment cannot be satisfied with the Enlightenment. We need to become enlightened about the Enlightenment, which means to move through the Enlightenment and not to stop with the Enlightenment. I do think that it is of the utmost importance to understand the historical critical analysis of the Scriptures. I think that it is of the utmost importance not to be taken in by the premodern notion that the authors of the gospels sat with their ears cocked as the Holy Spirit whispered into their ears words that were rapidly transferred to their scrolls. We need to understand as best we can how those documents arose and what they are trying to say. Thus far I am modern. I think that thus far we should all be modern, otherwise we risk lapsing into some kind of fundamentalism or absolutism about the Scriptures. But I certainly do not want to stop there and say that is the final word. I would go on and describe what I called in *Against Ethics* a "poetics." I would say that the New Testament gives us a poetics. It provides a certain phenomenology, describing in nonobjectivistic language an experience that we would not have been able to record with a video camera, had there been video cameras in first-century Palestine. That experience centers on the person of Jesus, who clearly left an impact on everyone around him, including on us today, which is, I would say, a kind of revelation. I am interested in structures that overtake us, and which bring us up short—which, as Levinas says, traumatize us. The mark of the divine for me is twofold: first, the mark of the gift, of the excess of grace and love; and second, the mark of contradiction, of something that contradicts our own human tendencies, our own self-gratification and self-love. When something powerfully interrupts and contradicts our narcissism, then that is the other; in a religious language, that is the mark of God, the mark of the divine. When you go through the New Testament you experience this constant shock. Jesus shocks us with his associations, his defiance of the law, his turning toward the outcast, the constant contradiction of the wisdom of this world. Paul never met Jesus in the flesh. He says that what he learned he learned through a vision—we are going to have to take his word on that. But one of the things that he got right about Jesus, judging by what we know of Jesus on independent, historical grounds, shows up when he says that God chose the weak things of this world to confound the strong, and the foolish to confound the wise, and *ta me onta*, the nobodies and the nothings, to confound those who are. That captures this whole sense of shock and contradiction I am describing. Paul is using the language of what we call today "overcoming metaphysics"—he chooses the ones who are not to confound the ones who are, the ones who have *ousia*, the ones who have being and substance, and *exousia*, the authorities of this world. That contradicts our wisdom, our narcissism, our pride and love of power. That arrives like an intervention from without, an interruption of our own human, all too human selfishness and turns us toward the other one, which is for me a mark of divinity, which I see exemplarily realized in Jesus. It is a very Jewish and biblical idea, a revelation. Jesus did not invent it but he embodies it for us, now. But I also think that other traditions would have other exemplars, other figures who are paradigmatic figures for them. They never heard of Jesus, or they do not know much about Jesus, so Jesus is not part of their world or their experience of the divine. Jesus has a unique place for us, and for Christians, but I would not say that the exemplarity of Jesus is exclusive, that all the people in the world who lived before Jesus came into the world and all the people who live in the world now who know little or nothing about Jesus are in some profound way disadvantaged by that. I do not think that God prefers Jews to Muslims, or Christians to Jews. Jesus is a unique and special place of revelation for us but not an exclusive revelation. I think there are multiple revelations, as there are multiple languages and cultures.

Putt: One might argue that you have been writing a radically hermeneutical theology, and that the God that Jesus reveals for you is first a God of grace and forgiveness and second a God who suffers. You have come out explicitly in the conclusion of *Prayers and Tears* with a postmodern theopassionism, a theology of a suffering God. So, in these two areas, I think that you have moved past formal indication and have become a Meister Eckhart, a preacher preaching a particular God—of grace and suffering. Would that be a fair assessment of your perspective?

Caputo: First of all, this is something I have learned from you. You pointed out to me this theological movement called theopassionism, which made great deal of sense to me when you started to tell me about it . . .

Putt: Because you were already doing it.

Caputo: I was, in my own way, moving in that direction. The Hellenistic idea of God is, in many ways, supremely uninteresting and supremely uninterested in us, and I think we should each go our separate ways. This is a God produced by aristocratic Greek intellectuals, more of a useful intellectual hypothesis, who inhabits planets that move in a circle, passing his days contemplating himself, who constitutes a form of pure actuality. That becomes tremendously difficult to reconcile with the historically active, passionately involved God of the Hebrew and Christian scriptures. Medieval Christian theologians, who inherited this Hellenistic God, had to worry over how God would know that we exist, or why God would care about us, or be grieved over our sinfulness or respond to our prayers, because God is an unmoved mover. In this case my feminist friends will forgive me if I do not use gender-neutral language because this is a very masculine God. I would say the very last question we would ever think to ask upon reading the Hebrew or the Christian Scriptures is whether God knows anything about us or why God would care. I would say that if we had never heard of Greek philosophy, or Plato or Aristotle, that question would never have arisen in theology. It is a completely Hellenistic question. The one thing that was most markedly clear about the God of Jesus is that God has counted every tear and every hair on our head. One of the books that I very much enjoyed reading when I was working on *Prayers and Tears* was Abraham Heschel's *The Prophets*, which provides a biblical portrait of God that makes good religious sense to a reader of the Scriptures. If the God of the Greeks is very cerebral, Heschel describes a passionate God who is involved in human existence, a very stormy being who gets irate and weeps and loves us and gets angry with us, who even has a mean side on occasion. This is a much more vivid, living, and concrete portrayal of God, which is blocked by the notion of pure act and impassivity that marks the Greek conception of God. We need to think about God in other terms, to revision or reconceive God, beyond logocentrism and beyond phallocentrism. The biblical God, by the way, is not simply "wholly other." Clearly God is beyond us and we do not grasp God. There is an incomprehensibility about God, but God also makes Godself vividly known to us. But the notion that God is simply, transcendentally remote and wholly other does not capture the biblical experience of God.

Putt: But then you say all that within the context of *khôra*, of the flux, and then it becomes another hermeneutic.

Caputo: Indeed.

Putt: That puts us back into the tension that you discussed earlier—the tension of faith.

Caputo: That is faith. It is not a faith that simply arrives out of the blue, but a faith grounded in a certain experience and in a community. It is rooted—by which I do not mean to say that it has a foundation or demonstrative basis—in an experience, in a tradition, in a form of life that makes sense and to which we can attach ourselves. But it is indeed another rendering of our condition, one among others. Even in the sacred texts themselves, there are signs of this "other" rendering. Felix Sineculpa makes his voice known even in the Scriptures from time to time. When you read some of the things in Job, you find a contentious voice there—Job argues with God—arising from a sense of violation and absurdity, which is an echo of the play of forces in Job's life. It is what tests Job—What have I done wrong? Why is this happening to me? It is also there in the very Pauline reading of the binding of Isaac that Kierkegaard follows. Abraham is up against something that he just cannot make sense out of, which Kierkegaard stresses in *Fear and Trembling*. It is there in the very beginning of Genesis, in the description of the *tohu wa-bhohu*, the original chaos to which God gives form. You do not have the *creatio ex nihilo* of later theology but an irreducibly primary and formless stuff, an abyss, which God does not seem to have created but which God forms and shapes. So the notion of an irreducible element, which shows up in Levinas's *il y a*—and Levinas appears to be translating the *tohu wa-bhohu*—is present in the Scriptures right from the first line of the creation story. God appears as the one who gives order to the play, overpowers the forces, subdues the abyss.

Putt: There is a theological tradition that picks up on that—the formlessness and the void—and argues that if it were not for the creative power of God holding the cosmos together, it would fall back into chaos. So the chaos is always there, not as another God—you do not have to be a Manichean about it—but it is always there because it is the "other than God," the other of God's embrace, of God's love, and of God's power. Of course, some theologians would argue that the chaos can come out as a moral figure in sin, oppression, violence. That is the nothingness brought to expression in immorality.

Caputo: I see. That is certainly at the heart of Levinas's thought, the horror of the anonymous rumble. I think that it is a very powerful phenomenological image present right at the beginning of Genesis. It is at least as interesting as the later theological idea of *creatio ex nihilo*, which is a very powerful thought as well, because of the notion of radical creativity that it implies. *Creatio ex nihilo* is another important paradigm for us, a very biblical paradigm, as opposed to the Greeks, who are much more enamored of necessity. The very word "divine" for the Greeks meant unchanging, immortal, and permanent; they contrasted the divine to the mortal as what comes to be and passes away. But in the Hebrew and Christian tradition the divine is associated with transforming change, the capacity to create from nothing, or to form the chaos, to renew the heart, to make miraculous changes, to transform the natural world. It annoys me that the theological tradition has become so attached over the centuries to essentialism and the theory of substance. If you read the Scriptures carefully you do not find the very self-sufficient *ousia* of which we learn in Greek philosophy, but an utterly transformable stuff that is constantly undergoing miraculous metamorphoses. It gets created out of nothing, it gets transformed and changed, and God is intervening in it all the time. God does not show up in the Scriptures in the regularities of nature but in those interruptions of the regularities of nature, in the disruptions, by being a very disruptive sort of anarchic being. God does not show up just as an *arche* but also as an *anarche*. In this debate between essentialism and nominalism, it seems to me that God is on the side of nominalism. God does not treat things as if they had deep unchanging essences but as things that are utterly responsive to God's will. They get altered, changed, interrupted—all quite regularly. One of the regular features of the scriptural world is the irregularity, the interruptions and the transformability. I do not find the notion of natural law or the attachment to essences for which theology and philosophical theology has shown a predilection to be a very biblical, but rather a very Greek way to think about things.

Putt: I cannot give a citation or remember the author, but one writer put it this way: we humans are always trying to create necessity, and God is the *bricoleur* of freedom.

Caputo: Exactly. We are more likely to find a view like this in the early medieval theologians. By the time we get to the high Middle Ages, then the Greek sense of necessity is stronger. But the earliest theologians wanted to stress the primacy of the good over being and the sovereign freedom of God. They thought that God could easily scale the walls of necessity that the philosophers were building. I am thinking of someone like Peter Damian, who had very harsh words for the philosophers and thought they deserved to be committed to the flames. He was the one who coined the expression "handmaiden of theology." Damian thought that the "law of contradiction" formulated by the philosophers was a man-made law that did not hold for God, that God's freedom can just overwhelm the principle of contradiction. For example, Damian even thought that God could change the past. The only question for Damian is whether God wants to do it. Would it be good? God would not change the past if what happened in the past was good. God would never make an innocent man guilty. But God could change the past if it were good to do so; so he could make it that an evil deed had never been done. The only thing that restricts God is God's goodness, which is beyond being, above being, which is the tradition from which Marion takes his point of departure. Damian may have gone too far, because it may actually be the case that it is incoherent to talk about changing the past, but I like the spirit behind Damian's idea, by which I mean the "poetics." I do not think the logic actually holds, but the poetics behind it, the phenomenology, suggests transformability, renewability, forgivability, new birth, creation. These are powerful motifs in a biblical phenomenology that contrasts with the Greek sense of necessity, fate, inevitability, what could not be otherwise.

Putt: You mention forgivability, which is again another characteristic of the God revealed in Jesus. For you, God is a God of grace, of gift, and of forgiveness. This has been a recurring theme in your work for at least the past ten years. I think it also can be found in *Radical Hermeneutics*. It certainly is found in your unpublished article "Sacred anarchy," in "Reason, history and a little madness," in "Metanoetics," and most recently in *Prayers and Tears*. In all these texts, you write about gift and forgiveness, and now, interestingly enough, Derrida himself is also working with the notion of forgiveness.

Caputo: Yes. I have to say that my interest in forgiveness antedates my interest in Derrida on forgiveness. In fact, it seemed to me then that Derrida ought to pay more attention to forgiveness than he was doing at the time. It is a very characteristic or salient feature of the deconstructive view of things, in my view. I addressed it in *Against Ethics* in connection with Hannah Arendt on forgiveness in *The Human Condition*. It was Arendt, not Derrida, who was the first resource I drew upon to discuss forgiveness. She says that punishment, which is the opposite of forgiveness, pulls the strings of the social order tighter and tighter, locking us into narrower and narrower constraints and blocking freedom so that we are caught up in a vicious cycle. Forgiveness is the way to cut those bonds, to release us and free us and open up new possibilities. So in the same way that we have hope with respect to the future, we have forgiveness with respect to the past. Forgiveness opens or frees the past so that the past can be altered; the past cannot be physically changed in the way that Peter Damian thought it could, but it can be reinterpreted, reunderstood, recontexualized and given a new meaning. Forgiveness has a certain mysterious power to annul the past—not literally, but at least to annul the meaning of the past by which we are presently trapped. Insofar as the past is irreversible, we are trapped by it, victimized by it. So we have to be able in some way to reach back into the past and alter it.

Putt: Was it she [Arendt] who called Jesus a poet of forgiveness?

Caputo: Yes. She says he was the discoverer of forgiveness. For her, Jesus is a master teacher of forgiveness.

Putt: A genius who taught us about forgiveness. And you have elaborated on that idea in your work?

Caputo: Yes, because, if you argue for a notion of radical contingency, as I do, then the past becomes a problem, because the past, as Husserl describes it, is inalterable. The present moment flows off into the past, where it is retained and then assumes an inalterable place in the stream of retentions. We may forget the past moment but it has still flown off into the past in an inalterable, irremovable way. Then it is a kind of trap, a fate, a fatal entanglement. The past becomes our fate unless we can change it some way, and it is forgiveness that allows that. It is a characteristically biblical idea, but it is also an important political idea, as Arendt tries to show—in the dispute in Northern Ireland, in South Africa, in the Middle East, in Bosnia and Serbia, all over the world. Each side is required to forget and forgive the past. Somebody has to break the stalemate and at a certain point decide to trust a mortal enemy; each side has to let go, and somebody will have to go first to break the cycle. George Mitchell is a hero in Ireland because he somehow or another got these people in a position where they could start to let go, to forgive. So this is an important political idea, a concretely real idea, not simply a beautiful religious sentiment that we find in the Scriptures. It is real and it needs to be given reality; it is the most fundamental reality behind all political negotiations.

Putt: You and I have discussed before the tension in the notion of unconditional forgiveness, the "let it go, it never happened." Such is pure grace, almost a pure gift of forgiving. What effect does that have on the issue of responsibility and the seriousness of the offense that is being forgiven? In other words, what is the difference between pardoning and condoning? In your own work that tension comes to expression in your understanding of the forgetfulness of forgiveness over against Johann Baptist Metz's notion of "the dangerous memory of suffering." How do you hold to this almost pure forgiveness while at the same time recognizing that there are some offenses for which people need to be held responsible, that they simply cannot be forgotten as if they were nothing, because they were not nothing?

Caputo: With the Holocaust, we say "never forget," and that is important. I do not want to deny that. At the same time, part of the movement of forgiveness is forgetting. Forgiving is not the same as forgetting, but there is an element of forgetting in forgiving. Both the "forget it" and the "never forget" have to be held together in a tension that it is productive but not easy to accommodate; that is "the impossible." Part of the way in which the tension can be maintained is to see that the "forget it" is something that can never be said by the offender. We who give offense must always remember, never forget our own murderousness or violence, as Levinas would say. It is the one who is offended who is in the position to say "forget it." There needs to be a moment of that, of the "forget it," which is *the* impossible. Forget it, it never happened, and don't forget it did happen. So even after someone offends the other, the offended one says to the one who offends, "forget it." They really intend to do that, to get past it. But in fact you cannot forget it; it is always there, because the past really is physically inalterable. You cannot actually make something not to have happened. But then that is what forgiveness is; to be forgiven is not to be made innocent, but to be forgiven. You do not actually erase or annul the past—for then there would be nothing to forgive—but you want to forgive it. Then we must not forget the notion of the happy fault, the *felix culpa*, in the Christian liturgy for Holy Saturday. In the Christian economy, good comes out of evil and the fall of Adam occasions a redemption that far exceeds the fault and anything we deserve. So very often, what we have done wrong, in ways that we can never foresee, turns out to be felicitous. In the long run, it makes us better, makes us stronger, more sensitive. It opens up new forms of generosity that would never have come about if we had not been so mean and selfish in the past. So we do not want to have annulled it; we do not want to forget it because it can be productive. Our own meanness in the past can emancipate us in the future.

Putt: Your insistence on the "forget it" aspect of forgiveness aims at trying to keep forgiveness from deteriorating into a pure economy; that is, to maintain it as gift.

Caputo: Yes, and that is Derrida's contribution to the discussion. You need to graciously forgo what is "by right" "owed" to you. To forgive is to forgo retribution and repayment, and to that extent forgiving is giving a gift. I do not want to be paid back. Forget it, you do not owe me. But it cannot be a simple forgetting; it must be what Nietzsche calls an active forgetting.

Putt: Remember to forget.

Caputo: Exactly. But that goes along, as you say, with the dangerous memory of suffering, because we must also always remember. We must maintain the tension. When the Irish settle their disputes, they are also giving justice to the dead. Three thousand people have been murdered in the last thirty years in

Northern Ireland, not to mention all the suffering and death prior to this
present struggle. They are dead, and they are not going to participate in any
new government or enjoy its fruits. So in some important sense, if this new
government is successfully formed, it must give justice to the dead. Abraham
Lincoln said that these dead shall not have died in vain. We always must
remember the dead. The structure of mourning is an impossible structure of
memory and forgetting, which belong together in a kind of ethical tension.
They each need each other to be what they are.

Putt: We have been talking about Continental philosophy of religion, and
earlier you made the statement that all Continentalists in some way or
another have been influenced by phenomenology. Some phenomenologists
would accuse you of being a phenomenological heretic with all of these
discussions of theology, faith, Jesus, and forgiveness. They would indict Derrida, Caputo, and all others who work in the area of recent Continental
philosophy of religion for having moved too far away from the Husserlian
tradition. Do you think that this critique is valid? If so, how do you respond
to it?

Caputo: I do not mind being called a heretic. I enjoy the notoriety. I would
even like to think of myself as a kind of heretical phenomenologist, a post-
phenomenologist or a quasi-phenomenologist. In *Against Ethics*, I was critical of phenomenology on the grounds that it tended to privilege healthy,
hale, whole, athletic bodies. Nobody ever seems to get sick in phenomenology, nobody is ever crippled, or is missing a limb. In Merleau-Ponty's *The
Phenomenology of Perception* the model is the whole body, the holistic
body, and he uses Schneider, who has suffered a brain injury, or the
phantom limb phenomenon, as foils in order to describe a healthy and hale
body. From that point of view, the bodies that appear in the New Testament are very unphenomenological. They are not these hale, whole masculine athletes, but bodies laid low. So in that sense I want to be a dissident,
heretical phenomenologist and to do a phenomenology of wounded flesh
rather than hail the hale body of metaphysics and phenomenology. The
other sense in which I would like to pursue a kind of heretical phenomenology is this: like Derrida I am interested in those phenomena that are
constituted by their nonappearance. The appearance of this sort of phenomenon is a function of its nonappearance. That of course is paradigmatically presented to us by Husserl in the fifth *Cartesian Meditation*,
which, far from being heretical, is a canonical text. The very structure of
the appearance of the other person is of one who in an important sense
can never appear, whose appearance therefore can never be present and
hence must always be "appresented." If the consciousness of the other were
presented, it would be my consciousness, the alterity of the other would be

compromised, and the other would be turned into me. So the very condition of the possibility of the appearing of the other is that the other not appear. Now that very interesting phenomenon, first described *ex cathedra*, in the seat of phenomenological orthodoxy, represents the formal structure of the idea of the *tout autre*. The wholly other is always the one whose very appearance is constituted by nonappearance; if it ever appeared, then it would not be the wholly other. St. Augustine says the same thing about God: if you understand it, it is not God. Now even though this issues from Husserl himself, it represents a kind of perverse or contrarian tendency within phenomenology which is pushing phenomenology to its limits, in the direction of pursuing phenomena that do not satisfy the phenomenological appetite for appearance, presentation, and intuition. I want to radicalize this tendency within phenomenology to take up what does not appear, in the same way that in *Speech and Phenomena* Derrida radicalized Husserl's discovery of the capacity of signifiers to operate in the absence of intuition. Husserl always wanted those intentions to be fulfilled, but Derrida said that in fact Husserl has shown how intentions work *without* being fulfilled, how they can operate as empty intentions. Of course, Marion wants to do exactly the opposite: he wants to radicalize the tendency of these intentions to be *fulfilled*, to be saturated by givenness. What interests Derrida, on the other hand, is the way these intentions can operate without givenness because that extends their reach. We can speak in the absence of what is not present; if we could not, speech would be clumsy and impeded and we would only be able to speak about things that we would be able intuitively to confirm on the spot. That would defeat the whole point of a signifier. Why measure a signifier by the standards of presence when the very idea of a signifier is to be able to operate in the absence of what it signifies? That is its whole advantage. Derrida takes phenomenology off in a certain direction which was not what Husserl had in mind, since Husserl privileged completion and fulfillment. Derrida pursued another possibility, and you can say that represents a heretical version of phenomenology. But that is all right because it extends phenomenology's reach. Derrida remains, as we all remain, indebted to Husserl. We love to go back to Husserl, again and again, and that is true even of deconstruction, which is rather more a phenomenological inquiry than an analytic one in the Anglo-American sense. But it is a dissident phenomenology, which is also true of Jean-Luc Marion, whose dissidence is in the opposite direction, of pure givenness. I would say that Derrida's heresy is more fruitful. Marion's heresy falls in line with a very powerful dogma and dogmatics of a more authoritarian sort, which is a very odd form for heresy to take.

Putt: Then do you think it is possible to have a phenomenology of God?

Caputo: I think that phenomenology provides the most successful, important, and meaningful way to think about God, with the proviso that this would always be a phenomenology that confesses the limits of what we can say about God. A phenomenological approach to God is necessary and inescapable, not only for religion—I think the Scriptures represent a great phenomenology of our encounter with God—but also for phenomenology itself. I think that any adequate phenomenological description of human life would have to take into account the structure of our desire, but the name of God is the name of what we desire. Any phenomenology that does not include God, which names our desire beyond desire, our desire for something of which we can only dream, for which we pray and weep, would be an incomplete, imperfect phenomenology. A phenomenology of God is a great gift for theology, and it is inescapably necessary for phenomenology; it calls out for doing. But that phenomenology would take place in a situation in which we confess that we do not know who we are or what we mean when we say God. We do not know if God is a translation for justice or justice is a translation for God. So the first question of this phenomenology is "What do I love when I love my God?"

Putt: You address this with reference to Kierkegaard, and here the Kierkegaardian influence in your work comes out again. You refer this to what Kierkegaard says about the Incarnation, the appearance of God in the person of Jesus, and how the disciples responded to that appearance with reference to the mediation.

Caputo: The very appearance of Jesus is conditioned upon his nonappearance inasmuch as we need the "condition" in order to apprehend him as the Incarnation.

Putt: Yes. You talk about Kierkegaard's insistence that the disciples encountered the man Jesus.

Caputo: And what they could see was not God. Insofar as they affirm him as the Messiah, they do not see that. That is faith, which has to do with what we do not see.

Putt: So those disciples are not privileged over a contemporary disciple.

Caputo: That is the analysis of *Philosophical Fragments*. What I like is that Kierkegaard never confuses faith with knowledge or with any kind of miraculous intervention in the natural order. He does not think faith is based upon a divine gleam that the disciples detect in Jesus's eyes; that is paganism for him. Faith is of what does not appear. So this structure of nonappearing and of the unfulfilled signifier, of the empty intention, is the very structure of faith. That is ultimately my argument with Jean-Luc Marion. At first he gave everybody the impression that the saturated phenomenon was an overwhelming experience of God that religious people have and that everybody else is going to have to get. But as his position became sorted out more carefully, it became clear that he did not think that the saturated phenomenon could be identified by phenomenology, because as a phenomenon it was bedazzling and confusing. In order to identify and name what it is that addresses us in the saturated phenomenology, we need faith. But one of the things that givenness means, certainly in Husserl's phenomenology, is clarification: givenness clarifies intentions. But Marion tells us that this givenness is not clear and it needs to be given clarity or identity by faith. So we ultimately come back to the original situation described by Husserl, where we have an intention of faith that is not fulfilled because the givenness that pretends to fulfill it cannot fulfill it but needs to be clarified by the intention of faith. Then we are back to the situation of faith described by Kierkegaard and Derrida, where faith is an intention of something that we cannot see or cannot clearly experience.

Putt: This is something other than Husserl's principle of principles. It does not fall under that.

Caputo: The principle of principles does not get realized. The saturating givenness is too confusing for us to know what it is, so we need to move past it to an act of faith that identifies what it is. But it does not know that what is given is God, or grace, etc. It requires faith. That is the difference between theology and phenomenology for him. Phenomenology leaves us with a bedazzling phenomenon that theology identifies by faith. But that faith obeys the law not of givenness but of empty intention.

Putt: That is Derrida's *sans savoir*. May I ask you about your own confessional tradition? Why do more Catholics not invite you to speak? Are you a Catholic heretic as well as a phenomenological heretic? (Laughter)

Caputo: First off, it should not go unnoticed that I am often invited to speak before Catholic audiences. But I hear what you are saying. Insofar as my work with Continental philosophy had to do with the intersection of Continental philosophy with Aquinas and Eckhart, with the medieval metaphysical and mystical traditions, it evoked a favorable response among my fellow Catholics. It was on the basis of that work that I was elected president of the American Catholic Philosophical Association back in the 1980s. Insofar as my work was simply phenomenological and existential, that evokes a good response among Catholics. But the Catholic community has become suspicious of recent developments in Continental philosophy, of poststructuralism, of Foucault and Derrida. They find meager nourishment there, and so they are more suspicious of my current interests. So I have tried with the "Religion and Postmodernism" conferences that we have been having at Villanova with Derrida, and with *Prayers and Tears* and *Deconstruction in a Nutshell*, to show the way in which this movement is congenial to religious faith. But when you look for the resonances and the correlations in the Catholic Christian tradition with this more Derridean deconstructive postmodern religion that I am describing, I must say that you find yourself back on the doorsteps of Augustine, not Aquinas—which of course plays very well at Villanova, which is an Augustinian university. But then you and I may start arguing about whether Augustine was a Protestant or a Catholic! In my view, recent Continental thought asks Catholics to come back and reconsider Augustine.

Putt: Let me conclude by asking you to do something quite non-Derridean and nondeconstructive, if Derrida's idea is not to try to program the future but to await the incoming of the impossible. Let me ask you to think ahead. How do you see the future of "Continental philosophy of religion"? How do you see all of this playing itself out over the next decade, as we move into the new millennium?

Caputo: I am very sanguine about it. I think that the multiplication of translations, new studies, and conferences bears witness to a great surge of interest in it. I hope it is not what they call in the stock market a "spike" that will be followed by a sag. The "Continental Philosophy and Theology" group in the American Academy of Religion is very vigorous, a fledgling "Society for Continental Philosophy and Theology" has recently been formed, and I am trying to feature this work in "Perspectives in Continental Philosophy," the book series I edit for Fordham University Press. This work is nourished by Levinas and by the later Heidegger's critique of "onto-theo-logic," but it also draws upon philosophers like Derrida and Luce Irigaray, who are not to be confused with religious authors in the usual sense, but whose work has inspired fascinating deconstructive and feminist theologies. Jean-Luc Marion's *God without Being* has also given a great impulse to this movement and has stimulated widespread discussion, numerous studies and conferences. Marion's work really has been a gift to this whole discussion. To this we cannot avoid adding the Anglican movement called "radical orthodoxy," a very aggressive expression reflecting a very aggressive movement. Even if these people are, in my opinion, as much premodern or antimodern as postmodern, they have added an important conservative voice to this discussion. They go back to a very classical kind of Christian Neoplatonic metaphysics, but they do so in dialogue with Continental philosophy. There has been a kind of polygenesis of this movement, with many different voices joining in—Christian, Jewish, conservative, liberal, feminist, and so on. I am very hopeful that we will see a strong postsecular version of Continental philosophy take shape in the United States, drawing on an older tradition in France, and that the two will nourish each other in a kind of transcontinental cross-semination facilitated by email and transcontinental flights. That will provide a very salutary alternative to the analytic philosophy of religion that has dominated the scene in the United States. That is my hope, and I hope it is not merely a hope against hope.

Putt: Thank you.

Name index

Subject index